THE Road THAT Silver Built

THE MILLION DOLLAR HIGHWAY

BY P. DAVID SMITH

WESTERN REFLECTIONS PUBLISHING COMPANY®
Lake City, CO

© 2009 by P. David Smith
All rights reserved, in whole or in part

ISBN 978-932738-80-3

Library of Congress Number: 2009923551

Cover Photo: Jan Smith
Cover and Text Design Laurie Goralka Design

First Edition
Printed in the USA

Western Reflections Publishing Co.
951 N. Highway 149
P.O. Box 1149
Lake City, CO 81235
(970) 944-0110
www.westernreflectionspublishing.com
publisher@westernreflectionspublishing.com

Acknowledgements

Many thanks to Freda Peterson for her help in using the archives of the San Juan Historical Society.

I appreciate the help of Ann Barney and Heather Braem of the Durango Area Tourism Office.

As usual I am very grateful for the help of noted and prolific historian Duane Smith of Ft. Lewis College in Durango, Colorado.

I also need to acknowledge that Marvin Gregory and I did much of the research that appears in this book. That research was originally used for our book *The Million Dollar Highway* that was published in 1986 by Wayfinder Press.

DEDICATION

To my wife Jan, who stayed with me, even after our first drive (thirty-five years ago) over the Million Dollar Highway in a borrowed RV and in a driving rainstorm.

For further reading about the scenic and historic
San Juans please see our website
www.westernreflectionspublishing.com

TABLE OF CONTENTS

INTRODUCTION 1

Chapter 1
THE FIRST TWO BILLION YEARS. 10

Chapter 2
THE SILVERY (AND SOMETIMES GOLDEN) SAN JUANS 30

Chapter 3
OTTO MEARS AND HIS TOLL ROADS 54

Chapter 4
THE ORIGINAL MILLION DOLLAR HIGHWAY IS BUILT 79

Chapter 5
CHANGING TIMES. 109

Chapter 6
NARROW GAUGE RAILS INTO SILVERTON 137

Chapter 7
THE TOWN OF DURANGO AND A TRIP TO SILVERTON 165

Chapter 8
THE TOWN OF SILVERTON AND THE RAINBOW ROUTE 204

Chapter 9
THE RED MOUNTAIN MINING DISTRICT-
   MOUNTAINS OF SILVER 237

PHOTO ESSAY 267

Chapter 10
THE IMPASSIBLE CANYON AND THE CITY OF OURAY 284

EPILOGUE 324

BIBLIOGRAPHY 327

INDEX 331

Introduction

WAY UP IN THE ROCKY MOUNTAINS of Southwestern Colorado, just about as high as you can possibly go, is a small, paved highway that twists and turns like a drunken snake through mountains that are still thousands of feet higher than the road. It goes up and over three of the highest mountain passes in the state of Colorado. In most places there is no shoulder, there are guard rails missing in places that you would sorely like to see them, and the road passes through one of the deadliest avalanche areas in the Continental United States. The formal designation for this highway is U.S. 550, and it is the main north-south highway in all of Western Colorado – but the locals call it "The Million Dollar Highway."

"The Million Dollar Highway" – the name sounds bold, brash, and beckoning. This is not your ordinary road. You don't push your car up to seventy miles an hour, put it on cruise control, and settle back in the seat. On this highway the speed limit is twenty-five miles an hour over much of its seventy-five miles, and you may find yourself going slower than the speed limit on many stretches. The road is short, but the trip from Durango to Ouray takes two hours to drive without stopping and in good weather; and if you can, plan on a full day's trip, so that you might enjoy its many special and spectacular sights.

One thing is for sure, the Million Dollar Highway will be like no other road you have ever traveled. Early nineteenth century traveler Ernest Ingersoll wrote, "In no other location are so many lofty summits to be seen crowded together." President Herbert Hoover said, "The views on the Million Dollar Highway ... are the most scenic and spectacular I have ever seen either in this country or in any other." Author Josie Crum called the road "a hairraiser of the devil's own manufacture," and well-known television travel commentator Charles Kuralt proclaimed the route's scenery "the

A Bristlecone Pine stands watch over the San Juan Mountains. In many ways it is like the residents. It is one of the longest living trees on earth because it bends but doesn't break. It is usually found clinging tenaciously to rocky ground on steep slopes, almost as if it prefers a rugged life to an easy one.

Frank Rice Photo. Ruth & Marvin Gregory Collection.

most beautiful road in America." Yet the scenery and the highway are impossible to adequately describe. It is one of those places you have to see to believe.

The San Juan Mountains, through which the Million Dollar Highway travels, are so spectacular and awe-inspiring that they were the original, proposed location for Rocky Mountain National Park (eventually established near Estes Park). Evidently, the only reason that these amazing mountains were not chosen was that too much private land lay within its boundaries, as they contain about 10,000 mining claims under private ownership.

The first question that everyone asks is how did the highway get such a name? In fact, the highway has had many names over the years, and there are many legends and tales concerning its present name. One is that it cost more than a million dollars to build in the 1880s. It actually wasn't that expensive, although it did cost a phenomenal sum for the time. A tale exists that the highway got its name from one very distraught early traveler, who said, "I won't go back over that road for a million dollars." That sentiment may have been expressed many times, but it was not how the highway got its name. And then there are the rumors that the road was graded with waste from the early-day gold mills, which were notoriously inefficient in extracting precious metals, resulting in a road that was literally paved with gold worth millions of dollars. In fact, some mill tailings were used in the construction of the original road, but their value was nowhere near a million dollars. Early pioneers were not so naïve as to use tailings that had any appreciable value. One fact is true, but not the reason for the name – there definitely is a million dollars worth of scenery along the way. So how did the road get its name? Well, we will have to tell a little of its background before we get to that point.

There is yet another mystery surrounding the highway. It may sound odd, but the exact length of the Million Dollar Highway is somewhat in controversy. Because various sections of the road were built at different times, some historians feel "The Million Dollar" portion is really only the six miles of road from Ouray to Ironton Park (or at the very most, the twelve miles to the top of

Red Mountain); others contend that it is the twenty-six miles of road from Ouray to Silverton; and some argue that it is the seventy-five mile road from Durango to Ouray. Every now and then, the name for the road is even pushed by someone south all the way to the New Mexico state line or north to Montrose, Colorado.

And then there have been all the names for the road. The first was given it by Dave Day, editor of Ouray's *Solid Muldoon* newspaper. He called it the "Rainbow Route," a very fitting description. Later, at different times, the road was called the not so romantic "Durango, Silverton, Ouray Highway" (or the "DSO"), then the "Circle Route Highway" after the name of a D&RG Railroad tour, then a Durango name -- the "San Juan Way," then "The Chief Ouray Highway" (a name Montrose citizens gave it)," and then "Otto Mears Highway" after the little Russian who is credited with building the hardest portion of the highway. The federal government decided recently to call it part of the "San Juan Scenic Skyway, a 236 mile loop. Everyone seems to want to give this part of U. S. Highway 550 a name, and everyone wants to be included in "The Million Dollar Highway." Once you have driven this road, you will understand why.

I have called the highway "The Road That Silver Built." Once you know a little of its history you will understand why the road was built through some of the toughest country in all of North America and why it took almost fifty years for the whole stretch to be completed. Although the ravages of time, deep snows, and man have taken much of the original buildings and structures, there are still numerous reminders along the Million Dollar Highway of the attempts of early San Juan prospectors to conquer nature and take away a lot more than a million dollars of her riches — crumbling cabins and mills, abandoned gold and silver mines, ghost towns built hurriedly during the boom days, and what are some of the most challenging jeep roads in the United States, built originally to get to and from the rich mines. And then the road itself has an exciting history, both in its construction and through the events that have occurred on the road proper through the years.

The San Juan Mountains are rugged. This scene from the top of 13,218-foot Engineer Mountain shows jeeps pausing on Engineer Pass before they resume their journey to lower elevations. Although this is a four-wheel drive road, similar scenes can be seen along the Million Dollar Highway.

Bill Fries III Photo. Author's Collection.

There is also a very complete geologic history along the route. The trip begins with the "young" ten-million year old sandstone bluffs near Durango and ends with the two billion-year-old quartzite in the Uncompahgre Canyon near Ouray. However what was most important, geologically speaking, to the early prospectors was that this extraordinary land contained millions of dollars (billions in today's values) in rich ore.

Today, this primitive, inspiring country is usually prized more for its scenic beauty than its mining riches, but the road wouldn't be here if it hadn't been for rich discoveries of silver in the San Juan Mountains in the early 1870s. In fact, the history of the road blends with its awe-inspiring beauty to make it perhaps the most unique roads in the United States.

Besides being a scenic and historic wonderland, today's Million Dollar Highway also opens up a wealth of recreational opportunities. Summer use includes hiking, four-wheeling, ATVs, motorcycles, rafting, gliding, cycling, hunting, fishing, horseback riding, mountain biking, hang gliding, hot air ballooning, and more; and, in the winter, downhill and cross country skiing, snowboarding, snowmobiling, snowshoeing, tubing, ice climbing, ice skating, and other winter sports take over along the route.

The trip over the highway is a major adventure in itself, often compared to the thrill of a roller coaster. The ride starts slowly out of Durango for ten straight, flat miles through the Animas Valley; then the excitement picks up a little as the road curves and rises along the Hermosa Cliffs up to the Durango Mountain ski area, then it rises steeply to the top of Molas Pass and starts to radically twist and turn as it goes steeply down the other side. But the ride isn't over. The road goes up and down again over Molas Pass and then once again at Red Mountain Pass. The Million Dollar is the only highway in the United States that crosses three passes over 10,000 feet in less than thirty miles. A flatlander once asked a local how he could get through these mountains. "We don't go through them, we go over them," was the very serious reply.

Introduction

This roller coaster ride includes sharp switchbacks, steep grades, narrow curves (some without guardrails), and extreme drop-offs that have caused some passengers to close their eyes, catch their breath, and mumble a quick prayer — after perhaps cursing their spouse for getting them into this situation. Even with a death grip on the steering wheel, the driver usually feels a little more comfortable. If a passenger, take comfort that the driver doesn't usually drive off the road on flat land, so why should he or she suddenly do so here? Fortunately, the Million Dollar Highway is now, after 125 years, a fully paved, well-maintained, and year-round federal road that is the most-used north-south route in southwestern Colorado. If driven with a dash of discretion and common sense, the Million Dollar Highway can be easily and safely traveled by the average car and driver, if everyone can just relax.

If you are a little tense about driving the highway, there is one important point that may help you plan your trip. If you travel the road from north to south (Ouray to Durango), you will be on the inside of the road for almost the entire trip (the exception being a few miles of road out of Ouray). Taking the highway south to north (Durango to Ouray) will leave you on the outside edge of the road for most of the trip (the exception being the six miles from the north end of Ironton Park down to the City of Ouray.

Before taking the trip, a few words of caution are in order. Use the pull outs on the side of the road when you are driving. They may look unstable, but they won't break off and slide down the mountain. Don't drive and try to look at the scenery at the same time. Your passengers will greatly appreciate this act. Take it slow — enjoy yourself. Be especially careful in the winter, which is one of the most beautiful times to be on the highway, but there may be snow or ice. The local radio stations usually update the conditions of the highway every few hours or so in the winter if the weather is bad. Portable electronic highway signs will also warn you of bad conditions, highway construction, or road closures. If conditions really get dangerous, there are barriers that will close the road off — some of them are even activated by the highway department by remote control.

The Million Dollar Highway is open and can be safely traveled in the winter, but it is the most avalanche prone area in the continental United States. Because of this danger, there are avalanche experts who monitor snowfall along the route and close the highway when the avalanche danger is too high. The worst danger is in February, March and early April; but at any time during the winter, watch for avalanches. Don't stop in the winter in or near avalanche paths. They are clearly marked by signs alongside the road. Avalanches are always a danger, but a moving car is usually in its path for only a few seconds, making it extremely unlikely that anyone would get hit. Virtually all avalanche deaths and serious injuries have occurred to vehicles that were stopped in avalanche paths – usually snowplow drivers trying to clear a path or automobile drivers putting chains on their cars.

If the road is temporarily closed in the winter, it is normally because of high avalanche danger. The Colorado Highway Department waits until major snow storms are over and shoots down further slides with howitzers or explosives dropped from helicopters. Then the snow plows clear the road. The highway will be closed during these times. Usually such closures are for only a few hours, but on occasion the wait can be longer.

One final word of caution – there are many old wagon routes that still exist as difficult four-wheel drive roads, branching off the Million Dollar Highway in many places to even higher, more beautiful, and rougher territory. These roads are worth the effort to explore, because as much as there is to see along the Million Dollar Highway, there is immeasurably more waiting for those who venture into to the adjacent high country. However, these roads are only for the experienced off-road driver and properly equipped four-wheel drive vehicle. They will be mentioned throughout this book, but they are totally open only in the summer. If you don't want to drive off road yourself, then stay on the asphalt. There are plenty of four-wheel drive jeep tours in Durango, Silverton, or Ouray that feature these trips; their drivers relate much of the history along the way and will bring you home safely.

All of these warnings make the road sound dangerous, but generally speaking, there is very seldom any kind of trouble. In fact, the Million Dollar Highway is a lot safer than (although very different from) a big city freeway. The highway is not what many people are used to traveling, but that is the reason it is such an adventure. The unbelievable sights along its route will be enjoyed and remembered for a lifetime by all who travel it – probably drawing you back to explore and enjoy the San Juans for many years to come.

An avalanche roars down Hayden Mountain in the San Juans. They look like beautiful, fluffy snow, but they travel at hundreds of miles an hour, creating a vacuum that can suck the air from a person's lungs, and when they stop they are as hard as cement and filled with rocks and pieces of trees.

Author's Collection.

Chapter 1

THE FIRST TWO BILLION YEARS

THE MILLION DOLLAR HIGHWAY travels directly through the middle of the majestic San Juan Mountains of Southwestern Colorado, which are among the newest to be formed in the Rocky Mountains, and are therefore some of the steepest and most imposing mountains in the world. The San Juans are the largest single mountain range in the United States and cover about one-eighth of the State of Colorado and a large portion of northwestern New Mexico. They are also the most mineralized mountains in Colorado, and therefore contain some of the richest mining regions in the United States. Literally tons of gold, silver, zinc, lead, copper, and other valuable metals have been taken from San Juan ground, and most geologists agree that there is still a large quantity of minerals yet to be mined. The valuable mineral riches and the rugged terrain of the San Juans established a conflict for the early American prospectors – the ore overflowed in this country, but it was almost impossible to get supplies and machinery into their mines and doubly hard to get the valuable, but extremely heavy, ore out. From this adversity came the eventual building of what came to be known as "The Million Dollar Highway."

The geology of the San Juans is very complex and cannot be explained in detail in the space allocated here; but to understand

Chapter 1: THE FIRST TWO BILLION YEARS

the scenery along the Million Dollar Highway, it is first necessary to have at least a rudimentary understanding of the physical makeup of the mountains that surround it. The oldest rock exposed in the San Juans, and that which might be called the "foundation" of the mountains dates from the Precambrian era of about two billion years ago. Over a billion and a half years of relative inactivity in what is now the San Juans allowed the Precambrian rock to be worn down to a flat plain. The Needles and West Needles Mountains north of Durango and the Uncompahgre Gorge near Ouray are composed of this very old rock.

Over the millennia several shallow oceans covered much of the central portion of what is now the United States. These oceans left sediments on their bottoms that were hundreds of feet deep. About sixty-five million years ago, as the San Juan region began to rise, the seas and sediments at the upper portion of the "San Juan Dome" were washed down into the lower territory at the edges. Erosion worked on this one hundred mile-wide dome, creating canyons, and also increased the sedimentary depth in the lower areas even more. Gradually, these sediments were compressed into thick layers of sedimentary rock. The lush vegetation that had grown around the swampy edges of the oceans eventually decayed and became the coal beds of the San Juans. Fossils of vegetation, shells, and other sea life can be frequently found throughout the San Juan Mountains because of these early seas, even though the land is now a thousand miles from the nearest ocean.

Then, from about forty to twenty-four million years ago, numerous volcanoes erupted. They covered the San Juan Dome with an average of 4,000 feet of ash. Eight thousand cubic miles of volcanic debris was spewed out over the dome, which still continued to push up until it was over 26,000 feet in elevation at the center. Much of the rock we now see in the San Juans is this dull, dark gray volcanic tuff. The immense rise in elevation caused cracks and crevices throughout the dome, and yet the fine ash filled in and leveled out the terrain. The increase in elevation was so immense that it caused the Continental Divide to bulge many miles to the

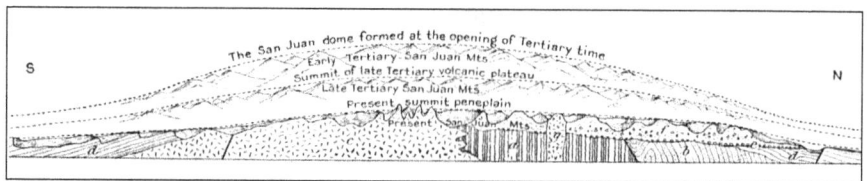

The San Juan Dome was 26,000 feet high but was reduced in size by millions of years of erosion. Now the highest peaks are "only" a little over 14,000-feet.

Reprinted from Wallace Atwood, *Eocene Glacial Deposits in Southwest Colorado,* USGS Professional Paper 95-B.

west. In some places in the San Juans, the volcanoes collapsed on themselves after "blowing out" massive amounts of material. This left deep circular depressions called "calderas" that were anywhere from a few hundred feet to fifty miles across; but today's mountains had still not been formed.

Surprisingly, the rugged, primitive nature of the San Juans came not from the fire and brimstone of volcanoes nor the fantastic thrusts and collapses in the earth's crust, but rather from ice – the melting, grinding, and continual push of huge, heavy glaciers that formed high on the cold slopes of the San Juan Dome. The area was so high and so huge that three different periods of glaciers occurred – the Cerro, the Durango, and the Wisconsin. The last of these glaciers were still around until about 10,000 years ago – just "seconds" in geological time. The scratches from the rocks that the glaciers carried with them can still be seen on exposed bedrock in many places in the San Juans. These huge, heavy glaciers formed deep gorges, high mountain parks, and steep-sided mountains as they slid downhill, tearing away the rock and exposing one of the most complete records of geological history found anywhere in the United States. Nineteen layers of rock formations are visible along today's Million Dollar Highway.

Although not nearly on the same scale, further erosion occurred from wind, water, and chemical reactions, giving the San Juans its jagged, unpolished roughness of today. All of this activity made the San Juan Mountains very steep and extremely rugged. Hubert Bancroft, famous historian of the nineteenth century, declared the San Juans to be:

> The wildest and most inaccessible region in Colorado, if not in all of North America. It is as if the great spinal cord of the continent has bent upon itself in some spasm of the earth, until the vertebrae overlapped each other, the effect being unparalleled ruggedness, and sublimity more awful than beautiful.... In the midst of a wild confusion of precipitous peaks and sharp ridges are a few small, elevated valleys, or as the early trappers

This view of Potosi Mountain near Ouray, taken from Governor's Basin, shows how rough the San Juans can be. In the winter, the gulch running down the center of the photograph is an avalanche path. The snow field near the bottom is near the Ruby Trust Mine, which has been hit several times by avalanches.

Marvin and Ruth Gregory Collection.

would have designated them, "holes," but which are without much relevancy denominated "parks" by modern Coloradans.

Because the San Juan Mountains are newly formed in geologic terms, erosion has not had a chance to completely wear them down, or even round them out and polish them as in most mountainous parts of the United States. Even after millions of years of erosion, the land that remainst is still high (mean elevation is 10,400 feet), and the mountains are still lofty (more than a hundred San Juan peaks are over 13,000 feet, and fourteen exceed 14,000 feet). In fact, about a quarter of all mountains in the United States that are over 13,000 feet are located in the San Juans, and 210 miles of the Continental Divide twist through the region.

The scenery along the Million Dollar Highway is not only spectacularly rugged but is extremely varied and breathtakingly colorful. The bold colors of the minerals vary from the dull grey of volcanic ash, to the greens of various copper compounds, to the bright reds of decomposing iron pyrites, iron oxides, or sandstone. Sprinkle in the dark greens of fir and pine, the blue green of spruce, and the fiery red and brilliant orange of the fall aspen and oak brush, and you have a symphony of hues that dazzles even the imagination of the artist.

But it wasn't the imposing scenery that brought prospectors to the San Juans – it was evident by the 1880s that the greatest mineral treasure chest in Colorado lay in these mountains. Generally, the rich San Juan ore had been injected into the local rock when volcanoes and uplifting fractured the local landscape. Magma, gas solutions, and mineralized water solutions were forced from deep in the earth upwards into the softer rocks, cracks, or crevices in the earth's crust. The valuable minerals cooled in the fissures as "hard rock veins" or layered in the softer rock in "pools," in what is called "replacement deposits." In most cases the richest ore was the first to be pushed into the rocks and crevices, so these more valuable minerals were, for the most part, left higher in elevation than later deposits. Erosion and chemical processes then exposed many of

Chapter 1: THE FIRST TWO BILLION YEARS   15

these veins, where they lay as an open treasure chest for millions of years – just waiting for prospectors to arrive and locate them.

Some of these veins are less than an inch wide, while others are more than a hundred feet across. Some are extremely rich, and some are almost worthless. And the nature of a particular vein can change within itself – a fabulously rich vein may become very poor just a foot or two further along its path. A vein may travel for miles and then just disappear, or a vein may be only a total of a few feet long. A vein may go down for hundreds of feet or just a few inches. There is no way to determine the economic worth or the size of an entire vein until it is explored by diamond drilling or mined. However, the volcanic activity in the San Juans did cause many of the veins to become highly mineralized. Most of that wealth could be found in an area of the San Juans that would be defined on maps by a right-angle triangle that runs through the present-day towns of Silverton, Ouray, and Telluride. This area

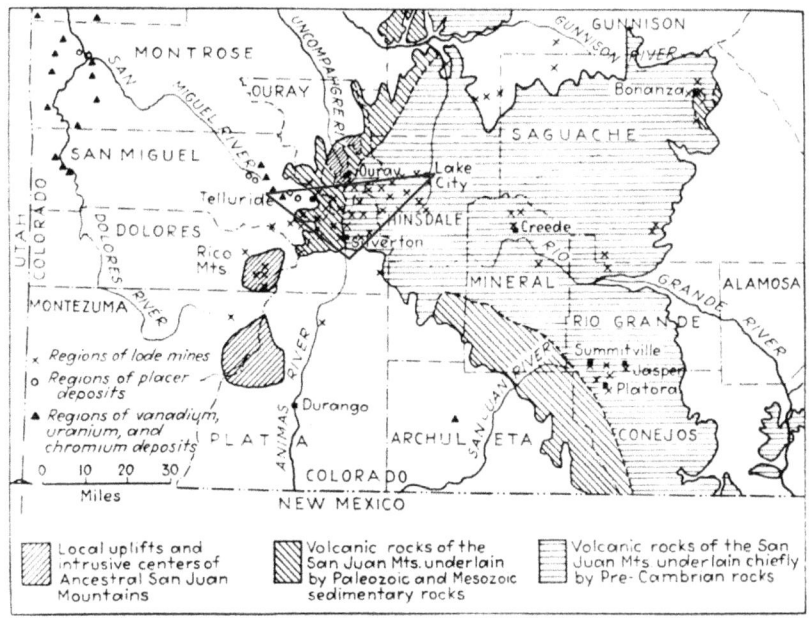

From Burbank, W. S., Camps of the San Juans, *Eng. Mining Journal,* 1935

came to be known as "The San Juan Triangle." Eventually almost 5,000 square miles (or about half) of the San Juans were incorporated into mining districts – and most of these were in the San Juan Triangle. (Three exceptions were pockets of rich ore at Rico, Lake City, and Creede.)

Since most of the Million Dollar Highway was built to service the rich mines of the San Juans, it might be well to take a moment and explain a few mining terms. "Prospectors" looked for rich ore and then usually sold their mines without doing any extensive work. "Miners" worked the claims but usually had no ownership in the property – they were being paid hourly. "Capitalists" bought

The early reports of gold and silver prospects in the San Juans were grossly over-exaggerated. This Harper's Weekly *drawing supposedly shows how easy it was to spot gold and silver veins in the mountain.*
Author's Collection.

the claims (or at least a partial ownership) from the prospector and infused money into the project to help buy equipment and pay the miners.

"Mills" crushed the ore and made some preliminary separation of the valuable metals from the waste rock. However, the minerals were usually found mixed together, and some waste rock was still present (sometimes at a rate of up to 50%). "Smelters" heated the ore and divided it into basically pure parts of gold, silver, copper, lead, and other valuable metals. All of these metals were usually found together in the ore from most San Juan mines, although their proportions might vary radically from mine to mine.

It is also important to note that the values given for ore are hard to compare, as different sources (including the mine themselves) often gave different weights of ore produced and different dollar amounts for the value of the ore (which did vary greatly because of fluctuating metal prices). It is especially hard to compare nineteenth century values against those of the twenty-first century, as the monetary worth of gold and silver in the last half of the nineteenth century was miniscule when compared to the values of these minerals today. For example, at the time of the writing of this book, silver sells for more than twenty times as much as it did before 1900, gold is over seventy times higher, and copper is a hundred times more valuable. To further complicate matters, the mines sometimes gave their values without pointing out that the ore was hand-sorted or that they were referring to the concentrate left after the ore was crushed and the waste rock removed. Sometimes the ore values were assayed, and sometimes they were only estimated. All this makes it very hard to determine the actual value of ore taken from a particular mine, and it is often impossible to compare ore values between mines. Values will therefore be given to merely give an indication of worth.

Although we refer to them as "The San Juan Mountains," the San Juans (called the "San Juan" in the nineteenth century) are not a single mountain range, but rather several mountain ranges – including among others the Sneffles Range, the San Miguel Mountains, and the Needles. This last range is the closest to the center of the ancient San Juan Dome and is therefore one of the highest, the most precipitous, the most primitive, and the most uninhabited in the nation. The different sub-ranges of the San Juans run in every direction, sometimes even running into each other and sometimes standing apart from the other ranges (such as the Wilson Range near Telluride). This makes it hard to calculate just how much territory is taken up by the San Juan Mountains, but in Colorado ten to twelve thousand square miles is a good estimate. A good portion (about a fourth) of the San Juans is in the northern part of New Mexico, pushing down almost to Taos and Abiqui, which are just north of Santa Fe. If the larger estimates of the area of the San Juans are used, and the portion in New Mexico is included, the San Juans total almost 20,000 square miles. That's bigger than Massachusetts, Rhode Island, and Connecticut combined. The roughness of the territory and the spread of ragged mountain ranges also meant that the San Juans were not settled from the same direction or all at once, but usually one mining district at a time.

Even though they are high and rugged, the San Juan Mountains are heavily forested – in fact, the San Juans incorporate all or part of five National Forests. The Million Dollar Highway travels through two of them – the San Juan and Uncompahgre National Forests. The San Juan National Forest, which the Million Dollar Highway passes through between Durango and Red Mountain Pass, is the largest National Forest in the state of Colorado with one and a half million acres of land. There are twenty-three varieties of evergreens in the forest (almost every variety in the state). Varieties of pine, spruce, fir, aspens, alder, box elder, willow, and cottonwoods are the most common trees. Timberline in the San Juans is about 11,500 to 12,000 feet, depending on the orientation of the slope. Above 12,000 feet, the vegetation is alpine tundra, which consists of mosses, low shrubs, and grasses. Please don't destroy the tundra by driving any type of vehicle on it. It could take hundreds of years to grow back because of the harsh climate at this high elevation.

Chapter 1: THE FIRST TWO BILLION YEARS ❋ 19

Even today, it is easy to imagine the problems that the early prospectors had to overcome to get through the San Juan Mountains. Yet good transportation was necessary to get supplies in and get the ore out.
Jan Smith Photo.

The San Juan climate is as rugged as its mountains. When asked what the weather was like in the San Juans, one early pioneer said "we have nine months of winter and three months of very late fall." Another local disagreed, as he felt there were only winter and the Fourth of July.

Spring comes late in these high mountains, so visitors are usually surprised to find snow on the ground in May and June and an abundance of San Juan flowers in what is mid-summer on the plains. With the many life zones in the mountains, spring slowly progresses up the slopes all summer long. The abundant spring and summer storms foster hundreds of species of wildflowers, from the Pasque flower at lower elevations in March to Columbines in the high mountain meadows in July. Daisies, roses, lilies, lupines, and paintbrush are just a few of the many varieties of native wildflowers.

Even dandelions seem acceptable here. In the late summer, the process reverses itself, as fall weather proceeds down the mountains.

The mighty Rio Grande River's headwaters are in the eastern San Juans near Stony Pass, and many of the major tributaries to the Colorado River come from the western San Juan Mountains. Four million acres drain into the southwest flowing Animas River, and it has forty major gulches in the San Juans– all of which are included in mining districts. The Uncompahgre and Gunnison Rivers also drain vast amounts of water from the northern San Juans west to the Colorado River.

Wildlife is abundant in the San Juans. Watch for them on or near the road, but don't approach them, as they are "wild" animals (as in dangerous). Especially don't stop if you hit an animal, as they can then be especially dangerous. Leave young animals alone, but call the Division of Wildlife if you feel they are orphaned or in distress (most phone numbers and addresses that you might need are at the back of this book). Large wildlife in the San Juans includes mountain lions, bears, moose, deer, foxes, elk, bobcats, and lynx. Smaller species include marmots, pika (some reports say they are becoming extinct, but we still see a lot of them in the San Juan high country), beaver, chipmunks, squirrels, and rabbits. There are also hundreds of varieties of birds, including bald and golden eagles.

Thousands of years ago Prehistoric Native Americans found this jumble of precipitous mountains to be hard to navigate, but evidence of the Clovis and Folsom cultures (who lived 7,000 to 13,000 years ago) has been found throughout the San Juans – even near the tops of the highest peaks. There were still glaciers in the high mountains when the earliest humans arrived. They were nomadic hunters, and some of the best hunting was right at the retreating edge of the glaciers. Their initial prey included the wooly mammoth and the saber-toothed tiger.

The Basketmakers, who were an early period of the agricultural Anasazi (a Navajo word for "Enemy Ancestors" and now also referred to as "Pueblo Ancestors"), were in the San Juan Mountains as early as 200 B.C. Among many other places, their dwellings have

Chapter 1: THE FIRST TWO BILLION YEARS

Although the government survey parties were generally very scientific, this scene of Rocky Mountain sheep surprised by the surveyors, which purports to be "extremely accurate," is in fact very exaggerated.
Frank Leslie's Popular Monthly. Author's Collection.

been found north of Durango near Fall Creek, throughout the Animas Valley, and within the present-day city limits of Durango. In fact, Durango was such a favorite spot for the Basketmaker and later the Anasazi, that in 1885, travel writer George Croffutt commented that ancient ruins were scattered everywhere around the new Durango town site. Anasazi arrowheads and pottery have been found throughout the nearby mountains and valleys.

The Ute Indians appeared on the scene about 1300 A. D. They came from the north and may well have been the reason that the Anasazi exited to the south at the same time. The Utes loved what they called "The Shining Mountains," but they didn't live in them year-round. They were nomadic and only spent time in the San Juans Mountains in the late spring, summer, and early fall, hunting game and gathering edible plants. The rest of the year the Utes were in the lower valleys that surround and cut into the San Juans, or in other parts of present-day Colorado, Utah, and northern New Mexico.

The Utes were brave and ferocious warriors and didn't hesitate to defend their homeland from other tribes. They made friends with the Spanish, who came into their territory from the south and from whom they obtained the horse and later firearms. The horse made life immeasurably easier for the Utes, and the firearms gave them a decided advantage over their Native American enemies. The Utes took command of their own destiny and occasionally, when they felt they were mistreated, they massacred entire Spanish settlements. Early American explorers found the Utes to be generally friendly, but they were known to occasionally attack small bands of white travelers. This hostile attitude became much more common as more and more whites tried to move into Ute territory.

Given the Ute's 500 years of habitation, well-worn trails were found throughout the San Juans by the earliest white explorers. These trails usually were broad and clear of vegetation because of the travois and tepee poles the Utes pulled behind their horses. The Ute trails were often upgraded into early "roads," as they were

After they obtained the horse, the Ute's life was much easier. This photo shows the breezy, brush wickiup used in the summer, and the much warmer tepee used in the winter. The photo was taken in 1899, but could easily have been 1799 except for the women's clothing.

Photo Courtesy Colorado Historical Society, F25,709.

generally the easiest and quickest way through the mountains. Interestingly, the main Ute trail into the San Juans from the San Luis Valley was up Rock Creek. Numerous pictographs have been found along the broad and well-traveled trail. Yet the whites made little use of the route.

Even though the Utes totally controlled their land, Spain claimed the San Juans from the time the area was visited on its southern edge by Coronado in 1541. His scribes recorded deserted Anasazi cliff dwellings. The entire San Juan region was included in Spain's Province of New Mexico (established in 1598), and the Spanish founded Santa Fe as the provincial capitol in 1609. Some

Spaniards were undoubtedly in the San Juan Mountains by the early part of the seventeenth century. The predominance of Spanish names (even "San Juan" is Spanish for St. John – probably John the Baptist who lived in the wilderness) furnishes hard evidence of the early Spanish habitation.

The eastern flanks of the San Juans spread out into the southern part of the San Luis Valley. In early times, the Utes, Navajo, and Apaches drove the ferocious Comanche from this valley, but they would return occasionally to kill and pillage. The "official" Spanish explorers spent most of their time in the valleys, like the San Luis, as opposed to "unofficial" prospectors who combed the mountains for gold and silver. Juan de Ornate and 300 families, soldiers, and priests followed the Rio Grande to Taos, New Mexico in 1608. He then sent his nephew Juan Zaldevar and fifty soldiers even further north. They explored some of the San Luis Valley and the very eastern San Juans, and Ornate himself went up the Rio Grande (its headwaters are in the San Juans near Silverton) the next year. By 1630, Spanish settlers inhabited the area along the Rio Grande near the present-day Colorado-New Mexico border.

By the late seventeenth century there were probably a few Spanish settlers living on the eastern slopes of the San Juans in the San Luis Valley and also just south of present-day Durango. The Pueblo Indian Revolts of 1680 ended Spanish occupation in what is now southern Colorado and northern New Mexico until de Vargas re-colonized Santa Fe in 1692.

It was 1761 before Juan de Rivera was sent to check out rumors of gold and silver in the San Juans, another sign indicating that previous Spanish adventurers had done prospecting in the San Juan Mountains. Rivera found a few Spanish settlers on the Animas River just four miles below present-day Durango at a good ford of the river. He also reported Spanish ranchers in the area. Rivera went up the Dolores River and along the west side of the La Plata and San Juan Mountains as far north as the Gunnison River, then traveled east up that river and over Cochetopa Pass, and back down the west side of the San Luis Valley, where he named many of the mountains and rivers in that part of the eastern San Juans. He crossed the Rio Grande near present-day Del Norte and then went south to New Mexico, thereby completing a full circle around the San Juans.

The famous Escalante-Dominguez expedition crossed the Animas River only four miles south of present-day Durango in 1776. It was probably the same ford that Rivera had used fifteen years earlier. The Escalante-Domingues expedition did not mention ranches or settlements in the Animas Valley. No one knows if the ranchers and settlers had been scared away by Utes or if they were known to be there and were not considered unique enough to be worth reporting.

At that time the Animas River's full name was "Rio de las Animas Perdidas" or "River of Lost Souls." Some historians propose that the name came from early Spanish settlers who drowned trying to cross the river in high waters, but others are convinced that the name was given the river by the members of the Escalante-Dominguez expedition, who were referring to the unknown nature of the land upstream. The river is now simply called the "Animas," in part to avoid confusion with another Rio de la Animas Perdidas near Trinidad on the eastern slope of Colorado, which is now called the "Purgatory" or "Purgatorie River."

The European concept of San Juan geography was very vague until Rivera circled the San Juans and Escalante-Dominguez traveled its western flank. Usually there was just a blank spot on the maps before that time. However the Rivera and Escalante expeditions gave Spain a pretty good idea of San Juan typography by the late eighteenth century. Escalante and Dominguez had a cartographer with them who drew a very accurate map. It included a lot of territory that the expeditions didn't pass through, so the information must have been obtained from Native Americans or other whites who had traveled into the areas not covered by the 1776 expedition.

Escalante wrote of rich ore in the La Plata Mountains (Spanish for "Silver Mountains"), where "years ago people came from New

ESCALANTE AND RIVERA EXPEDITION ROUTES

- - - - Juan de Rivera Expeditions 1761-1765 *(Note: Rivera's Diary has never been found. We can only speculate on his route(s).)*
———— Dominguez-Escalante Expedition 1776

Mexico and examined them... and carried away ore." There is a very good chance that he was referring to today's San Juan Mountains as the Sierra de la Platas are shown on his map as being on the east side of the Animas River. Almost a hundred years after Escalante and Dominguez (in 1867) Randolph Marcy, Inspector General for the U. S. Army, evidently made the same mistake when he wrote: "It is said that there are gold mines in the La Plata Mountains near the Animas River, and that they cannot be worked without the protection of troops." The Animas River is in today's San Juans and not in today's La Plata Mountains.

Although there were undoubtedly Spanish prospectors in the San Juans in the seventeenth, eighteenth, and early nineteenth centuries, their struggles are unrecorded, since they chose to go secretly so they would not have to give one-fifth of all they found to the crown.

In 1779, Don Juan Baptista de Anza, Governor of New Mexico Province, went after a small but deadly group of Comanche led by Cuerno Verde (Greenhorn), who had been raiding Spanish settlements. De Anza and 600 men went up the entire eastern side of the San Juans, trying to stay hidden so as to surprise the Comanche in the Sangre de Cristo Mountains across the San Luis Valley to the east. Local Mexicans told him that Mexican settlers were now all the way up the Rio Grande to near its headwaters.

It wasn't until the 1820s that the name "San Juans" was used for the region; since all of the Spanish maps made prior to that time refer to the mountains as "Sierra de las Guillas," ("Mountains of the Cranes"), or just the broader term "Sierra Madre," which was the Spanish name for the Rocky Mountains. Sierra de las Guillas was a reference by Spanish settlers to the thousands of cranes that migrate through the San Luis Valley on the immediate eastern side of the San Juans. The term "Rocky Mountains" was first used on American maps in 1794. Lewis and Clark adopted the name, and it became common used by Americans thereafter.

French trappers, prospectors, explorers, and traders were in the San Juan area by the 1790s as Spain had deeded "Louisiana" to France in 1763. The problem was that the San Juans were so remote that no one was sure where Louisiana's border was located in the Rocky Mountains. In 1800 Spain again took control of the San Juans, but many of the French mountain men continued to hunt and prospect after this time. There was considerable mining done by the French in the San Juans in the late eighteenth century around Wolf Creek Pass, and some French prospectors undoubtedly made it over to the Animas River. When the United States made the "Louisiana Purchase" from France in 1803, it received all land north and east of the Arkansas River. Once again, the problem was that the land was still basically uncharted, and the Americans supposedly did not know where the Arkansas River's headwaters lay. Spain did, and sent colonists into the San Luis Valley to make sure that the French and Americans would stay off their land. Spain even built a fort near La Veta Pass in 1819, but it was abandoned the same year. The San Juans passed from Spain to Mexico when the later gained its independence, but the San Luis Valley and eastern part of the San Juans were soon lost to the Republic of Texas, which even sent troops to guard its land in this area. Finally, the San Juans went to the United States when Texas became a state, thereby making five countries and the Ute Indians the legal owners of the San Juans at one time or another.

The core of the San Juan Mountains was so high and so rugged that many of the early "official" European and American expeditions considered them inaccessible, winter or summer, and like Rivera and Escalante-Dominguez, they skirted them once they could not find an easy route through them. The only white men going into the core of the San Juans were trappers from 1810 to 1844, who usually traded at Bent's Fort on the plains or with Antoine Rubidoux at his fort near present-day Delta, Colorado, or at Abiqui, Santa Fe, or Taos in New Mexico.

When Mexico received its independence from Spain in 1821, it encouraged rather than discouraged trappers to visit the San Juans. Some of these trappers came up the Uncompahgre and the Gunnison Rivers from Robidoux's Ft. Uncompahgre, and others went up the Rio Grande from the San Luis Valley. In 1833, Col. William Walton and a party of "trappers" went up the Dolores River to Trout Lake seeking gold as well as furs. Until 1844, when Ft. Uncompahgre was destroyed, Antoine Leroux, Kit Carson, Charles Autobees, Tom Tobin, "Uncle" Dick Wootton, Antoine Robideaux, and others spent time trapping off and on in the San Juans.

The rather cumbersome sounding West Branch of the North Branch of the California Trail (used by many early trappers and merchants) ran from Santa Fe up the far eastern edge of the San Juan Mountains in the San Luis Valley, over Cochetopa Pass, and then followed the Gunnison River west along the northern edge of the San Juans. The main route taken by most early Spanish explorers going to California was a hundred and fifty miles south and ran along the southern edge of the San Juans and then north up the

Chapter 1: THE FIRST TWO BILLION YEARS

Dolores River (to the immediate west of the San Juans), and over the Uncompahgre Plateau to the Uncompahgre River. Neither of the routes went into the heart of the San Juans.

From 1848 to 1850 Colorado was in unorganized United States' territory, then from 1850 to 1861 eastern Colorado was in Kansas Territory and western Colorado was in the Territory of Utah. During this time the United States was very actively exploring transportation routes to California, but no one found a successful route through the San Juans. With the mad rush of hopeful prospectors to the Pike's Peak area in 1859, the Rocky Mountains white population exploded so much so that the Territory of Colorado was created in 1861. Most of the 1859-1860 prospectors found that claims had already been filed on all the potential mining districts on the eastern slope of Colorado. Many returned home disappointed, but a few hardy men started to explore what later became western Colorado.

Chapter 2

THE 'SILVERY' (AND SOMETIMES "GOLDEN") SAN JUANS

IN THE SPRING OF 1859 American prospectors rushed to what soon became the Territory of Colorado, where gold had been discovered in Clear Creek near present-day Denver. It was only a few months before there were claims filed all along what is now known as the "Front Range." However, there was nowhere near enough gold to be split among almost 100,000 men, many of whom had bet everything they had that they would "strike it rich." Within a few months over half of the men went back home disappointed, but many others refused to give up and traveled further into the Rocky Mountains to look for their fortunes. Some prospectors chose to travel southwest, as it was apparent to the thorough observer that there was a mineral belt that ran in that direction. By late summer of 1859, American prospectors were entering the San Juan Mountains of southwest Colorado.

Chapter 2: THE 'SILVERY' (AND SOMETIMES "GOLDEN") SAN JUANS ❖ 31

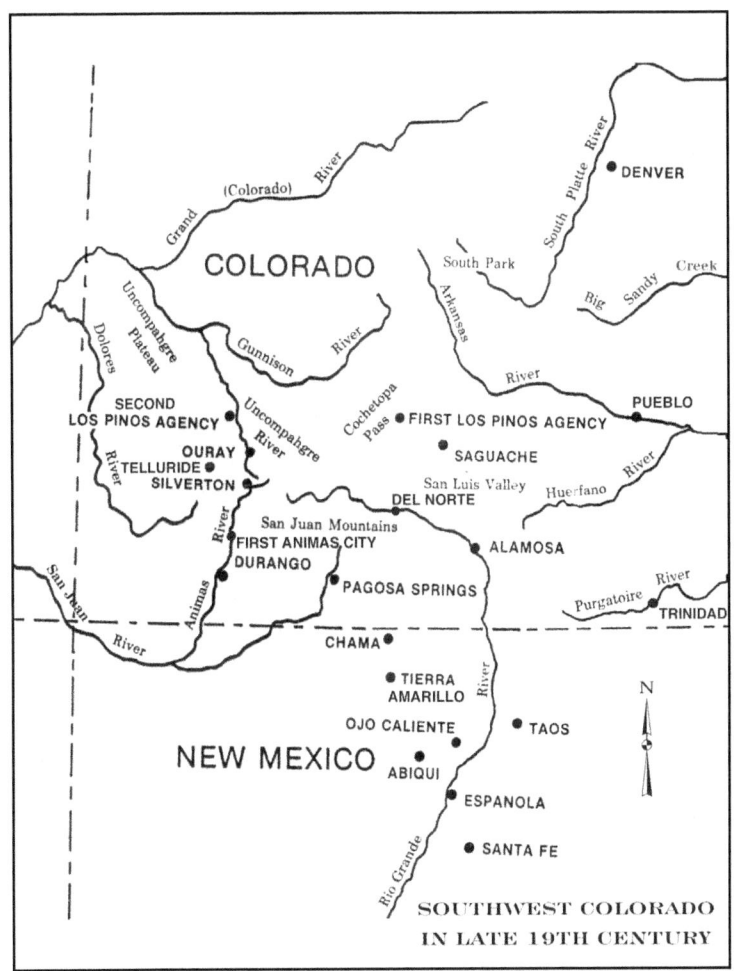

There are many conflicting accounts concerning these hopeful men; but as best as can be determined, the true record follows. In August of 1859, a group of unsuccessful Pike's Peak prospectors worked their way into the Arkansas River Valley, then over Poncha Pass into the San Luis Valley, over Cochetopa Pass, down the Gunnison River, and up the Uncompahgre River. Albert Pfeiffer and Henry Mercure spent a few weeks just downstream from present-day Ridgway and reported that they had found signs of gold in the river. It was a lucky discovery, but also very limited. Although there wasn't a lot of placer (or free) gold in the San Juans, one exception was north of present-day Ridgway, where glaciers had brought out considerable gold from the hard rock deposits at Gold Hill near Ouray.

One group of about 100 men from the Denver area heard rumors of the gold strike and started for the San Juans, but most dropped out as the going got rough. Only about sixteen men made it to the eastern edge of the San Juans in the San Luis Valley, and then they too turned back. It took true determination and grit to prospect in the wilds of the Rocky Mountains in those days.

In August, 1860, in the second half of the Pike's Peak Gold Rush, Charles Baker, a former California gold-placer prospector, made the first recorded entrance into the park in the center of the San Juans that would eventually bear his name. He and six others were among the prospectors who had given up on finding new gold discoveries near Denver and Pikes Peak; and, having heard the rumors of gold in the San Juans and with the financial backing of S. B. Kellog, they (like the Mercure and Pfieffer party) traveled over Cochetopa Pass. However, Baker's group went up the Lake Fork of the Gunnison and eventually headed south over what later came to be called "Cinnamon Pass."

Baker was a strange man, who reportedly had other motives besides personal wealth. As opposed to many of the men in Colorado who were trying to escape the impending Civil War, Baker was evidently a hard-core Confederate who hoped to claim a mineral rich southern Colorado for the South. He also hoped New Mexico would join the Confederacy, or in the alternative be quickly occupied by Texas when the impending war broke out. The rugged and wild country around what came to be known as "Baker's Park" was in the middle of Ute Territory, so the members of Baker's party were said to have kept one eye on the ground looking for gold and the other on the nearby mountains looking for Utes.

Unfortunately, few signs of gold were actually found. The group didn't grasp at the time that the small amounts of placer gold that they found had been brought out of the nearby mountains by glaciers or erosion. Later the accepted practice would be to follow the gold "float" back to its source at a vein.

In 1860 the accepted southern route to the San Juans from Taos or Santa Fe was to travel up the Rio Chama from where it joined with the Rio Grande, through the early Spanish settlements of Abiqui and Tierra Amarilla (both settled by the mid-1700s) to the present-day Pagosa Springs (there was only the hot water springs and no town at this time), and then proceed west to the Animas River. Abiqui was founded in 1754, and it was a major "jumping off" point for travelers going either north to the San Luis Valley or west on the California or Old Spanish Trail. After about 1810, Abiqui and Taos were accessed by the "Trapper's Trail," which ran from Bent's Fort, northeast of La Veta Pass over Sangre

Sangre de Cristo Pass, also known as "Trapper's Pass," was the entry way into the mountains. From Bent's Fort, travelers would go through the Sangre de Cristo Mountains into the San Luis Valley, then south to Taos, Abiqui, or Santa Fe.

From an 1855 sketch by J. M. Stanley. Author's Collection.

de Cristo Pass, then southwest through the San Luis Valley. After the United States won this territory in the Mexican-American War, Fort Massachusetts was built by the United States to protect American travelers, and then replaced by Ft. Garland in 1858. By 1860, Mexican-American settlers were already at Del Norte and La Loma on the western edge of the San Luis Valley.

Abiqui became a wintering and supply spot for the prospectors, trappers, and traders in and around the San Juans. It had grown to a population of about 3,600 by the 1820s and was the third largest settlement in New Mexico Province at the time. In the 1840s, it was also a military post and a Ute trading center. Taos was another very important trading and supply center for those traders, prospectors, and explorers going into the San Luis Valley and perhaps further north over Cochetopa Pass or east over Sangre de Cristo or La Veta Pass.

By October, 1860, Baker had sent out glowing but false reports that gold was being found at the rate of twenty-five cents a pan; and, presumably because of his Confederate sympathies, he encouraged future prospectors to enter the San Juans from the south, and not from the north or east. Other prospectors had joined Baker and reported back to Denver that they were finding small amounts of gold, and that the Utes seemed to be generally friendly. The *Rocky Mountain News* of October 12, 1860, carried an article about Baker's Park, which optimistically declared, "the metaliferous development of (Colorado), if not all of North America, reaches its culmination point in that region." Baker also wrote a full report of his 1860 trip that was printed in the November 29, 1860 *Santa Fe Gazette*. He claimed to have found extensive gold placers that he believed to be much richer than those in the 150-mile stretch from Boulder to Pikes Peak. Baker made the grossly exaggerated prediction that "there will be not less than 25,000 Americans engaged in mineral and agricultural pursuits (in the San Juans)…within a year, perhaps double that number." These totally unsubstantiated reports set off a small stampede of prospectors over the next few months — all headed into the San Juans from the south.

Chapter 2: THE 'SILVERY' (AND SOMETIMES "GOLDEN") SAN JUANS ❦ 35

Even though the Ute Indians, who lived in the San Juans for 500 years, were "legally" given their land in 1863 and 1868, Americans ignored the legalities in their search for gold and silver, especially in the San Juan Mountains.

Harper's Weekly, Oct. 25, 1879. Author's Collection.

The *Santa Fe Gazette* also printed the reports of Albert Pfeiffer and H. Mecure of their prospecting in the San Juans in the early summer of 1860, that they had found many gold deposits. In 1861, they came back to the San Juans from the south, and Baker used their information to help establish the most practical southern route to Baker's Park – then claimed the route as a toll road.

One very possible reason that Baker sent out such glowing reports was that he was evidently as much a financier and land speculator as he was a prospector. There is some evidence that Kellog, Baker, Pfieffer, and Mecure were acting together in speculation of great and rapid growth in the San Juans. There were conflicting reports of gold in the San Juans. A prospector who signed his name "G.W." wrote Williams Byers of the *Rocky Mountain News* after his return from the San Juans in late 1860: "If this is humbug – and there is little doubt about that – it is a severe one, and disastrous to many." But even G. W. had the eternal optimism of the prospector, as he also reported that his next year's search for gold and silver in the San Juans would certainly be better.

(G. W. well could have been the man in the story about a prospector who died and went to heaven, but when he got to the Pearly Gates was told by St. Peter that Heaven already had its quota of prospectors. The man thought a while and then started a rumor that there was a gold strike in Hell. When he checked back with St. Peter, he was told that he could come in now as many of the prospectors had left to look for gold in Hell. The prospector thought another minute, then replied that he would have to pass, as he would like to check out the new rumor himself.)

By late 1860, Baker had already laid out the first town site ("Baker City"), organized a mining district, and chartered the toll road from Baker's Park to Abiquiu, New Mexico Territory. He was in the middle of Ute Territory and absolutely nothing had been built, but Baker obviously had grandiose plans. On the other extreme some parties who knew Baker well, reported behind his back that he was a mad man, trying to draw attention and glory to himself.

On December 14, 1860, S. B. Kellogg, Thomas Pollack, and F. R. Rice started on another trip to Baker's Park, leading several hundred prospectors from Denver, including some who had their families with them. Several smaller groups also started out during the winter of 1860-61. People joined and left this group as they slowly made their way towards the San Juans. A few of the smaller expeditions apparently went into Baker's Park for short times during the winter but reported that they found nothing of any great importance. Most of these prospectors left to the south and reported that Baker's proposed toll road from Abiqui was actually being worked on during the winter – but not by Baker (perhaps he had sold his interest or his financial backers had taken over.)

Because of the snow, cold, and lack of roads, it took the large group of prospectors from Denver almost three months, via Sangre de Cristo Pass and the San Luis Valley, to reach a level and fertile spot in the southern San Juans where the Animas River emerged from the Animas Canyon. There they stopped and built cabins and named their small settlement "Animas City." It was a very good location for a town, and a logical spot for a bridge to be built over the Animas River. Crops could be grown at this elevation, and what later became known as "Pinkerton Hot Springs" was nearby. Timber and game were also abundant. The site was about twelve miles north of present-day Durango.

Because of the excitement to get to Baker's Park and strike it rich, the whole group spent only a short time in Animas City. Even though it was still winter, the lure of gold was too great. The prospectors built Baker's Bridge over the Animas River and headed on towards Cascade Creek. Reportedly eight to ten of the men left their families in the log cabins at Animas City. Because of the deep snow, the main party stayed for a few weeks in late March at "Camp Pleasant," which was located slightly south of the present-day Durango Mountain ski area near Castle Rock, where they found a good spring for drinking water. The prospectors probably didn't know it, but Colorado became a United States Territory in February, 1861.

In early April, 1861, the group at Camp Pleasant sent scouts on to Baker's Park, and they found that the upper end of the nine-mile, hour glass-shaped park was already being actively prospected. Baker and a few other men had bypassed the large group and were working a spot at the far north end of the park, about eight miles north of present-day Silverton (somewhere around where Howardsville and Eureka were eventually built). When the scouts returned, the large group left more of their families at Camp Pleasant, and most of the men went on to Baker's Park. The new arrivals quickly spread out and panned the streams in and around the park, but they were only able to find small amounts of gold. In fact, they averaged only fifty cents a day in gold compared to the ten dollars (twenty-five cents a pan) that Baker had claimed.

The group's hardships were beginning to take a toll, and several people even died. By May, some of the group returned to

These prospectors are looking for a little "color" in their pan. While California prospectors did well using this technique, it didn't work in the San Juans, where the gold was still locked into hardrock veins. Early prospectors could pan all day and might find only fifty cents in small gold flakes.

Postcard from Author's Collection.

The first prospectors in the San Juans were on Ute land and were not supposed to build permanent structures, so they used tents and camped as seen here. However, this required them to leave in the winter for lower elevations.

Harper's Weekly, Nov. 10, 1883. Author's Collection.

Camp Pleasant or Animas City, and others had already left these camps and were on their way back to Denver. The prospectors who remained were so disappointed that they convened a miner's court to try Baker for fraud. He was almost hung because of his exaggerations, but legend has it that he saved himself by panning gold on the spot and finding enough "color" that the other men dropped the matter and went back to work. Nevertheless, the vast majority of the group soon left the San Juans, most by mid-summer via Stony and Cunningham Passes, which were now known to be shorter routes to get back to Denver.

Even Baker and a few other diehards left Baker's Park by winter, since their supplies were exhausted. Word had come that the Civil War had started; so, being Southerners, they left to the south via Mineral or Bear Creek, and then went down Cascade or Lime Creek – the then accepted southern routes in and out of Baker's Park. Although Baker went directly to New Mexico and then back East to the Civil War, several members of his party wintered for a time at Animas City before leaving the San Juans.

The Denver papers began to publish reports that nothing of interest had been found in the San Juans, that it was very hard to travel in that area, and that Utes were killing white prospectors. Several of the disgruntled prospectors that had been to Baker's Park reported that traders in New Mexico were spreading the rumors of gold discoveries in the San Juans to try to spur on sales of overstocked goods. However the stories told by the men coming out of the San Juans were very conflicting, so it was very hard to tell exactly what was happening. And it must be remembered that the newspapers of Denver, who now declared the "San Juan Excitement" to be "Humbug," were protecting their own turf by trying to keep men in the Denver area, since many of the original "Pike's Peakers" were heading to other parts of Colorado or back East. Many men who had actually been to Baker's Park were now calling Baker a "maniac" or "lunatic" to his face for leading them and their families into an area that was so dangerous and now seemed so worthless. The prospectors complained of the altitude, the cold, the snow, the short prospecting season, the lack of agricultural land, the lack of game, and, most of all, the lack of adequate transportation to and through the San Juan Mountains.

The San Juans were therefore ignored or forgotten for almost a decade, but the stories that the early prospectors later told were responsible for other mining expeditions being formed, once the clues of the gold flakes and a heavy black sand that was also found in abundance were reconsidered. There were riches to be had in Baker's Park, and some of it had already been found. Most of the early prospectors had been looking for gold nuggets and didn't follow the fine gold flakes to the source. They also either missed, or more likely ignored that the black sand in their pans was galena – a silver and lead ore. If they knew that the black sand contained silver, they may have intentionally passed it over, as silver was only worth about one-twentieth of an equal amount of gold and would be very costly to transport to smelters because of the weight added by the lead in the galena.

Meanwhile, thirty-five miles to the north of Bakers Park, a few prospectors had come back to the present-day Ridgway-Ouray area in the spring of 1861. One group even spent the winter of 1861-62 in the little bowl that now holds the City of Ouray. The party, which included O. H. Harker, came by way of Ft. Garland in the San Luis Valley and then went over Cochetopa Pass. Harker was later quoted as saying that "it took nerve and staying qualities to prospect in the San Juans in those days." It was certainly a true statement, and the Ouray area was ignored for over a decade.

There was another major problem that prevented the able-bodied men who remained in Colorado from prospecting in the San Juans. All of the soldiers in Colorado were now fighting in the Civil War. Colorado was a part of the Union; but the war was basically going on back East, so both Union and Confederate sympathizers left Colorado. This meant there were very few, if any, soldiers available to protect prospectors. The Utes made a treaty with the United States in 1863, in which they agreed to be peaceful and were allocated the land west of Colorado's Front Range. As most Native Americans, they had little or no concept of ownership of land when the United States deeded them the property they had already lived on for five centuries. The Utes now demanded that under United States law the whites must stay off Ute land; and because so few able-bodied white men were in Colorado, the Americans played it safe and avoided Ute territory.

However the prospectors didn't like their situation. As geologist F. L. Ransome put it: "At a time (the 1860s and early 1870s) when every gulch in the Sierra Nevada was a scene of picturesque activity, the Indians and the mountain sheep were as yet undisturbed in their possession of the San Juans." Three years after the Civil War ended, in an 1868 treaty, the Utes gave up the San Luis Valley, but kept control of the San Juan Mountains. The Utes had at first tolerated the few whites who trespassed on their land; but, as the number of white prospectors grew, they often required payment from Americans who were on their land, or in some cases they simply killed the American prospectors outright. One early San Juan merchant, piece by piece, gave away a whole wagon load of supplies in an attempt to keep the Utes peaceful; but, afterwards, the Utes demanded more payment or that the party of whites must leave their land or be killed. This was not an idle threat; one estimate (probably exaggerated) was that Utes had killed ten percent of all the whites in the San Juans up to this time. Many of the killings were on the road between Abiqui and Animas City (Baker's "preferred" route). No wonder that the prospectors soon chose the treacherous Stony Pass trail from the San Luis Valley instead of the trail along the Animas River from the south.

Prospectors and trappers weren't the only Americans in the San Juans during the 1850s, 1860s, and early 1870s. The United States government sent several official military expeditions to explore the land that had been won in the Mexican-American War in 1848. Some of the first government explorers who ventured into the San Juans met with odious fates. In 1853, Captain John W. Gunnison and his group skirted the San Juan Mountains over Cochetopa Pass and then passed along the northern edge. Lt. Edward Beckwith, who traveled with Gunnison, reported about Cochetopa that "no mountain pass ever opened up more favorable for a railroad than this." Piute Indians killed Gunnison shortly after he passed into present-day Utah. Only Beckwith and three men escaped. The Gunnison massacre was one of the worst U. S. Army defeats by Native Americans in the American West up to that time, and it didn't leave a very good impression as to the friendliness of the natives along this route.

In 1858 Senator Thomas Hart of Missouri contacted fur trapper Antoine Leroux to determine the best way to go through the Rockies. Leroux, quite correctly, suggested the route from Bent's Fort over Sangre de Cristo Pass, Cochetopa Pass, and down the Gunnison to the Old Spanish Trail. John C. Freemont was sent to check out the route. but he did not go over Cochetopa Pass for some unknown reason. He failed in an attempt in December, 1848, to cross through the La Garita Mountains (northeast of the San Juans) despite being led by the well-known and respected western mountain man Preacher Bill Williams. Freemont lost ten of his men and all of his 120 mules to deep snow, extreme cold, and hunger. He ended up backtracking and going around the San Juans to the south. He later described the San Juans as "the highest, most rugged, most impracticable, and inaccessible of all the Rocky Mountain Ranges, inaccessible to trapper and hunter even in the summer time."

The northern route around the San Juans was used again after the "Mormon War" (which actually was just the threat of a war) by Col. William W. Loring, when he was traveling from Utah to Ft. Union in New Mexico on July 19, 1858, with Antoine Leroux as his guide. After his fifty wagons and 350 men passed over the northern portion of the California Trail, it might have been packed into what could be called "a road." Trapper Jim Baker led Captain Randall Marcy and sixty-four men over Cochetopa in December 1858. They came very close to perishing in the deep snows that had already piled up on the pass by that time of year.

Chapter 2: THE 'SILVERY' (AND SOMETIMES "GOLDEN") SAN JUANS ❋ 43

The Freemont expedition later published this gloomy looking drawing showing the La Garita Mountains, where some of them lost their lives and all of their animals died from hunger and freezing cold.
Author's Collection.

The Cochetopa route should have become accepted as the way to get around the San Juans if not through them. Cochetopa Pass was definitely the easiest route over the Continental Divide for a hundred miles to the north or south and therefore had a well-worn Ute and trapper trail. Why the Americans didn't choose to use it more remains somewhat of a mystery. Both Gunnison and Freemont (on a later expedition) went over Cochetopa Pass and declared it to be passable for a railroad. However, the route was evidently not used for such because no one at the time figured out a successful route through the Black Canyon, about twenty miles to the west or over Blue Mesa to the south of the Black Canyon. Later the D&RG Railroad's engineers surveyed a route that ran its rails through the Black Canyon to a point where they left the canyon at Cimarron. The rails then went over Cerro Pass to the Uncompahgre Valley.

Lt. Col. E. H. Bergman, while scouting the southern edge of the San Juans for a site for the location of Ft. Plummer in 1867, came upon the remains of the first Animas City and reported that "we are astonished to find the signs of civilization and the indication of the presence of white men ... scattered profusely through

Cochetopa Pass (which means "Pass of the Buffalo" in Ute) was used for thousands of years as the main route for Native Americans going over the Continental Divide in what is now central Colorado. This sketch shows a Spanish prospector or trader on the route in 1855.

Sketch by R. H. Rem. Author's Collection.

Chapter 2: THE 'SILVERY' (AND SOMETIMES "GOLDEN") SAN JUANS ✣ 45

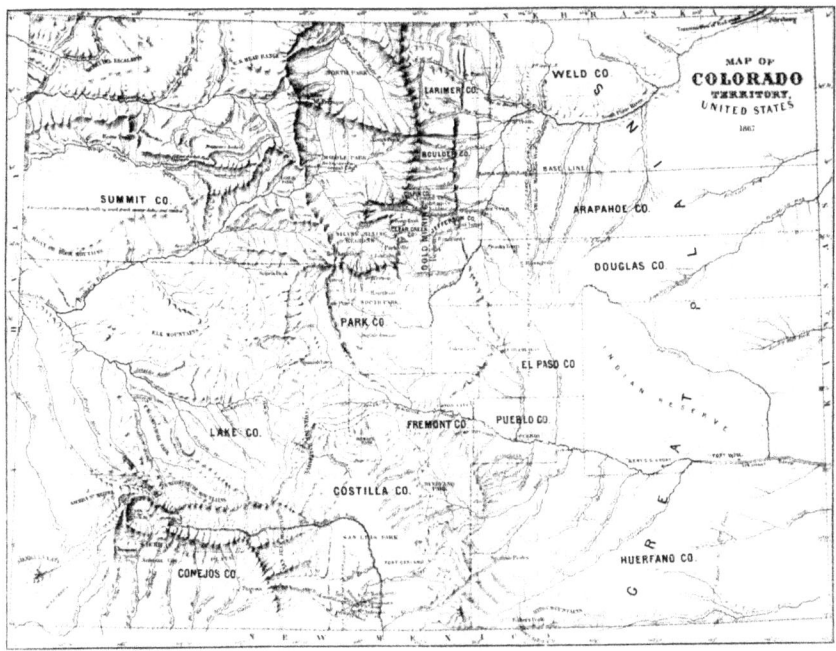

This 1867 map shows that Americans were generally familiar with the San Juans (in the lower left corner), although they got a little of the topography wrong. Baker's Park is shown as totally surrounded by mountains with the Rio Grande leading up to it.

From J. P. Whitney, *Colorado, In the United States of America.* Author's Collection.

some fifty half-decayed log houses...." The cabins were probably not in bad repair, but they had no roofs, since tarps had been used for that purpose and were later removed. The cabins could not have been in "half-decay" after just a few years in Colorado's dry climate. Bergman also reported that the Ute Indians were not friendly. He felt the settlement had been abandoned quickly (he somehow even gave the date of July 3, 1861) because of a Ute scare. Household, mining, and cooking tools and utensils were left behind, but more than likely to make it easier and quicker to get back to the front range.

Again, it is interesting to note that Bergman said that Animas City was in the La Plata Mountains, giving credence to Escalantes reference to the San Juans as the "La Plata Mountains." The Utes had burned Baker's Bridge, so Bergman couldn't cross the Animas River at that point. However, the bridge, if burned, was reconstructed on the same spot, perhaps when Baker and others returned in 1868 to do more prospecting. (Baker was killed shortly thereafter by Indians in Arizona.) Bergman suggested the site of Animas City for Fort Plummer, but a location at Pagosa Springs eventually won out.

There were also many official geological expeditions to the San Juans. J.J. Newberry was there in 1859 for the U. S. Geological Survey. Lt. E. F. Ruffner and J. J. Stevenson were checking out the gold and silver situation in 1873 (mainly by interviewing prospectors); and the Hayden Survey made a detailed geologic study and survey in 1873-74, publishing wonderful, detailed geological and typographical maps of the San Juans in 1877. Some postulate that these maps did as much for the development of the San Juans as any other single action.

It was 1870 before other members of the 1860-61 prospecting party, now generally known as "the Baker Party," returned to the San Juans. They had learned in the meanwhile that they needed to look for hard rock veins instead of gold nuggets, and that the black sand in their pans was silver; but they soon discovered that even though silver and gold were present in considerable quantities, it was a difficult and trying challenge to wrench the precious minerals from their hiding places. This new concept was evident to Special Agent William Arny, who was in the lower Animas River area in May, 1870, checking out white conflicts with the Utes. He wrote that "on the stream are good placer gold diggings and in the mountains above are rich gold and silver quartz deposits."

What was required was what is now called "hard rock mining." The ore had to be blasted or laboriously picked from the hard rock, then brought to the surface, crushed, sorted, and eventually bagged and shipped to smelters to extract the rich minerals. This process was costly, and the most expensive factor in the whole procedure was the transportation of the ore through the remote, rugged, and steep terrain – much of which was still owned and

Chapter 2: THE 'SILVERY' (AND SOMETIMES "GOLDEN") SAN JUANS ✣ 47

occupied by the Ute Indians. In the winter, there would be the added challenge of transporting the ore through deep snows and potentially hazardous avalanches.

In 1870, Dempsey Reese, Miles Johnson, Abnah French, and Thomas Blair, members of the original Baker Party of 1860, discovered rich silver veins and a sizeable gold vein in what came to be called "Arrastra Gulch." The party brought the ore down from their mine by a 1,000-foot tram, and crushed the ore in an arrastra they built. They then panned the crushed rock for gold. An "arrastra" is a Spanish device. It is an enclosed circular stone bed with a post in the middle and a horizontal arm (leg) attached to an animal, which walks around the outside of the bed pulling a heavy stone or stones attached to the arm. The heavy stones smash the ore that has been put into the circle. The men named their discovery the "Little Giant Mine."

Early San Juan prospectors panned for gold, but these men are working a hardrock claim, blasting a shaft into the rock, and then removing the loose rock to follow the vein.

Harper's Weekly, November 10, 1883. Author's Collection.

News of this rich new mine spread fast, and by the late summer of 1870 there were about fifty prospectors in Baker's Park, with most of their attention focused on Arrastra Gulch. That fall the men working at the Little Giant Mine returned to Santa Fe for the winter and while there had their ore assayed. The samples were found to be quite rich, so Reese and French returned in the spring of 1871, this time with financial backing from the Governor of New Mexico Territory, and with six other men to help them with their work at the Little Giant Mine. Late that year they sold part of their mine to E. M. Hamilton, who as partial payment ordered a "prefab" crushing mill shipped to the mine. The mill was transported over Stony Pass in 1872 in the first "wagons" to make the trip. When the mill came over Stony, the freighters supposedly snubbed the wheels, made the wagons into sleds, and brought the heavy equipment down by gravity, using ropes wrapped around trees for brakes. After the mill was assembled the next year, the concentrated ore was reported to assay at $1,000 to $4,000 a ton – even with the high freight rates, it was worth carrying to the smelter. A small cluster of cabins called "Bullion City" was erected at the mouth of Arrastra Gulch – the first settlement in the core of the San Juans. The Reese party's action in seeking "capitalists" to financially back them in their venture was something that San Juan prospectors would resort to on a regular basis in the future.

Although the discovery of gold at the Little Giant was exciting, it was short-lived and really not that profitable. In 1871, the mine only produced twenty-seven tons of gold ore worth about $150 per ton. In 1872, it produced $12,000 in ore out of a total of about $15,000 shipped out of the entire San Juans. A lot more ore was probably produced by other mines, but it was not yet economical to ship it out. The Little Giant was only mined for a few years after 1872 with a total production of a few hundred tons. The pay streak in the Little Giant vein was small, and disputes arose over title to the property since it had been filed on before the land belonged to the United States, so the property was basically abandoned.

Chapter 2: THE 'SILVERY' (AND SOMETIMES "GOLDEN") SAN JUANS

By 1871, virtually all of the prospectors in Baker's Park were looking for hard rock lode claims. One party of about fifty men had come in to the park as soon as the snow melted enough for travel. The Utes were naturally very upset about the large number of prospectors, as well as the arrival of the ore-crushing mill, followed a little later by a sawmill. They asked their Indian agent to get the trespassers off their land. The federal government, amazingly, did take steps to warn prospectors to stay out of the San Juans, but many of the gold and silver hungry men came anyway. The Utes were typically thought of as savages who were standing in the way of progress. This was during the time of "Manifest Destiny" in the United States, and citizens of the period felt it their duty to crush what they felt were "less than human" natives.

Because it became a major freight and supply center for the San Juan discoveries, the population of the settlement of Del Norte increased substantially. The town was surveyed and platted in 1872, across the Rio Grande from the slightly older settlement of La Loma. Del Norte would eventually become the major supply point for Silverton, Lake City, and Summitville (another new San Juan discovery near Wolf Creek Pass). Del Norte was also a place where many of the prospectors went to spend the winter. The town boomed even more in 1874 after the Brunot Treaty went into effect and by 1875, 1,500 people lived permanently in the town.

By the end of 1872 there were hundreds of prospectors in the San Juans, and as more and more valuable discoveries were made, the federal government decided to change its tactics and try to get the Utes to sell their land. Meanwhile United States troops were sent to patrol the San Juans and try to prevent trouble between the two groups. Later, it was revealed that one of the government's main goals was to determine just how much gold and silver was in the San Juan Mountains, so that officials could decide if it would be worth the trouble to get the Utes to move out.

Even though the Utes continuously protested the intrusion of the miners, by July of 1873, the ore-crushing mill was operating at the Little Giant Mine, and it had become one of the best-known mines in southwest Colorado. The Utes kept constant pressure on the 300 or 400 prospectors in the San Juans to get off Ute land. No major incident occurred, but the Utes vehemently and continuously demanded that the United States remove the whites. The miners, therefore, erected no permanent buildings and lived in tents and brush structures.

Ouray, chief of the Utes, had originally balked at giving up more Ute land. Ouray was an interesting combination of cultures. He had grown up near Abiqui, New Mexico, where (as was common at the time) he had been sold by his family into slavery to a Spanish couple during his younger years. There he learned fluent Spanish, became a friend of Kit Carson, and learned firsthand the might of the United States war machine during the Mexican-American War. Ouray first became prominent when he was a translator for the 1863 Ute treaty, then later he was appointed by the whites as the first overall Chief of the Utes. Somehow Ouray was actually able to assume this position among his people.

Ouray asked why the white "chief" couldn't control his men. He wanted to know why the white chief wasn't man enough to keep his promises. He reminded the Americans that two previous treaties (in 1863 and 1868) had promised that this would be Ute land "forever." They were good questions, and created an unusual and frustrating position for the Americans to be in. Usually Native Americans fought rather than negotiated with the Americans. If the United States won a "war" with the Indians, they could simply take their land. But under United States law, this land belonged to the Utes.

Finally, Otto Mears and Felix Brunot, two of the negotiators for the Americans, came up with the idea of finding Chief Ouray's lost son (who had been stolen by the Arapahoe many years before) if Ouray would promise to give up the San Juans in return. The idea worked. Ouray's son was found and Ouray convinced the rest of the Utes to give up the area. What now seems an insignificant point to whites may have also made a huge difference in the Ute's change of heart. Under the treaty, the Utes would be allowed to

Chapter 2: THE 'SILVERY' (AND SOMETIMES "GOLDEN") SAN JUANS ❦ 51

Chief Ouray of the Utes was known for his peace-keeping abilities, which ran a fine line between being a traitor or a far-sighted visionary who kept his people from total destruction by the whites.
　　　　　　　　　　　　　　　Main Street Photography. Author's Collection.

continue to hunt, fish, and gather food in the San Juans, which had always been their main use for the mountainous territory. They would also receive $25,000 per year as payment for the land. Ouray is quoted as saying, "We are perfectly willing to sell our mountain land, and hope the miners will find heaps of gold and silver; and we have no wish to molest them or make them any trouble. We do not want they should go down into our valleys however, and kill and scare away our game." It is even possible that the Utes had no understanding that they had lost "title" to their land, since Native Americans had little concept of "owning" the land, and they would be able to continue to use it as they always had. This important hunting, fishing, and gathering provision was later ignored by the United States during the entire twentieth century; but in 2008 the Utes (pursuant to the Brunot Treaty) were again allowed to fish and hunt in the San Juans without regard to state or federal law.

Under the new treaty, Ouray was further given $1,000 a year for personal use. Negotiator Otto Mears had proposed this as a necessary and important provision. But did Ouray sell out his people? Or was he farsighted enough to know it was futile to fight the whites? Mears said Ouray deserved the money for the time spent in negotiating the treaty. It is a point that is still debated among historians; but in September, 1873, the Utes signed the Brunot Treaty, although it was not until March, 1874, that the treaty was officially ratified by the U. S. Senate and took effect.

Unfortunately, a national recession in 1873 cooled down mining activity, as money tightened and property values fell. It hurt, but didn't kill mining activity in the San Juans. The question of legal title to the land was now resolved. Title problems did arise for those claims filed on before the United States owned the land, and also on claims that lacked the necessary assessment work by prospectors who did not tend to their development work because of Ute threats or because U. S. soldiers had run them off the land. When the Utes were no longer a problem, there was a rush of prospectors to the San Juan region—most of whom traveled from Del Norte, up the Rio Grande, over treacherous Stony Pass, and down Cunningham Gulch to Howardsville at the upper end of Baker's Park. By the end of 1873, over 1,500 mining claims had been staked in or around Baker's Park. However all of the mineral riches being discovered and filed on would be worthless unless decent wagon roads could be built to get supplies into the San Juans and to get the ore out to the smelters. Or to put it another way and quoting a writer of the time—"The natural wealth of the mineral deposits in this vicinity seems to be proportionate to its inaccessibility."

Chapter 3

OTTO MEARS
AND HIS TOLL ROADS

AS THE POPULATION OF THE SAN JUANS increased and new mining claims were discovered, so did the need for a good transportation system. It was in this area that the San Juaners would face their biggest challenge. As noted Colorado historian Duane Smith wrote: "The San Juans demanded year-round, fast, and economical transportation. Until that was achieved, it would never attain the destiny that seemed to be ordained." A local paper of the time gently put it: "(the San Juans) are somewhat deprived of easy transportation."

The 1870s were a time of mining exploration and of the location of some of the best prospects in the San Juans. By the end of the 1870s, almost every major mine, except those in the Red Mountain District, had been discovered, but most of them had not been developed. Some valuable ore had been produced in the San Juans by the end of the summer of 1874, but very little of it had been shipped out. The area was found to be too remote and the

Chapter 3: OTTO MEARS AND HIS TOLL ROADS

terrain too rugged for economical transportation. One prospector of the day complained to *The Denver Tribune*: "The San Juans are the best and worst of mining country I've ever struck. It has more and better minerals ... but you can't get at it ... and when you're in, you're corralled by the mountains, so you can't get the ore out." Frank Hall, early Colorado historian, wrote: "There was little

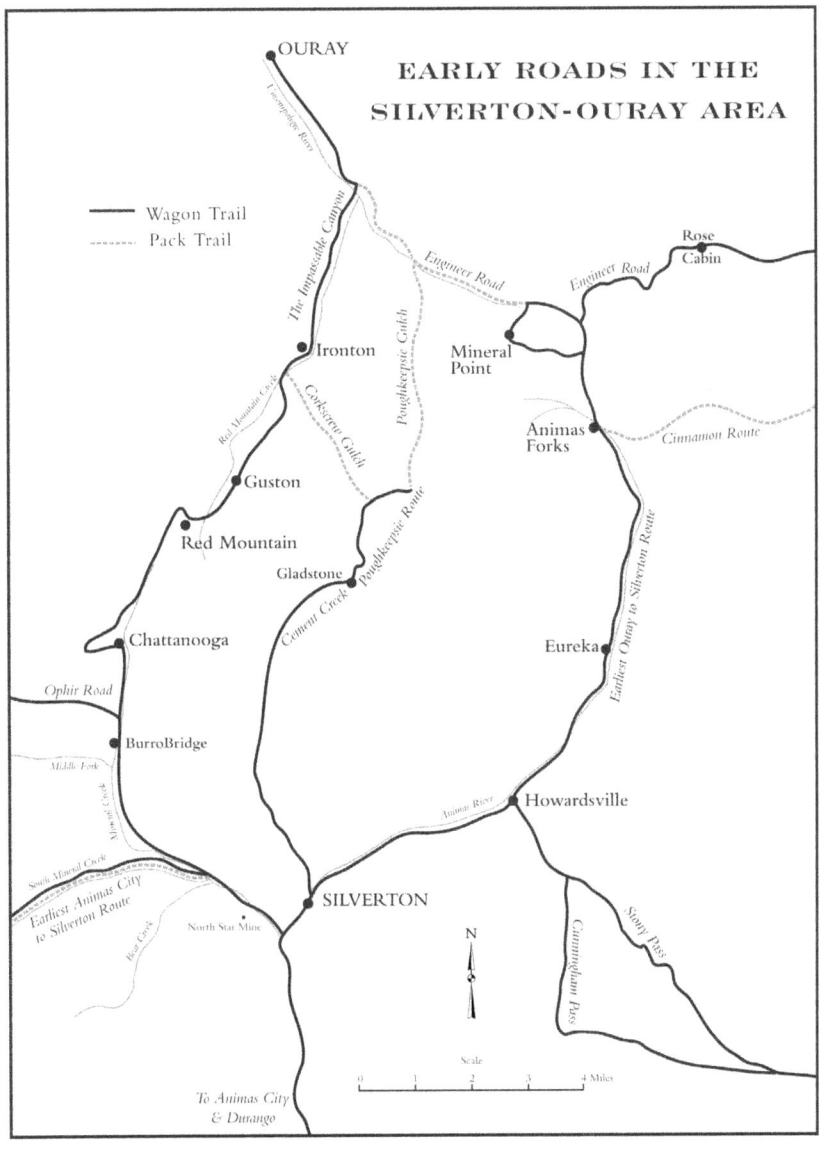

encouragement to produce ores, for a large part of their value was consumed in conveying them to the distant market."

Franklin Rhoda, assistant topographer of the Hayden Survey of 1874, quickly recognized the importance of Baker's Park and the problems of getting in and out of the San Juans.

> The great and important feature of this region is the far-famed Baker's Park. Small in area and quite unimportant in itself, it would be utterly disregarded if situated in any other part of Colorado; but, located as it is, surrounded on all sides by the most rugged mountains in the Territory, if not in the whole Rocky Mountain system, this little area of flat land becomes an object of curiosity and interest. When looked at as the center of the great mining district, it becomes an object of great practical importance. But not until one has crossed over the several passes leading out of it can he feel a proper regard for this spot, so carefully guarded by nature from the invasion of men.

At the same time Rhoda declared Stony Pass to be "well-marked" and "the most practical at present for entry (to the San Juans), but local wagons couldn't cross it." Rhoda was probably referring to Cunningham Pass, as there was some confusion about the names of the passes at this point on the Continental Divide. Cunningham was sometimes called "Rio Grande Pass" and was located about a half mile south of what today is called Stony Pass. To make the confusion even worse, Cunningham Pass was also at times called "Stony Pass." Most travelers commented that Cunningham was very torn up, muddy, and steep. Constant travel in all kinds of weather kept it in horrible shape. Stony Pass, although a little steeper, was rocky, which gave the pack animals better footing. Pole Creek, on the east side of the Continental Divide, often stopped traffic to both passes when its waters were raging with snowmelt in the early spring or during heavy summer rainstorms. In the spring, freighting outfits could often only wade the creek in the early morning hours, if at all. After a summer storm, it was necessary to wait for the water to go down.

Chapter 3: OTTO MEARS AND HIS TOLL ROADS   ❋ 57

Noted frontier photographer William Henry Jackson, who was with Rhoda, wrote in his diary: "What can possess those people we pass to go into that place (Baker's Park) this time of year (September 1874). Passed burro trains and wagons. Smashed up wagons there (Stony Pass)." Travel writer Ernest Ingersoll was another member of the Hayden survey party and later wrote of Stony Pass, "Eight years ago (1874) I let my mule down into Baker's Park by hitching its ivory tail around successive snubbing posts (tree stumps)." Some in the Hayden survey reported that they weren't able to find the Stony Pass "road," and that the only way to get a wagon down the pass was to disassemble the wagon and carry it over in pieces on the backs of mules.

In 1874, Rhoda also checked out and described the Animas Canyon, leading south out of Baker's Park, and felt it to be so rugged "that travel through it must long be a matter of great difficulty,

W. H. Jackson took this photo of the Rhoda Division of the Hayden Survey encamped just above Howardsville and Cunningham Gulch in September, 1874.

Photo Courtesy of Colorado Historical Society, WHJ 2897.

though it is said that some miners have passed up from the plains to Baker's Park by that route." Rhoda also mentioned the route going south up Sultan Mountain, "which is the roughest and most dangerous of any route leading out of the park, and even in the best summer weather is unsafe for pack or riding animals." That was saying a lot, and ironically he was referring to the route that the Million Dollar Highway now takes.

The first prospectors may well have traveled *to* the San Juans with wagon, but they only traveled *into* the San Juans over old Indian or game trails, and on foot or using horses, mules, or burros. Oxen (which were preferred for heavy loads on the plains) were tried but were unable to travel well in the San Juans. Burros could go anywhere a man could go while walking, and a single burro could be trained to follow his master like a dog. Burros were most often used to transport the early prospector's supplies and bring out small amounts of ore. The little beasts of burden were very patient and sure-footed on the narrow trails and would eat almost anything. They would never stray very far at night and would often come back into camp on their own in the morning, looking for food or salt. Individual burros carried about 150 to 250 pounds (depending on their size, age, and health), but they were often grossly overloaded. Burros were also fairly inexpensive on the frontier (ten to thirty dollars).

Pack burros were usually driven like sheep, in groups of up to thirty or forty animals. Often the burro punchers used a dog to help keep the burros together and steer them. The dog would follow commands to take the burros left or right and would usually nip at their heels to get them to go the direction that was desired. Travel writer Ernest Ingersoll wrote: "Goods and merchandise of every kind were brought in on the backs of the tough and patient little Mexican burro, toiling across the terrible heights under burdens almost as bulky as themselves."

Some prospectors preferred mules to burros, even though they required hay and grain for food. Mules could carry 300 to 350 pounds of supplies or ore and were usually tied fourteen to sixteen

Chapter 3: OTTO MEARS AND HIS TOLL ROADS

All the provisions needed at the mines or San Juan settlements were brought by mule trains or pack burros before there were roads. Often they had to cross deep snows when crossing the high passes.
Harper's Weekly, June 19, 1883. Author's Collection.

in a row, with a muleskinner riding his own horse or mule and leading the whole group. Sometimes another muleskinner would follow at the rear of the line. Horses, although generally faster than a mule, were not usually used as pack animals, since they were not as surefooted and lacked the strength and stamina of mules or burros.

Whether it was burros or mules, this early form of transportation was terribly expensive, and a massive support system was necessary to meet the needs of the packers – barns, corrals, blacksmiths, and livery stables; and local ranchers and farmers were needed to grow hay and grain for the horses and mules. The burros or the pack mule trains worked reasonably well for prospectors who were only trying to bring in their supplies or send a little ore to the smelters to be assayed, or perhaps for a man doing a little early development work. However, once capital was infused into a mine, vast quantities of ore would need to be shipped to smelters, and boilers, crushers, ore cars, pumps, and other heavy, bulky items would need to be brought in. This would require substantial freight wagons traveling over true wagon roads.

A wagon road also meant stage travel, which in turn meant that more investors (who usually didn't live the rough life of a prospector) could come into the San Juan Mountains. Mail could be shipped faster and more regularly, and "express" packages could be used for items that needed to be shipped quickly. Magazines, cigars, hardware, and many other items that otherwise would not be available could be shipped in by stage; and heavy or bulky items like furniture and pianos could be brought in by freight wagons. Stage travel was considered a much more "civilized" way to travel, especially for women and children, but it was still a long and rough ride. One danger early on was stage robberies, which occurred regularly on the early San Juan roads. Deadly accidents were also all too frequent.

The average freight rate to get ore from the San Juans to the smelters (usually in Pueblo at this time) by burros or mules in the mid-1870s was about $100 per ton – thousands of dollars per ton in terms of today's dollar. As a result, only the very richest ore could be sent out, and it still had to be milled or hand sorted ahead of time with as much waste rock as possible chipped away in advance of shipping. Even after all these efforts, it was hard to make a profit from the ore after huge transportation costs were paid.

Several methods were used to attempt to reduce the weight of the ore being shipped. Early on, the prospectors tried arrastras, hand sorting, or picking away the waste rock by hand. Later, "concentrating mills" were built at or near the mines to crush the ore and take out as much waste rock as possible. However this basically allowed only the richest ores to be processed, and as much as fifty percent of the valuable minerals in the ore ended up being tossed out on the waste dump. Quite a few of these dumps were later reworked at a good profit when cheaper transportation and better mill recovery were available.

Chapter 3: OTTO MEARS AND HIS TOLL ROADS

This photo shows the reason why the San Juans had to have wagon roads. Boilers like this could not be brought in by mule train or burros. It took twelve huge draft horses to move this equipment. The driver didn't have a seat — he just sat inside the boiler.

Marvin and Ruth Gregory Collection.

What was needed were wagon roads, or even better, a railroad. In some places, the mines tried to build their own roads; or a stage company might try to clear a path that it could travel over. The San Juan Mountains, however, were so steep and rugged that a good wagon road was not possible without a very large expenditure of money. There were no public funds available for such large expenditures. A few public "roads" were being started in the San Juans, but if they were finished they were usually so rough that most travelers thought they were on a trail and not a road.

One solution was to bring the smelter to the mines, but they needed coal to operate effectively, and smelters worked better at lower altitudes. In Lake City, the editor of *The Silver World* wrote in his September 18, 1875, issue that although Lake City had several good smelters, that it was not a smelter that was critical to the San Juan country. "The greatest and more immediate want is the necessity of thoroughfares and highways." Even *The New York Times* got its two cents in: "The best and almost only way (to the San Juans) is by pack animals."

One way to try to solve the road problem (at least for a few months) was to wait for winter. Travel in the 1870s could actually be easier at that time of year, when snow and ice filled in the gullies and covered up the stumps, rocks, and logs. Freighters took off their wagon wheels and replaced them with runners. Some large bulky equipment was actually delayed in shipment until that time of the year, when shipping was easier (or even possible).

Toll roads, although not the ultimate solution, were the best way to solve year-round transportation problems quickly in the San Juans in the 1870s. Although road building was especially costly in the steep, rocky, and rugged mountains of Colorado, it was an expenditure that could be justified by men who could make enough profit in return. Since toll roads went where they were needed, the history of toll roads is to a great extent the history of the development of Colorado's mining districts and towns. Often they were privately financed by the sale of stock. Investors were given the exclusive rights to charge a toll to those using the road, usually for a period of about twenty years. (As it turned out, the counties involved bought out many toll roads much earlier than their charters expired.)

The system worked pretty well, considering that there were no federal or state funds available for road building in the new Territory of Colorado; and the new counties where the roads were needed were usually much too poor to afford much, if any, road construction. Toll roads were usually built relatively fast, as the investors wanted to get a return on their money as quickly as possible. On the other hand, the general population was not too excited about paying tolls. All kinds of schemes were devised to get out of it. Some travelers sneaked by; others said they had no money and would pay later; others just rushed through the tollgate without paying and kept going.

Colorado's toll road laws had several phases. From 1861 to 1867, thirty-eight toll roads were licensed directly by the legislature, but only two of these toll roads came even remotely close to the San Juans. (Both routes were from Canon City to the Rio Grande River in the San Luis Valley). In 1867, the law was changed to require that a much more specific route be located, terminuses had to be established and named at each end, toll gates could be no closer than every ten miles, and the rates charged had to be approved by the counties involved every two years (if needed there was an appeal process to county court). In 1877, another legislative act required rates to be posted at the tollgate, and if a road was not believed to be in good shape, a complaint could be filed with the local Justice of the Peace. If found guilty of neglecting the maintenance of his road, an owner could be fined. The new law also required that companies must begin work and spend at least $500

Tollgates were usually established at a likely spot where travelers were funneled through the gate. Most locals griped about this system, but eventually the road would become public.

Harper's Weekly, Sept. 3, 1881. Author's Collection.

on construction costs within ninety days of being chartered or their right to the toll road would be forfeited. Instead of a specific route, the road now had to be surveyed.

Unfortunately, there was little coordination of toll road building. Each one of the San Juan settlements or counties took a different tactic on their toll roads. For example, Silverton was "accessible" from Animas City by several routes. Baker's Bridge became the tollgate for the first toll road, but for many years there was no wagon road all the way to Silverton. You just went as far in a wagon as the road had been constructed at the time and then switched to mules or burros. It didn't make sense to locate the Silverton tollgate entrance any further south than Baker's Bridge at Animas City, as the Animas Valley was too broad and flat to funnel traffic into the toll road. An early toll road was tried through the Animas Valley, but it was declared a private road within a few years as it received very little business since travelers could just take other routes down the broad, level valley.

The earliest Silverton wagon toll road from Animas City extended up the hill to Rockwood. From there, it followed Elbert Creek through the area now covered by Electra Lake, and then (until 1879) ended around the present Durango Mountain ski area and Cascade Creek. Before 1879, it was from Cascade Creek to Silverton that difficulties began. There were several routes to choose from, but none of them were easy.

Two of the routes from Cascade to Baker's Park in the early 1870s were the "impassible" Animas Canyon and the dangerous Sultan Mountain trail that Rhoda described. A third route went up Cascade Creek, then down either Bear or South Mineral Creek. This last trail was longer but public. None of the routes were passable by wagon. Another very rough toll road was built in 1875 between present-day Rockwood and the top of Coal Bank Hill, a distance of sixteen miles; but it was then left unfinished for decades, and in the meanwhile it was still necessary to use the old Ute pack trails through Lime Creek to travel the additional fourteen miles into Silverton.

Chapter 3: OTTO MEARS AND HIS TOLL ROADS 65

Cunningham and Stony Passes remained the accepted routes into Silverton, even though it was impossible to get a wagon over them without using it like a sled. It was a very hard route, even for a man on foot. Miner Alfred Camp wrote that he came all the way down Stony on foot. "This experience will hardly be forgotten as for several hours we scrambled and slid as best we could to get down – fortunately without breaking our necks." Then looking back he saw, "an almost impassible road winding upwards." He felt it was "as hard to get an empty wagon out as to bring a loaded one in." Chains and ropes were still used to tie wagons onto tree stumps. The really bad part of Stony was the section about a mile down from the top on the Cunningham Gulch side of the pass. In 1875, it was "upgraded" to a barely passable wagon road. Squire (W.D.)

This Harper's Weekly *drawing shows early-day Silverton in the background from Greene's Smelter on Cement Creek. The mountains weren't quite as rugged as shown in the drawing.*

Author's Collection.

Watson lowered wagons by ropes tied to stumps for $2.50 a wagon (about a day's wages for most men) through a 200-foot portion of the trip. From 1874 to 1879, Watson had an inn and stable at Grassy Creek on the Rio Grande side of Stony Pass. He would follow the wagons going up to Stony and was reported to do a thriving business in the summer. The solution for most freighters was to take their loads out of the wagons and carry the freight down Stony or Cunningham Passes on burros or mules to their destination, but it was costly and time-consuming to do so.

W. B. Dickerson wrote a letter to the *Rocky Mountain News* in November 1874, stating "one begins to curse the (Stony Pass) road immediately after he leaves Antelope Park (the last large park going up the Rio Grande River), and, though rough roads have been experienced before, at the summit of the range, roads that are not roads at all are encountered."

Yet just how desperately important good, year-round transportation was to the locals can be sensed from a May 6, 1876, issue of the Silverton *La Plata Miner*:

> *Last Tuesday afternoon our little community was thrown into a state of intense excitement by the arrival of the first train of jacks (burros), as they came into sight about a mile above town. Somebody gave a shout, 'turn out, the jacks are coming, and sure enough there were the patient homely little fellows filing down the trail. Cheer after cheer was given, gladness prevailed all around, and the national flag was run up at the post office. It was a glad sight, after six long weary months of imprisonment, to see the harbinger of better days, to see these messengers of trade and business, showing that once more the road was open to the outside world.*

The "Stony Pass Road" (whether by Stony or Cunningham Pass) left the San Luis Valley at Del Norte, went west to South Fork, then up the Rio Grande River to Wagon Wheel Gap (there was no town of Creede at this time), into Antelope Park, and continued up the Rio Grande to its headwaters near Stony or Cunningham Passes. Although the Stony Pass Road was 110 to 115 miles long, the first ninety miles to Antelope Park were relatively easy going, and soon there were many small settlements and ranchers along the way. There was a big cabin and several warehouses at the point on the upper Rio Grande where most freighters switched to mules and burros. (This spot is now at the end of the dirt road that follows the Rio Grande.)

Two major advantages of the route over Stony Pass were that the D&RG Railroad was supposed to arrive soon at Alamosa about thirty miles east of Del Norte; and, after 1873, the United States had purchased all of the land the prospectors were traveling through, so the Ute Indians should not have been a problem. It was really only the ten or so miles over the passes that were difficult and dangerous. But it could take several days to get through this section. The Stony Pass road was bad, but the nearby road at Cunningham Pass was much worse. Both fell about 2300 feet in two miles, but Cunningham was almost always muddy, torn up, and slippery. Cunningham Pass was eventually abandoned because the snow melted earlier in the summer on Stony Pass, and it wasn't nearly as muddy and slick. However in the winter, travelers on snowshoes or skis usually felt that Cunningham Pass was a little shorter and easier to travel.

There was also an attempt to go north out of Baker's Park. Silverton and Lake City both made efforts to connect with each other. Saguache and Lake City merchants wanted the supply business, and Silverton mines wanted to get ore to Lake City's Crooke Smelter, which was getting the best results of any smelter in the area. Lake City was located near the eastern and northern edges of the San Juans, yet the route to Del Norte was still a long, rough, and circuitous 125 miles and required traveling up or down Slumgullion Pass – a slippery, steep road often made of corduroy (logs laid side by side) that nearly tore the wagons and passengers apart.

Like Animas City and Ouray, Lake City became an entry point into the San Juans and was soon a large town. Because of its relatively easy access and the fact that it received freight from both Saguache and Del Norte, Lake City had many amenities that were not available in other San Juan towns. Cigar stores, newspapers, nice restaurants, and reading rooms were spread throughout the town. Most of its citizens were reported to be young, educated, and robust. Its initial surge of prospectors was essentially American born; although European miners soon followed them to the mines as more extensive development began.

It was, however, a poor, uneducated foreigner, Otto Mears, who was the man ultimately involved with developing most San Juan roads (he eventually had 383 miles of toll roads and several railroads). Mears did so much that he eventually became known as "the Pathfinder of the San Juans." As Frank Hall wrote: "The influence that has been most important in opening highways in the (San Juans), provided outlets for isolated, struggling, and thinly populated camps, was the courage and energy displayed by Mr. Otto Mears.... He is simply a sharp, shred, sagacious man of business; with remarkable foresight, marvelous energy, and power of direction."

Although he was often cursed for bad roads and high tolls, Mears was a true visionary and built his roads at an acceptable rate of progress; and when they were finished, they were passable. Also in Mears' defense, Colorado mountain roads to this day are not always in good repair because of summer floods, winter avalanches, constant freezing and thawing, heavy traffic, and often not enough money for upkeep.

The life of Otto Mears was a Horatio Alger story come true. He was born in Kurkland, Russia, on May 3, 1840. His father was English and his mother was Russian, but both of his parents died by the time he was four years old. His maternal uncle took him in, but when he did not get along well with the other children in that family, he was sent to England at age nine. He went to Ireland at ten and that same year was sent to New York. He soon was passed on again, this time to relatives living in California, but by the time he got there they had left for Australia and he was on his own at age eleven. From 1851 to 1859, he did various jobs to stay alive. From 1859 to 1861, he was in the California gold fields, and then he entered the Civil War by enlisting in California. The Union Army sent him to New Mexico, where he served under Kit Carson. He fought Texas Confederates and was also a part of the "Long Walk" of the Navajos to Ft. Sumner, New Mexico. Mears got his first financial break in the army. He was in the quartermaster corps and was responsible for making bread for the army. He was given one pound of flour to make one pound of bread, and he obviously didn't need that much. So he sold the leftover flour for an eventual profit of $1500. When he was discharged at Las Cruces, New Mexico, he had been promoted to the rank of captain. He then went to Santa Fe, where he worked for a while. Then he went to Conejos (which was the Ute Indian agency at the time), where he built a saw mill and a grist mill in partnership with Lafayette Head – who was later appointed the Ute Indian agent.

In 1866, Mears decided there was not enough tillable land near Conejos and leased 200 acres near Saguache, where he grew wheat. When the new County of Saguache was formed in 1866, he became the first treasurer, which he said was no big deal as there probably weren't eight residents of the county at the time and everyone got some type of political job. He also started a general store that year and ran a pack train to get his supplies in over LaVeta Pass. He brought the first threshing machines to the San Luis Valley and made other innovations in local wheat farming. His first wheat crop was twenty bushels of wheat an acre. When the army at Ft. Garland dropped the price it was paying for wheat from twelve dollars per hundred pounds of flour to five dollars, Mears decided to take his wheat to California Gulch (the predecessor of Leadville), since they were paying twelve dollars per hundred in that new mining location.

In 1867, Mears tried to get his wheat over Poncha Pass to a grist mill in Granite, Colorado, where it was processed into flour for the booming area of California Gulch. This was before there was a road over Poncha Pass, and one of his wagons tipped over on the way down and much of his grain (which was being carried unsacked in his wagon bed) was ruined. Territorial Governor William Gilpin happened by the scene on his way between a Baca land grant that he owned in the San Luis Valley and the City of Denver. When Mears complained about the lack of a road, Gilpin suggested that Mears spend five dollars, get a charter, and build his own toll road. Mears was (as historian Duane Smith put it) "ever alert for opportunity." He incorporated the fifty-mile Saguache to Nathrop road in 1867 and finished the road in 1868. Later, when the Leadville excitement erupted, Mears made enough to repay himself for the construction of the whole road in three months, and he was reported to have made over $100,000 in tolls during the entire Leadville boom.

Otto met his German wife at Granite, Colorado, and married Mary Kampfshulte on October 17, 1870. In 1871, he formed his second toll road company, which ran to the Ute Indian agency on Cochetopa Pass; and then he formed the Saguache and San Juan Toll Road with Enos Hotchkiss and other Saguache businessmen to extend the road to Silverton; but, it was 1872 before the construction of the road was started. He also expanded his mercantile business and started the *Saguache Chronicle* newspaper in 1872.

Since Mears had acted as a treaty translator and now spoke fluent Ute, he recieved the contract for supplies at the Ute agency; but he could also charge others (including soldiers and agency employees) for using his road. Native Americans, by the way, were almost never charged a toll – a way to keep them friendly. Mears toll road career began to soar because of the rivalry between the San Luis Valley towns of Saguache (at the north) and Del Norte (at the south), each wanting to become the main route or the "Gateway" to the San Juans. Mears extended the Los Piños Agency Toll Road and started building his third toll road from the Ute agency to Lake City in 1872-73. Mears' "Saguache and San Juan Toll Road" eventually covered 125 miles. It was one of the easiest and safest ways into the San Juans, but also one of the longest. From Cochetopa Pass it ran over Los Piños Pass (to the west), then down the Cebolla River to

Chapter 3: OTTO MEARS AND HIS TOLL ROADS

This Harper's Weekly *illustration by Harry Fenn was taken from a Charles Goodman photograph and supposedly shows the rugged terrain around the first Ute agency at the top of Cochetopa Pass. However in real life it is not this rugged, so Fenn took some liberties with his drawing.*
Author's Collection.

present-day Powderhorn, then south and west to the Lake Fork of the Gunnison River, and then up the Lake Fork to Lake City. Like most of his routes, it was traveled by pack animals before it could accomodate wagons. The Barlow and Sanderson Stage eventually ran three times a week along Mears' route from Saguache to Lake City, the first stage arriving July 11, 1875.

Mears was beginning to realize the advantages and profits from running complimentary business ventures, so at this time he also moved into the freight business, using mules, burros, and even oxen. He had a real advantage since he could run his freight teams and wagons over his toll roads at no charge. This further allowed him to open additional general merchandise stores that could earn a greater profit because of the "free" freight. Eventually Mears invested in mines, railroads, and other businesses, but everything turned on his transportation business. Unfortunately, Mears lost much of what he had in the Silver Panic of 1893, as his interdependent businesses collapsed one after another. During his lifetime, Mears was a negotiator with the Utes in the treaties of 1868, 1873, and 1880, politician, telegraph owner (the first in Western Colorado), and he built the first irrigation ditch in the San Luis Valley. He even helped contract the state capitol building in Denver. His portrait in stained glass is in the Senate Chamber in the state capitol building in Denver in honor of his many contributions to Colorado.

When Mears' Saguache-Lake City toll road met the Lake Fork of the Gunnison River, he also built a short, twenty-five mile road to Cimarron. It was 1873 before his toll road got to the site that would eventually become Lake City. In August of 1874, his partner Enos Hotchkiss started to build a road up the Lake Fork of the Gunnison River and over Cinnamon Pass to Silverton. Hotchkiss was one of the founders of Lake City and located the Hotchkiss Mine, which later became the famous and rich Golden Fleece. Not to be outdone, Del Norte's merchants built the Lake City and Antelope Park Toll Road, which arrived in Lake City over Spring Creek Pass and down the Slumgullion Slide on November 22, 1875. One stage passenger commented: "The first day out of Del Norte the access is so gentle you feel yourself on level ground;" but went on to describe the descent down Slumgullion: " With a jerk and a jolt, and a pitch, down, down you go until you think you have reached the bottom of all things. Down, down till the bottom of all things seems an elevated peak, and down, down till you lose all sense of everything but the awful downwardness of life – and here you are at Lake City." By the summer of 1877, there was daily stage service to Lake City for as long as the weather permitted. Most of the travelers continued on from Lake City to Silverton, Ouray, or other towns deeper in the San Juan Mountains.

The Mears' forty-mile "road" over Cinnamon Pass to Silverton was one of his few failures. The difficult parts of the route were from the end of the Lake Fork Valley to the beginning of Burrows Park, from the upper end of Burrows Park to where the Tobasco Mill was eventually built, and the final harrowing descent into Animas Forks. Franklin Rhoda of the Hayden Survey saw Mears' surveyors

Chapter 3: OTTO MEARS AND HIS TOLL ROADS   ✤ 73

at work and wrote, "How the people of Saguache ever expect to bring a wagon road up this I cannot see. On account of the surrounding bluffs there is very little opportunity to wind the road up it, while the miry nature of the soil (near the top) will require vast sums of money to be spent after the grade is obtained before the road can be made passable. The fall from the pass down to the Three Forks of the Animas (Animas Forks) is very sudden." Rhoda had previously tried Engineer Pass (not an easy route in itself), where he took the opportunity to go up Nellie Creek and climb Uncompahgre Peak and then turned back and tried Cinnamon Pass. Mears continued with a trail over Cinnamon Pass to Baker's Park, but the trail was not passable by wagons, as it was reportedly only a slight upgrade from an old Indian trail and went so high (13,009 feet) that it was only passable a few months of the year. One traveler over Cinnamon in 1876 wrote "After we left Lake City, we traveled over some of the worst roads I have ever seen. Only the trees, stumps, and rocks which would have made the road absolutely impassible had been removed, but no thought had been given to the comfort of the traveler."

In September 1875, Mears was still working on the Lake City-Silverton toll road over Cinnamon, but in the winter of 1875-76 he got the mail route over his toll road to the new Ute Agency on the Uncompahgre River. The west end of this route closely followed the northern branch of the California Trail. After unsuccessfully trying dog sleds and men on skis, Mears ended up carrying the mail himself in the spring, when the snow was slushy and the route was almost impossible to traverse. He was evidently afraid that he might lose the mail contract, and there was a very heavy fine for failure to get the mail through.

In 1875, when the Town of Ouray had been founded, it was extremely remote, and there was an immediate demand for roads to replace the narrow, dangerous Indian trails down Uncompahgre and Bear Creeks that had been used to get into the place from Mineral Point. A. W. Begole, E. C. Bradley, and J. T. Jones began a toll road north out of Ouray to Los Piños on November 3, 1876, but a year later little work had been done. Otto Mears bought them out and finished the road in 1877. This gave him a route from Saguache to Lake City to the second Ute Agency to the Town of Ouray. Cochetopa Pass had proved too high for anyone, Native American or white, to live on year round. He started the route to the new Los Piños off the point where the toll road he had previously constructed from Saguache to Lake City met the Lake Fork of the Gunnison River. His road then went over Blue Mesa, west to the Ute Agency near present-day Colona, and then south along the Uncompahgre River to Ouray.

After the road was completed, the trip by wagon from Ouray to Saguache could take two weeks. The road was rough, so rough that its patrons constantly complained that a toll shouldn't be charged. Mears' tollgate in Ouray was near the present-day swimming pool,

The post office at the Los Piños II Ute Agency, near present-day Colona on the Uncompahgre River, was made of adobe. The whites were mainly the crew that watched the Ute cattle.

Photo Courtesy of Colorado Historical Society, F-7358.

Chapter 3: Otto Mears and His Toll Roads

and a fence ran out to the river on one side and the canyon walls on the other so as to funnel travelers into the toll keeper. The toll, as usual, was high – twenty dollars (equivalent to hundreds of dollars today) for a six-mule team and wagon to Saguache, and the road was so bad that it took a six to eight animal team to conquer the steeper parts. Mears finished the road in 1878, and Ouray was finally linked to the outside world by a wagon and stage road, even if it was of somewhat dubious character, very lengthy, and passed through Ute territory.

In 1877, he "finished" the road over Cinnamon (most people would not travel on it in a wagon). In 1878-79, Mears built the sixty-mile Marshall Pass Toll Road off his Poncha Pass Toll Road; and a year later he sold it to the D&RG Railroad for $40,000. This was the first really big money that he got for any of his projects to that date.

In 1879, Mears also built a toll road from Gunnison to the Cebolla River to tie in with his Saguache to Lake City Road. This was followed by the 1880 Durango to Ft Lewis (near Pagosa Springs at the time), a Dallas to Telluride in 1880, and six-mile extension off this last road from Vance Junction to Ames in 1881 (to serve Ophir). With all this activity, he had built the majority of the roads in the San Juan Mountains at the time.

After the Meeker Massacre in 1879, Mears personally obtained the signatures of 1,400 Utes on the 1880 Treaty that moved the Utes out of Colorado. He did so by paying each Ute two dollars, which he later insisted was not a bribe, as the Ute would rather have two dollars in hand than the promise of much more from the U.S. in the future (they may have been very wise). He even submitted a bill to the U.S. government for the money and was reimbursed. When the government troops were no longer needed after they moved the Utes out of Colorado, Mears even charged the army for moving their men across his Ouray to Saguache toll road. Mears was especially interested in building his roads where he knew there would be considerable government travel, for which he was always well paid.

This photograph was taken in 1874 when the Utes were in Washington, D.C. Ouray and his wife Chipeta are at the center of the front row. Otto Mears is the man on the right in the center row. The other whites are treaty negotiators or Indian agents.
Photo courtesy of Colorado Historical Society, F-24385.

Later Mears built three railroads as well as his toll roads. Arthur Ridgway, one time Mears employee and, later, chief engineer for the D&RG Railroad, wrote – "eccentric, visionary, impetuous, indefatigable, generous, human, sympathetic, charitable – all combined in one personality made it impossible to say that as a man he was this or that or the other." Mears died on June 24, 1931 at the age of ninety-one.

As mentioned, Mears had made efforts to upgrade the Cinnamon road, but it was so bad that an 1876 issue of the *San Juan Prospector* declared, "There is no wagon road between Lake City and Silverton." Lake City merchants, mill and mine owners, and investors were determined to connect Lake City with a wagon road to Silverton. In 1877, they built a road up Henson Creek that

Chapter 3: OTTO MEARS AND HIS TOLL ROADS   77

crossed at Engineer (12,800 feet) and Yvonne (12,250 feet) Passes and went down to Animas Forks. In August, 1877, the first stage made it over Engineer Pass, and the road became the accepted route to travel by wagon or stage between Lake City and Ouray or Silverton; but it was still a very rough road that was usually used for only a few months during the summer and early fall.

The easiest part of Mears' toll road from Lake City to Silverton (and the only part truly completed by him for wagons) was the section of basically flat ground between Animas Forks and Silverton. Not only was the terrain easy, but the county contributed money to help Mears build this part of the road. He was paid $600 ($150 for the section between Silverton and Howardsville, $150 for Howardsville to Eureka, and $300 for Eureka to Animas Forks).

William's Tourist Guide to the San Juan Mountains in 1877 suggested that anyone coming to the San Juans from out of state take the stage from LaVeta to Del Norte, which took fifteen hours. (It was probably the Barlow and Sanderson six-horse stage.) The guidebook also mentioned that the stage from Canon City to Del Norte took twenty-five hours. It did not even mention Mears' Saguache to Ouray route. From Del Norte to Lake City was thirty-six hours, including an evening stop at the "Widow Jennison's place." The guide mentioned that it was shorter to go directly from Del Norte to Silverton but it suggested the traveler go by way of Lake City, as it was the easiest route. The guide book suggested horse or private conveyance from Lake City on.

Freight was carried from Canon City (the end of the railroad at that time) over Mears' toll roads – Poncha Pass to Saguache to Ouray for ten cents a pound. On the return trip, ore was carried for eighty dollars a ton. When the D&RG reached Montrose in 1882, wagon freight and passengers were switched to the railroad. Dave Wood was the main freighter into Ouray, and Barlow and Sanderson ran the stage. In early 1887 the D&RG began a branch to Ouray, completing the effort in October of that year.

By 1877, four toll "roads" had been created to Silverton over Cinnamon Pass, Engineer Pass, Stony Pass, and from Animas City to Cascade Creek, but none of them were easily accessible by wagon, and none were passable in the winter. All of them had sections of extremely steep grades. Only the road that Mears built from Animas Forks down to Silverton could be traveled with relative ease (it later became the roadbed for his Silverton Northern Railroad), but this road only tied together several little settlements in Baker's Park and didn't reach the outside world. The San Juans still needed a good road into its mining districts, and Otto Mears greatest achievement was yet to come.

The arrival of the first stage was always a momentous event. It brought friends and relatives, mail and express, but mostly it was a sign that civilization had arrived at a camp.

Harper's Weekly, November 10, 1883. Author's Collection.

Chapter 4

THE ORIGINAL MILLION DOLLAR HIGHWAY IS BUILT

EVEN AFTER OTTO MEARS built his toll road into Ouray from the north, Ouray County worked on a public road to the south and east up what is the present Engineer road. This route was chosen over what could have been a more direct route to Silverton via the Red Mountain because of what Franklin Rhoda had called "a deep box canyon where the fall is very great (and) travel for some distance is both difficult and dangerous ... traveling is very nearly impossible." Then, because Rhoda felt the canyon "bars all egress" – he felt it required no further description. Rhoda also noted the route from Silverton to Ouray up Cement Creek, over Hurricane Pass, down to Lake Como and Poughkeepsie Gulch, and then down the Uncompahgre River to Ouray needed no description, as it was also basically "impossible." The route chosen by Ouray County up the dangerous, high, and roundabout Engineer trail wasn't much better. Rasmus Hanson declared "a man risked his life on it. It was not safe to ride a horse over. When slippery it was not safe to walk on it." Several men were actually killed when they fell off the dangerous trail.

Because of a lack of finances Ouray County could only afford to put a few men to work on the project, and with the slow progress up the lower Uncompahgre Canyon and Engineer roads, the

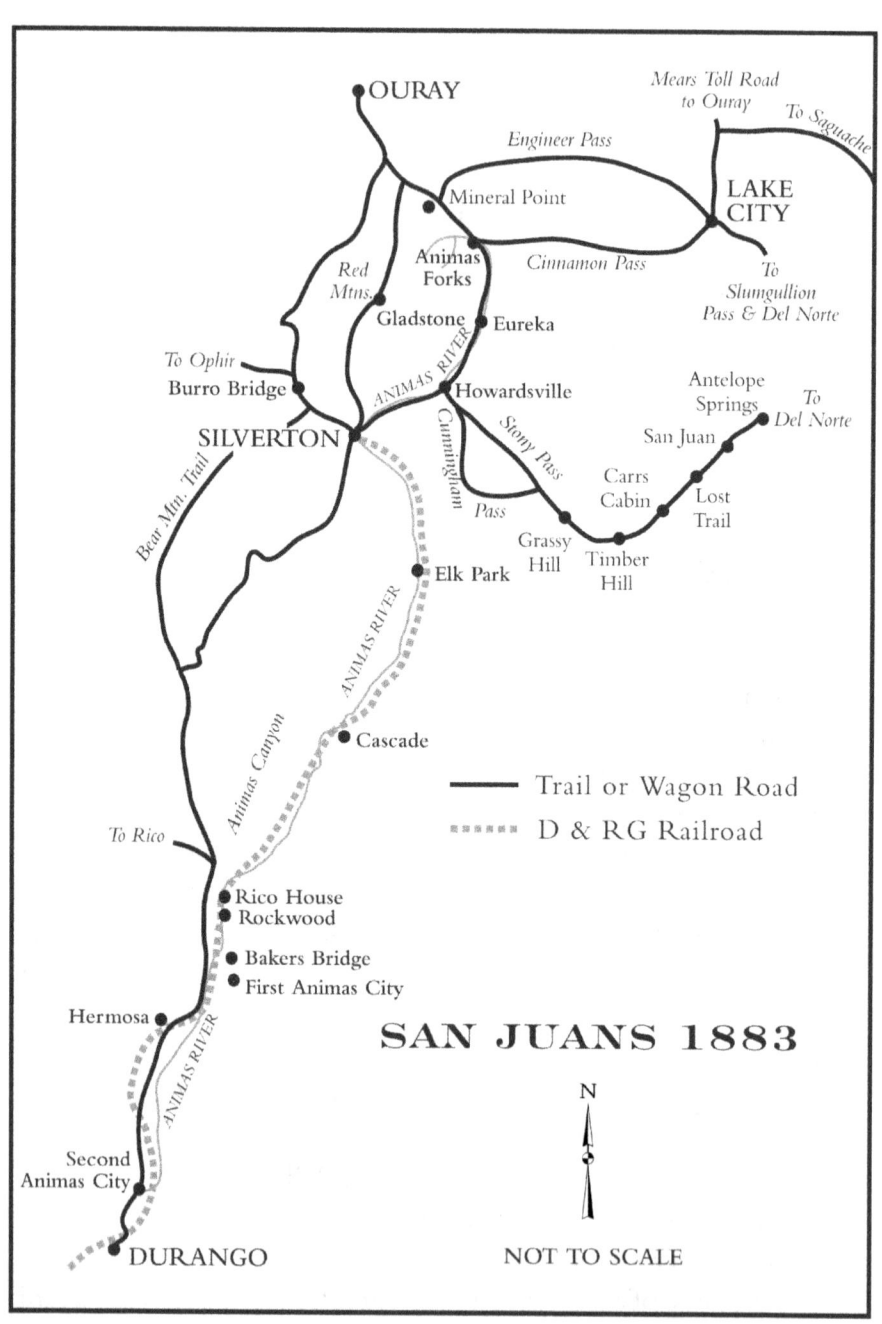

Chapter 4: THE ORIGINAL MILLION DOLLAR HIGHWAY IS BUILT ✤ 81

Otto Mears' toll route north out of Ouray was to remain Ouray's main access during the 1870s. However Mears' toll road had its own problems as it was a long roundabout route that went directly through Ute land. By treaty the whites had the right to cross the land, but it was a nerve-racking and dangerous trip that many people refused to take.

By 1878, Ouray County had given up on its attempt to build a public road south and east from Ouray; and, perhaps in response to the Lake City merchants success in getting to Silverton, a toll road company was formed by Ouray merchants to try to connect Ouray to Silverton and Lake City over the Engineer Road. The Ouray, Mineral City, and Animas Forks Road Company's route was much shorter than Mears' Saguache to Ouray road and was not in Ute Territory; but the first few miles went through the "impassible" Uncompahgre Gorge. A few more men were added to the road crew, but it was soon obvious that the merchants would have to spend a lot more money and hire a lot more men to finish their project quickly. The Ouray merchants chose to give up their project within a year, and the County of Ouray continued with meager efforts to complete the road.

In the meanwhile, the economy in the San Juans picked up considerably, and good transportation became much more important. The Bland-Allison Act of 1878 provided that the federal government should purchase silver as well as gold to back the U. S. dollar. For a while this helped the silver industry and eager speculators began to buy and sell mineral interests in the silver rich San Juans. The speculators brought money with them, which allowed for the purchase of needed equipment for the San Juan mines and for construction of roads and railroads to get the ore out. But road construction was expensive in the San Juans, and this translated into high rates that were going to have to be paid by consumers.

In April of 1880, the Ouray and San Juan Wagon Toll Road Company was formed to make another attempt to build up the Engineer road. There was some progress over the next two years, although it was very slow because finances were always a

This part of the Million Dollar Highway, now called the Ruby Cliffs, was a section of the road that caused all kinds of trouble with construction for the City of Ouray and the San Juan Wagon Toll Road Company. Note the man in the center by the road.

W. H. Jackson photo. Author's Collection.

Chapter 4: THE ORIGINAL MILLION DOLLAR HIGHWAY IS BUILT ❦ 83

problem. The plan was still to build along the Uncompahgre River up to Mineral Point and Animas Forks, then down the river to Silverton or over Engineer Pass to Lake City. A branch road to Red Mountain was planned for later. All that existed from the previous road building efforts was a small path along the river between Bear Creek Falls and the point where the Uncompahgre River entered the Uncompahgre Gorge. The trail then went up the steep side of the canyon to what is now the Engineer road and forked at Poughkeepsie Gulch. The toll company hired several dozen men, raised the route out of the river bottom, and made some progress, but all they accomplished was a partial trail; not a foot of the route was passable by wagons.

Although the citizens of Silverton were also building a road north toward Ouray, they were side-tracked by new mining discoveries near present-day Rico, Ophir, and Telluride. San Juan County desired the milling, smelting, and transportation business of those towns and decided to give a charter to James Mountain for construction of the Silverton and Ophir Toll Road over Ophir Pass. He asked for and was given the existing public route from Silverton to Burro Bridge (which Mountain had built as a public road for the county), and in early 1881, thirty men started to work on the Ophir toll road. By July 1, Mr. Mountain had a toll gate up at Burro Bridge, even though his toll road wasn't nearly finished. From Burro Bridge, Mountain followed one of the most heavily traveled Indian trails in the San Juans. He had done a great job from Silverton to Burro Bridge, and did an good job from Burro Bridge to the top of Ophir Pass; but he was evidently running out of money and built a narrow road almost straight down an extremely steep scree slope on the west side of the pass. (That part of his road didn't follow the same path it does today.) The road officially opened in August, 1881, after a stated expenditure of $15,000, but the west side of the pass was so bad that some questioned whether Mr. Mountain had done any work at all. A cry went up immediately that the road on the west side of the pass had to be upgraded. Toll was two dollars for a wagon with two horses

The Ruby Cliffs and the narrow, original road are photographed looking south. The Uncompahgre River is to the right and Mt. Abrams rises in the background. The original road to Engineer went up the draw near the center of the photo, to the immediate left of Abrams.

Photo Courtesy Colorado Historical Society, F-23,853.

Chapter 4: THE ORIGINAL MILLION DOLLAR HIGHWAY IS BUILT   ❉ 85

or mules, fifty cents for a saddle horse, and twenty-five cents for a pack animal.

But events were about to occur that would turn the Silverton merchant's attention away from Ophir and Telluride. In 1882, a boom unparalleled in the San Juans occurred at the Red Mountain Mining District. When the rich discoveries were made, Ouray County took over the Ouray and San Juan Toll Road project and chose a route to Red Mountain along the Engineer Road to Poughkeepsie Gulch, over Hurricane Pass, and down Corkscrew Gulch. Extra men were put to work on the route, but winter was setting in and even after spending $42,000, the road was nowhere close to being finished. In fact, at the rate the workmen were going, it would take many more years to complete the job.

The Ouray and San Juan Toll Road officers had voluntarily given up their interests in the road because they realized that, although they had the exclusive rights to build from Ouray to Red Mountain, they did not have the funds to build the road quickly, which would have meant a major economic loss to the merchants of Ouray. Ouray County officials also realized they didn't have the funds needed. Otto Mears was eventually asked to take over and supply the necessary engineering expertise, capital, and men for the project. However, his fee would be high – 540 shares of the initial 1,000 shares of the toll company, which would give him total control of the company and the toll road.

Meanwhile efforts were still being made to reach Silverton from the south. In late 1879, Joseph Wallace, James Wightman, and others finished "The Animas Canyon Toll Road." It had taken two years to build at a cost of $60,000. It followed the most logical year-round route into Baker's Park from the south. The Animas Canyon Toll Road's charter stated that the road's purpose was to bring people, coal, and produce to Silverton from Animas City. The charter was issued December, 1879, so the toll road only existed as constructed during 1880, 1881 and the first part of 1882 before the D&RG Railroad arrived. There was initially no stage on the route, but passengers and freight were carried in wagons. It is possible the road was secretly backed by the D&RG, which had already surveyed this route before the toll road was even chartered. By having a toll road, they "saved" the route for themselves. Toll on the road was six dollars per person from Silverton to Baker's Bridge. Even in the winter pack animals and sleds could usually use the Animas Canyon route.

It was basically a good road. From Animas City going north, the road followed the older toll road to a little past Rockwood, then went through the area now covered by Electra Lake, and then plunged down Little Cascade and Cascade Creeks, losing 800 feet of elevation in one-and-a-half miles (an average 12% grade). The road then basically followed what is the present-day railroad grade up the Animas River until it reached the northern toll gate just south of Silverton near the Champion Mine. It was an easy route except the portion up or down Cascade and Little Cascade Creeks. When traveling uphill to the south, the stage and wagons usually had to add two extra horses to their teams; and even then, passengers often had to walk and the driver had to change to fresh horses just one and a half miles later at the top of the hill.

Travel writer Ernest Ingersoll came over this road in 1882. He complained that it was very rough from Rockwood to the bottom of Cascade Creek, but was pretty decent as it followed what would be the railroad grade that was then being built into Silverton. He mentioned that Stony Pass was still being used as a rough, but passable wagon road. He also mentioned that even in the summer the mail came in over Cunningham, and not Stony Pass, probably to make connections with the Highland Mary Mine. A Mr. Howard carried the mail in a sixty pound knapsack, traveling on twelve foot snowshoes (skis) most of the year. Ingersoll also traveled over the Ophir Toll Road on his trip, but he did it on horseback, as the stage wasn't running yet.

In 1879, Bill Harwood and a crew of forty men from Del Norte completed an upgraded toll road over 12,594-foot Stony Pass that was better than the old toll "road" (if it could be called a road). It could be traversed by wagons, but was still very steep

Chapter 4: THE ORIGINAL MILLION DOLLAR HIGHWAY IS BUILT ❋ 87

in places. However, Silverton could honestly claim that it was now accessible by wagon from the east. The new road dropped freight prices from Silverton to Del Norte to thirty dollars per ton. Freighters still claimed the trail to be so rough that "every ten feet there was a stone projecting from six to eighteen inches, and frequently on the opposite side of the road a hole from six to eighteen inches deep with a tree stump in the middle."

In 1879, a wagon road was also completed along the relatively easy eight miles up Cement Creek to Gladstone, and then was extended up a rough, steep slope to the head of Poughkeepsie Gulch, where a pack trail led north to Ouray. The road was constructed to access some rich discoveries in Poughkeepsie Gulch (many of which were owned by H.A.W. Tabor) – the Old Lout, Alaska, Alabama, and Saxton Mines to name a few. The eight mile road to Gladstone later became the roadbed for the Silverton, Gladstone, and Northerly Railroad.

The public road from Silverton up Mineral Creek to Burro Bridge has also been extended as far as Chattanooga, with a pack trail that led to the Red Mountains; and there was another trail that led out of Ironton Park up Corkscrew Gulch and tied into the Gladstone to Poughkeepsie Gulch Road. Although there was no wagon road to Red Mountain, this meant there were two pack trails into the area from Silverton.

In early 1881, when the railroad still had not reached Durango, the stage ran from Durango to Silverton at a cost of ten dollars per person. However, the road was described as being in "deplorable condition." Freight traffic decreased remarkably during this time, when many of the Silverton area mines started to stockpile their ore, waiting for the D&RG Railroad to arrive before shipping. One exception was the North Star Mine that sent its ore over to the owners' mill in Lake City. The first actual stagecoach with a four horse team that made it from Durango to Silverton via the Animas Canyon was in May, 1881.

In the early 1880s, when it became obvious that the railroad would take over the toll road's route through the Animas Canyon, a man named Weir and an unknown partner started a toll wagon road approximately six miles up the steep cliffs from Silverton to Molas Lake (then called Fish Lake), basically following an old Ute trail. The road was finished in 1882 and was operated by Weir until 1905, when he sold it to the county for $1,500. The idea had originally been to extend the Weir road to the old toll road from Animas City to the top of Coal Bank Pass, however money ran out, and it was not possible for a wagon to go further than Molas Lake. This still left a big gap in the middle that was only a trail, and a bad one at that. One major problem was the tangle of dead trees in the Lime Creek Burn. In 1877, The Reverend George Darley traveled "on one part of that trail known as 'Old Coal Bank Hill.' When a long way up, my horse fell while jumping to catch a footing, and rolled more than fifty feet. I was walking behind and came near being carried down with him. The trail was certainly rough."

The Pioneer Stage Company was started at this time by H.A.W. Tabor, who was now totally convinced that the San Juans would be the next Leadville. His Pioneer Stage ran a regular route from Animas City to Silverton and on up to Animas Forks. After the railroad reached Silverton, the stage continued to travel the section from Silverton to Animas Forks (and points in between), and it also later ran to Ouray and along several shorter routes. The stage ran an ad that claimed "We have put on one of the finest buckboards ever on a road, between Animas Forks and Silverton ... connecting with the Rocky Mountain Stage to Lake City."

After 1880, the Brewster Stage Line started running over Stony Pass. Passengers departed from Alamosa on the Barlow and Sanderson Stage Line's "Southern Overland Mail and Express" on the route to Lake City, but at Antelope Springs changed to Brewster's stage and followed the Rio Grande and Animas toll road from Antelope Springs to Silverton by way of Stony Pass.

The Town of Silverton thought it had conquered its transportation problems when the D&RG's first train puffed its way into Silverton on July 13, 1882. When the D&RG arrived, freight rates fell to as low as twelve dollars per ton, and passengers and freight

Chapter 4: THE ORIGINAL MILLION DOLLAR HIGHWAY IS BUILT ❖ 89

could go all the way to Denver without changing trains (although it took almost thirty hours). Silverton's economy boomed because it was now economical to ship low grade ore to the smelters, and at this time the only rail route out of the entire San Juans was at Silverton.

For a while the stage and wagons tried to run alongside the railroad track in the Animas Canyon, but that practice was soon discontinued. Since the railroad used the bed of the wagon toll road for much of the way through the Animas Canyon, it virtually eliminated wagon traffic to the south towards the new town of Durango, which had been built two miles south of the second Animas City. Most people didn't care about toll roads, since shipping and travel were so much cheaper and faster on the railroad than in a wagon. Unfortunately, Ouray and Lake City still had no

Early reports from the San Juans made it sound like there were mines everywhere, as shown in this exaggerated drawing. In fact, most mines were only small holes in the ground. It would take money to make them into real mines.

Harper's Weekly, July 18, 1874. Author's Collection.

railroad. Even though the D&RG had promised branch lines to the towns, it bypassed both of them by about thirty-five miles to the north.

When it became evident in the late summer of 1882 that a major new discovery had been made in the Red Mountains, both Ouray and Silverton fought to be the main supplier for the new mining district. Silverton concentrated its efforts on getting the D&RG to extend their railroad from Silverton to Red Mountain. In the meantime there was the trail from Chattanooga directly up Mineral Creek. The Silverton paper claimed in its end of the year summary of 1882 that a *good* wagon road existed all the way to Chattanooga and from there a *good* trail ran to Red Mountain, but if the road and trail were really that good, they deteriorated quickly in the spring of 1883. Only mules and burros went up to Red Mountain from Silverton, and the packers themselves were the main source of any improvements made to the trail.

The new mining district desperately wanted a wagon road. The Congress Mine (in San Juan County) offered $2,000 to help defray the expenses of anyone who would build a wagon road to its mine. *The La Plata Miner* of January 13, 1883, suggested that San Juan County match that amount. The same paper also scoffed at the idea that Ouray would ever build a road to Red Mountain. "The people of Ouray say they will build a road to Red Mountain. How absurd and ridiculous. The people of Ouray began seven years ago to build a road to Mineral City and have not gotten it completed yet."

However, this time the people of Ouray had a card up their sleeve – they were going to hire Otto Mears to help build the road the six miles through the Uncompahgre Canyon to Ironton Park. Initially, it looked like Ouray made the wiser choice, because the D&RG eventually decided that the route to Red Mountain was impractical for a railroad. On the Ouray side of the pass, Otto Mears declared that the route for a wagon road from Ouray to the Red Mountains would be extremely difficult but possible, and he immediately set to work planning the details.

Chapter 4: THE ORIGINAL MILLION DOLLAR HIGHWAY IS BUILT   ❋ 91

Mears enlisted his friend Fred Waslen to help him with the task of building one of the most difficult roads in all of Colorado. One of their first projects would to get the route out of the bottom of the Uncompahgre Canyon at Ouray on the far north end and move it higher up (to a level near today's highway). This reduced a 30% grade to a 20% grade. Mears then decided that the quickest way to build and the best route at the south end of the six miles would be to go alongside Red Mountain Creek directly through the Uncompahgre Canyon to Ironton Park– the route declared nearly impossible by the Hayden Survey. Mears' engineers had suggested that he totally abandon the idea of going up Engineer, over Poughkeepsie, and down Corkscrew, thereby taking many extra miles off the route. Ouray County's *Red Mountain Review* of March 3, 1883, announced that this time the people of Ouray were serious about building a road, and it predicted that at least a trail would be built to Ironton Park by June, 1883. However it did take several more months for Mears and the County to come to terms in writing. Most of the road from Ouray would have to be blasted into the center of the high cliffs, thereby creating a shelf road. To cut the road through these sections would mean that men were sometimes let down on ropes from the tops of the cliffs. After drilling their holes, the dynamite fuses were lit, and the worker's life depended on the men above quickly pulling him up and away from the blast.

By late March, the County of Ouray had blasted in many places along the Uncompahgre cliffs. In places, like just north of Bear Creek Falls near today's tunnel, the road was very steep, causing the Silverton paper in February to write with just a little exaggeration that "the road is down a fearful grade, so that in the most favorable seasons of the year the mountain sheep pause and tremble to walk the precipitous trail, and in the winter it is practically impossible except for the most daring and heroic mountaineer." A statement in the March 17th paper that "you can only get to Red Mountain from Silverton" followed. On the other hand, the *Red Mountain Review* stated "The road is being blasted in many places and will be ready in the spring" (remember spring is about May or June in the high country).

By late April (with the County still working on the road, but presumably with Mears' advice, a trail that was barely passable by horses or pack animals was completed to Ironton Park, presumably along the creek from the Engineer cutoff. The Silverton and Ouray newspapers broke into a barrage of confusing and inconsistent statements about the road. The April 28, 1883, *Red Mountain*

Some sources identify this image as being on the Million Dollar Highway. Others feel it is the road to Yankee Boy Basin. Either way, it shows how a rough trail was blasted from the sheer cliffs and then widened into a road.
Photo Courtesy of Ft. Lewis College, Center for Southwest Studies.

Chapter 4: THE ORIGINAL MILLION DOLLAR HIGHWAY IS BUILT ❖ 93

Review stated that the new road from Ouray was basically complete and the road would change from the east to the west side of the canyon at Ironton Park. The *La Plata Miner* of May 26, 1883, wrote "the five men working on the road between Ouray and Red Mountain were congratulating themselves the other day upon their good fortune of getting employment for life."

By June 14, 1883, Mears had total ownership of the Ouray and San Juan Wagon Road and work began in earnest. Mears brought hundreds of men in to finish the job. Work went on as long as there was daylight, seven days a week. By July the shelf trail had been blasted into a road wide enough for a wagon to travel all along its path from Bear Creek to the Engineer cutoff. By July Mears had also built his tollgate at Bear Creek. The placement of the tollgate allowed Mears to collect toll from those going up or down the Engineer Road, as well as those going to Red Mountain. Once the road reached Ironton Park, it was supposedly up to Ouray County to build it through the level, but boggy, park to the town of Ironton and then on up to the Red Mountain mines. Unfortunately this decision slowed completion of the road considerably.

On June 16, the *Red Mountain Review* stated that "the road from Ouray is supposed to arrive in two weeks." And then again in August, "the wagon road to Ouray is fast approaching completion. This time it was the County's portion of the road in Ironton Park that was the problem. The *Western Slope Congress of Colorado* wrote: "The stage road from Ouray to Ironton is one of the marvels of the region. In places it is merely a notch carved into the vertical rocks that wall in the Uncompahgre River.... In places it is like looking into the jaws of death."

Things got a little ahead of themselves when in September, 1883, Mears announced that he had just completed arrangements for a tram from Ouray to Red Mountain, which would use mule power to pull the cars up and gravity for downward travel. The *Montrose Messenger* reported that "the grading of the road is almost complete and the bed will be wide enough for a wagon road to run alongside the tramway." Someone was really dreaming here! The finished road was barely wide enough for a single wagon or carriage in most places. If two vehicles didn't see each other in time it could require some real ingenuity, as it was hard to get a team to back up, especially with a loaded wagon. In some places a man in a buggy would have to unhitch his buggy and pull it up on the side of the road to let an ore wagon pass. Along most of the road two vehicles couldn't pass, necessitating some wagons to back up as much as half a mile without turning around.

Anyone who thinks the Million Dollar Highway is narrow today should take a look at this photograph. This may be part of the original county road before it was upgraded by Mears. It is hard to see how an ore wagon could make it through this stretch.

Photo Courtesy of Colorado Historical Society, F-15140.

Chapter 4: THE ORIGINAL MILLION DOLLAR HIGHWAY IS BUILT   ❧ 95

The tollgate above Bear Creek Falls and the little "hotel" that Mears had the toll keeper, Harvey Lewis, build were the subject of this Harper's Weekly *drawing. Because of the cliffs, photographs often couldn't show the bridge, the cabin, and the falls at the same time.*

Author's Collection.

There were still large rocks, and potholes that some said a burro could drown in on a rainy day. It was narrow, steep, and crooked, but it was access, at least to Ironton Park. In October 1883 it was reported that the trail from Ironton to Red Mountain still had not been finished by the County as promised. Otto Mears was called on to finish the road to the mines. With winter coming on, famous freighter Dave Wood promised to use sleds to get to the mines if he could contract ten or twelve wagons or sleds of ore or supplies a day.

Despite the delays in getting the road open, even access by pack trail helped the mining district greatly. It was like a great, dammed-up flood of travel was released and could finally flow to and from Red Mountain. A large amount of ore was shipped out of the district by burros and mules, and hundreds of prospectors made their way to Red Mountain from Ouray along the new trail. Although the Ouray papers constantly proclaimed the progress on the road, and the Silverton papers constantly proclaimed the lack of progress, by the end of the summer of 1883, the road from Ouray was nearing completion at a cost of about $190,000. It was now estimated that certain sections of the road through the Uncompahgre Canyon had cost $40,000 per mile – an immense sum for the time. The bridge over the Uncompahgre (at the present Engineer cutoff) was finished by Mears in September, 1883, and by October, the original "Million Dollar Highway" was basically complete for travel to the town of Ironton, although the main road to the mines was still under construction.

As soon as the road was opened, teams of six huge horses or mules (Clydesdales and Percherons were the top of the line) started pulling huge, heavy wagons with doubled steel wheels up

Although this photograph was taken in the 1920s, it shows the Mears road (lower) blocked by snow and the auto highway (higher up) still open near the Riverside Slide (in the canyon at the right).

Author's Collection.

Chapter 4: THE ORIGINAL MILLION DOLLAR HIGHWAY IS BUILT ❊ 97

Once the toll road got to Ironton Park there was still some major construction necessary. This 50-foot high bridge over Red Mountain Creek was near the Silver Belle Mine. Note that most passengers are up top to enjoy the views.

Photo Courtesy of Colorado Historical Society, F10,512.

and down the Million Dollar Highway. The wagons had bigger than average axles and extra large lumber formed the beds to hold the heavy ore. The wagons had heavy wheel brakes with extra long poles that gave the driver additional braking power. Sometimes a second man would ride in the wagon just to work the brakes on extra steep grades, and sometimes the driver would ride the left wheel mule with a jerk line going to the bridle of the right hand lead mule. Long strings of mules would also snake their ways through the canyons. Men using small whips were encouraging herds of burros up or down the road. Mules or burros were sometimes pulling long loads like lumber, pipe, or ore car tracks with one end dragging on the ground. Really bulky items like pumps, winches, or boilers we often placed directly on wheels on axles and were moved by six mules pulling at the lead and another six pushing at the rear.

Several large freight companies were soon working the road. In Ouray, John Ashenfelter maintained a large barn on Second Street and Eighth Avenue for his many pack and freight animals. At one time he had over fifty-six horse teams pulling his wagons as well as about 100 burros and fifty pack mules. He also kept about fifty horses for rent. Ashenfelter died in 1902, and his company was taken over by John McDonald, another well-respected freighter. Dave Wood worked all over Colorado but in his later life he settled down and worked mostly in Montrose, Gunnison, Ouray and Telluride. Wood advertised that he was "the largest freight outfitter in the west"--a claim that may well have been true. In Silverton it was probably Otto Mears or Louis Wyman who would handle most freight. Stagecoaches full of passengers (as many as possible up top to enjoy the scenery) sped down the Million Dollar Highway. Riderless horses might be making their way back to their stables (and food) at town after their riders had gotten off at a mine and trusted the animals to go home where there was food. And there were many men on foot (usually with a burro following) – a very acceptable way of travel in those days. Everyone was shouting and cajoling, making a real racket which added to the excitement of the day.

Chapter 4: THE ORIGINAL MILLION DOLLAR HIGHWAY IS BUILT

Even with the demand for "good" roads, and specifications having been strictly set by the county commissioners, the condition of Mears' toll road was deplorable compared to today's standards. In places the grades were steep. In most places it was rocky and narrow. But it was a road, and it did the job. Dave Day wrote: "The ride is one that America cannot duplicate, and the road the grandest and most expensive ever inaugurated and completed in the land of pluck and nerve – The Great American West." Freight prices for ore from Red Mountain to the D&RG Railroad in Montrose fell to around thirty dollars a ton. Otto Mears also got his money. The toll for the six-mile trip through the canyon was five dollars per team and wagon, two dollars and fifty cents for a passenger wagon, and one dollar for a saddle horse and rider.

Ouray had beaten Silverton to the Red Mountain Mining District. Silverton still hoped for the D&RG Railroad to build to the mining district from its side of the pass. In the summer of 1883 Thomas Wigglesworth of the D&RG had surveyed from Silverton to the Yankee Girl and Guston Mines for the D&RG Railroad and said the branch could be built. This caused all kinds of rumors that the D&RG had decided to build to Red Mountain. The only problem Wigglesworth had seen was around the Knob at Red Mountain Town. However, despite the favorable report, the owners of the D&RG officially declared that a railroad couldn't be built from Silverton to Red Mountain. The reason was not the terrain, but that the D&RG officials were increasingly focusing on their main lines to Utah and New Mexico, and branch lines weren't appealing at that time or (they thought) as profitable.

Once it became clear that the D&RG would not build to Red Mountain, San Juan County, like Ouray, tried to no avail to build its own wagon road. In March of 1883, San Juan County started building a free public trail from their road's end at Chattanooga to the top of Red Mountain. It wasn't a wagon road, and not even a good trail, but the editor of the Red Mountain Pilot (a Silverton paper) wrote: "the road is all that can be expected." The county spent $1,675 on the project – a large sum for a county trail at that time, but not nearly enough to get a good road; and the trail did not even connect to the old road from Silverton that ended at Chatanooga. It stopped at the bottom of the Red Mountain slope – a matter of only a couple of hundred yards, but the ground was very swampy and needed some major work. The road from Burro Bridge to Chattanooga was soon reported to be in horrible shape because of heavy use and melting snow. However, in order to get to the railroad, the Yankee Girl extended the Silverton trail from the top of Red Mountain Pass to its mine at its own cost.

In the summer of 1883, Joe Patton attempted to run a stage line from Silverton to Red Mountain; but he soon gave up the project because of the condition of the "road." The first wagon of any kind made it from Silverton to Red Mountain on June 20, 1883. The Chattanooga road was in such horrible shape that by the end of the summer of 1883, almost all traffic to Silverton from Red Mountain went east down a trail to Del Mino on Cement Creek and then to Silverton on the road from Gladstone. As winter "improved" the roads, traffic started going by way of Chattanooga again. The San Juan County commissioners tried to build a road from Gladstone to Red Mountain, basically over what is now the Corkscrew Gulch jeep road; but it was a very rough, steep trail that only a few wagons ever even attempted. The commissioners also upgraded the road from Silverton to Chattanooga. In the winter of 1883-84, very large amounts of heavy equipment were moved to Chattanooga from Silverton on sleds pulled by six and eight mule teams, but the final part of the route from Chattanooga to Red Mountain remained very dangerous and extremely steep.

In the fall of 1883, Otto Mears shifted his attention from the nearly finished construction of the Ouray-Red Mountain road to negotiate with the San Juan County commissioners for construction of a toll wagon road from Silverton to Red Mountain. In September he suggested that he would upgrade and finish the entire road for $25,000 plus the tolls he would collect. Most Silverton residents were vehemently against the move, as they felt

Chapter 4: THE ORIGINAL MILLION DOLLAR HIGHWAY IS BUILT ❋ 101

the monopoly of roads to Red Mountain would allow Mears to charge extremely high toll rates. The *Silverton Standard* later wrote "there was considerable agitation as (the local miners and merchants) felt that he was getting more than his share of the gravy, and tolls were exorbitant." Silverton merchants also pointed out that the road from Silverton to Chattanooga was now in pretty good shape. Instead of being intimidated, Mears increased his request to $40,000 in bonds plus the tolls. Nevertheless, the parties agreed in principle; but because winter was setting in, it would be almost six months before Mears could actually begin work.

The owners of the Congress Mine were so anxious to ship ore that they built their own "road" to a point on the county wagon road south of Chattanooga; but because of large rocks, mud, and stumps, it was only passable by sleds during the winter time. In the summer it was extremely slippery when wet. This road still exists as what is now called the Brooklyn Jeep Road. Meanwhile the citizens of Silverton voted to authorize $70,000 in highway bonds. The bond issue was totally open-ended, as it did not specify where the money was to be spent, although it was assumed that the majority would go to Mears' road to Red Mountain.

It wasn't until June, 1884, that Mears and the San Juan county commissioners came to a written agreement, which contained certain provisions that at first glance one might speculate the commissioners felt were needed given the supposedly poor construction of Mears' road from Ouray. The road grade was to be a continuous downgrade to Silverton, with no more than a 350-foot drop per mile (a seven percent grade), and it was to be wide enough for two wagons to pass at all points. No curve was to be so sharp that a six mule team could not exert its entire effort throughout the whole curve. The construction was to have proper drainage and also usable for winter travel. These provisions would provide a very good road when compared to other mountain roads of the time, but some opponents still protested that Mears was being paid a small fortune to only improve what was already there. Mears was doing more than that. The easy, wide grade up the mountain would be perfect for the railroad that Mears already had in mind – and he was getting San Juan County to pay for it!

Mears put 350 men to work on July 8, 1884. Most of the men were inexpensive Mexican or Navajo laborers. The only extensive work needed was the three miles starting at Muleshoe Curve at Chattanooga and up and over the mountain. This part of the road had to be blasted, and work stopped periodically when Mears' workmen hit ore bodies along the way. (Unfortunately the ore was not rich enough to mine.) The road was basically completed to the Yankee Girl Mine by November 1884; however, it was only finished after Mears requested and received an additional $12,000 cash "donation" from San Juan County for the road's construction in December, 1884. Winter had arrived, so the first stage from Montrose didn't make its run to Silverton until the summer of 1885. When the stage did make its first run, it was decorated, pulled by six white horses, and had travelled from Ouray to Silverton in just over three hours.

Now Mears had a six-mile toll road from Ouray to Ironton Park and a twelve-mile road from Silverton to the Red Mountain Pass. The section in the middle was technically a public road, but that didn't bother Mears, since he controlled the access from both ends. Mears had set his northern tollgate just outside Ouray at Bear Creek Falls. The south gate was at Burro Bridge (since the Ophir Toll Road still existed).

Both Ouray and Silverton could now access the new Red Mountain Mining District by wagons, but they did it over Otto Mears toll roads. In one year Mears was reported to have collected $100,000 in tolls, much of it from the army and the federal government. Much of the ore from Red Mountain was going to Silverton because of the arrival of the D&RG train in that town. Due to lower freight rates, the amount of ore being shipped from all over the San Juans picked up dramatically. Less than a million dollars in ore had been shipped from Ouray and San Juan Counties combined in all the years before the arrival of the train in Silverton (1860-1882). After the arrival of the train, there was more than a million

Chapter 4: THE ORIGINAL MILLION DOLLAR HIGHWAY IS BUILT ❦ 103

This part of the road was at the south end of the "impassible canyon" that the Hayden Survey wrote about. The debris in the foreground was from the Riverside Slide.

Photo by William H. Jackson. Courtesy of Colorado Historical Society, WHJ 2786.

dollars in ore shipped each year from the Red Mountain Mining District alone, and sometimes it was many times that amount. With the railroad's presence, capitalists began to turn their attention to the San Juans, and badly needed money started to become available for the development of the local mines.

The road from Ouray to Silverton was now finished in its entirety, but it was a much different road from that of today. It started near today's highway barn at Ouray, went up an eighteen percent grade, then back down to the river, and then back up a twenty percent grade so it could pass over Bear Creek Falls. The route, which was barely wide enough for one wagon, then crept south across the cliffs, went down almost to the river at the Riverside Slide, then straight up to Ironton Park (there were no switchbacks like today). Then the road went along the west side of the park (it is still there if you look carefully), back to the middle of the park about Ironton, and up the east side of the mountains through the Guston and Yankee Girl Mines to Red Mountain Town. The road to Silverton followed basically the same path it does today (the old road can occasionally be seen slightly above or below today's Million Dollar Highway).

As rough as the road might seem by today's standards, the people of Silverton and Ouray were "pleased as punch." Everyone felt the new wagon and stage road, with its awesome scenery, would soon dramatically increase the number of tourists coming to the San Juans. Dave Day's article in the December 6, 1884, issue of the *Solid Muldoon* is lengthy, but worth quoting:

> *It should be the policy of the various counties throughout the state to build and own their own wagon roads, but when they are without the means to build them, it is nothing short of commendable judgment on the part of the people to prevail on those having the means to build toll roads. A toll road is a long way better than a burro trail, and even if the rates of toll are rather high, shipping over a wagon road is always much cheaper than packing on mules and burros. The best illustration of this*

is found in the case of the new toll road to Red Mountain. Everybody knows that heretofore the cost of bringing a ton of ore from the Red Mountain to Silverton ranged from nine to fourteen dollars. The cost is now only about four dollars and thirty cents from the Yankee Girl Mine situated over one mile beyond the divide. The one factor that has contributed so much to the reduction in shipping costs is that the new road has been built on such a grade that a six mule team can draw about eight tons of ore in one load. The rates of toll are thirty cents on a ton, and this is included in the figure of four dollars and thirty cents a ton from the mine above mentioned…The branch from Ouray to Mount Sneffles costs thirty thousand dollars; Ouray to Montrose, twenty five thousand dollars; Telluride to Montrose, forty nine thousand dollars; and Silverton to Animas Forks—when finished— fifty thousand dollars.…

The advantages that Silverton will receive from the road just completed to Ouray, will not be alone in increased ore shipments, but in an increased number of visitors as well. The wonderful scenery along this road surpasses in wilderness and grandeur anything in the state, and as the beauties of the road are certain to be well known, it can confidently be expected that tourists will make the trip in preference to any other. The wildest scenery along the road is about sixteen miles from Silverton, and commences at a point several miles beyond Ironton. The first striking view on the road is at the point where it curves to the right before the Uncompahgre Bridge is reached. At this place an uninterrupted view is had of the Uncompahgre Valley and the Grand Mesa some fifty miles away. The mountains rise up for thousands of feet around you and you seem to be literally walled in except looking north. When Uncompahgre Bridge is reached another grand spectacle is presented. You are directly under masses of rock that tower two thousand feet above you, and looking up the Uncompahgre the wagon road to Poughkeepsie can be seen winding in and out until it appears no larger than a thread in the distance.

A mile or so beyond the Uncompahgre bridge can be seen some of the finest pieces of road work in this country set off by surroundings without parallel. The road has been chiseled out of solid rock, about one thousand feet above the bed of the usually turbulent and roaring Uncompahgre River, and about the same distance below the snow capped peaks. The mountains on either side rise up almost perpendicularly and not more than five hundred feet apart. Roaring cataracts leap from their sides, and present the appearance of being vertical bands of silver. A mile or so beyond, the celebrated Bear Creek Falls, and the point where the lover of the wild and beautiful in nature can tarry without becoming weary. Bear Creek rushes down a rocky defile with a greater angle than forty five degrees and at the point where the falls are formed, makes a leap of two hundred feet into a rock-bottomed basin below. This is a basin of almost perpetual rainbows, and they can be seen in rare brilliancy at nearly every hour of the day. Numerous other points of attraction occur between Bear Creek Falls and Ouray, but the crowning point of the grand scenery is just as you reach the promontory that overlooks the pretty little village of Ouray. The town nestles between beautiful terraced mountains that rise up on the east, south, and west, while stretching away to the North is the Uncompahgre Valley. The exquisite beauty of the scenery in the vicinity of Ouray, as well as along the road, really has to be seen to be appreciated, and descriptions, no matter how eloquent, invariably fail to do it even half justice.

And how much did the road cost to build? It was reported that from Silverton to the Yankee Girl Mine the road cost $56,937, the three miles from the Yankee Girl to Ironton $9,800, and the eight miles from Ironton to Ouray $143,200. Not nearly a million dollars, but well worth the price! In 1885 Fossett wrote that "one of the best mountain wagon roads in Colorado has recently been completed between (Silverton) and Ouray."

Chapter 4: THE ORIGINAL MILLION DOLLAR HIGHWAY IS BUILT ❋ 107

The Riverside snow tunnel became a tourist attraction. The six-horse Circle Route stage has just come through the tunnel. Other tourists are on the road that went over the slide. Note the large amount of debris.

Photo, Author's Collection.

The County of Ouray had twice given up on the road. Two previous toll road companies (in 1877 and 1880) had tried but failed. Otto Mears did what others couldn't, but he only operated the road until 1887, when he sold it for less than his stated construction expenses, and then unsuccessfully petitioned the Colorado legislature for reimbursement of the rest of the money. But don't feel sorry for Otto. With the tolls that he collected over the five years he ran the toll road, he made a very good return on his money.

The Million Dollar Highway was used summer and winter, although avalanches made winter traffic more dangerous and sleds were used instead of wagons. The Reverend J. J. Gibbons, an early-day Catholic priest in the San Juans, reported that a winter 1890s trip by stage from Ouray to Red Mountain was "in the usual way without anymore serious inconvenience than that of being obliged to shovel snow, open the road, and help drag out the horses from high drifts." The average speed of travel by stage over the road was said to be three to five miles an hour.

Almost from the day that it was finished, the Million Dollar Highway was touted as a "tourist's delight." The Circle Route Stage brochure for 1892 reported:

> *This wonderful road owes its construction to the genius, daring, and wealth of one man, Otto Mears, who has been for years the "Pathfinder of the San Juan region," building toll roads and opening the gates of prosperity to the many towns of this mountainous country... The old fashioned stage, with its romantic association, is rapidly becoming a thing of the past. A year or two more and it will disappear, except in rare instances, from Colorado.*

This statement was a little premature. Stages (including the Circle Route) would run for decades to come. Until the advent of the automobile, they were usually the only means to conveniently travel into any of Colorado's remote areas. But the automobile would change everything – including the Million Dollar Highway.

Chapter 5

CHANGING TIMES

AT THE BEGINNING of the Twentieth Century, many events caused a switch of transportation modes in the San Juans, which eventually led to the building of the Million Dollar Highway of today. Although the charter of Otto Mears' Silverton to Ouray Toll Road expired in 1900, the *Silverton Standard* reported that the road was taken over by San Juan and Ouray Counties in 1887. Other sources say Mears sold the road to the counties in 1891. The Colorado Department of Transportation confirms the 1887 date, but mentioned that the road was still being called "the toll road" in the early 1890s. Regardless of the actual date, why did Mears sell out so early? The answer is not known for sure, but it is possible that since Mears was getting ready to start building the Silverton Railroad from that town to Ironton Park, he felt it was no longer necessary to control the toll roads between Ouray and Silverton. He needed the toll road on the Silverton side of the pass to get the necessary grade for the Silverton Railroad. He had already made a good return on his money, and perhaps (but it is not likely) the criticism over high tolls was getting to him. Or perhaps he was being philanthropic. The real reason is probably a combination of all of these possibilities.

The Town of Ironton, eight miles south of Ouray on the Million Dollar Highway, looked pretty well past its prime in 1908. We are looking north down the mile long Main Street with the Albany Mill in the background at the bottom of the slope.
Photo Courtesy of Denver Public Library, Western History Department, F 12497.

At any rate, at the beginning of the twentieth century the Million Dollar Highway had become a public road. After the Silver Panic of 1893, the boom times were over and the Red Mountain Mining District began to decline sharply. The Silverton Railroad (built by Mears from Red Mountain to Silverton) was eventually abandoned, and even the D&RG's Durango-Silverton branch was having major financial troubles as mining declined. However, the biggest event, which changed not just the San Juans but the whole of the United States, was the advent of the automobile.

Chapter 5: CHANGING TIMES ❊ 111

The first car in Colorado was a homemade electric model made in 1895. The first factory-made cars started showing up around 1898. Only the most daring would venture onto a wagon road in an automobile in those days, and almost no one dared to go into the mountains in a car; although in 1901, a car made it to the top of Pikes Peak, even though the "road" was nothing more than a footpath. In 1902, there were 200 cars in Denver, but most were steam or electric powered. Gasoline-powered cars hadn't shown up until 1901, but quickly caught on.

In 1902, enthusiasts of the new-fangled invention started the Colorado Automobile Club. In July 1905, sixty-three Colorado counties formed the Colorado Good Road Association in an attempt to coordinate Colorado highway projects and raise money for the construction of better roads. The three counties along the Million Dollar Highway (La Plata, San Juan, and Ouray) were all members of the new organization. The use of automobiles was catching on fast. Rather than being intimidated by the hardship and costs of constructing good highways in the mountain areas, the people of the San Juans realized the importance of obtaining good automobile roads as quickly as possible. This was exactly the kind of territory that attracted tourists. National Parks were being started, and auto camping was beginning to become popular. Auto clubs, chambers of commerce, tourist businesses, even automobile dealers all demanded better mountain roads.

In 1893, the State of Colorado had allocated $15,000 to San Juan County for the start of a wagon road, as there was no wagon road of any kind from Silverton to Durango at the time; but by the time the project was finished it would be an automobile road. In 1907 the federal government decided that twenty-five cents of every dollar earned by the U. S. Forest Service should be dedicated to road construction within the forest boundaries. A major part of the route of today's Million Dollar Highway qualified for such funding.

Although it had very little initial funding, a Colorado Highway Commission was being considered in 1907, was formed in 1909, and was funded in 1910 for the purpose of setting automobile highway standards and getting better roads in Colorado. Because there was very little construction funding available, the Colorado Highway Commission decided that its main focus would be to coordinate and oversee construction work, and that they would leave scenic routes, such as the Million Dollar Highway, for the Forest Service to fund. However, southwest Colorado immediately received the attention, if not the money that it deserved, as Thomas H. Tulley of Durango, and Dave Day's son-in-law, was one of the first Colorado highway commissioners.

As a part of the movement toward good roads, San Juan County, in 1905, bought the Weir Toll Road, which ran up the steep cliffs south from Silverton to Molas Pass. The county then

The Million Dollar Highway in the "Upper Animas Valley" was at the end of its wagon era in the late 1910s when this photo was taken. Note how well the road has been graded.

Author's Collection.

used $1,500 in state funds to augment county funding and upgrade and extend the road over Coal Bank Hill to what remained of the old Wightman toll road of 1876 after it came up Cascade Creek from the Animas Canyon near present-day Durango Ski Mountain. This meant that for the first time since the D&RG Railroad built into Silverton in 1882, there was a complete (if not good) wagon road from Durango to Silverton, and it was a free public road. However, the road was very difficult to travel; so much so, that when not traveling by train, the Stony Pass Road was still usually preferred for travel in and out of Baker's Park. Then in 1909 and again in 1911 disastrous floods destroyed so much of the Silverton to Durango road that it was reported to be only passable to pack animals.

Another idea of how bad the conditions were on the Silverton to Durango Road can be ascertained from the fact that the first automobile to arrive in Silverton, basically under its own power, came by way of Stony Pass. On August 26, 1910, David Mechling (a former Silverton pharmacist and owner of the car) and John McGuire (editor of *Outdoor Life* magazine) drove a thirty-horsepower Croxton-Keeton (manufactured in Ohio but patterned after the French Renault) over 12,500-foot Stony Pass. They also brought their sons with them for the adventure. The trip had been planned for months in advance, after San Juan County Commissioner Louis Wyman invited them to make the trip in an attempt to promote the need for more and better highways in the San Juans. Their trip wasn't made without its snags: Mechling and McGuire had to build part of the roadway during their journey; they had to ford the Rio Grande numerous times; they had many flat tires and several mechanical breakdowns; they had to stop quite a few times to roll boulders out of the road; the automobile had to be pulled part of the way by horses; they had to stop many times going down Stony to let the brakes cool; and the 110-mile trip took five days from Del Norte in the San Luis Valley to Silverton.

Two women and a man waving an American flag met Mechling, McGuire, and their sons at the top of the pass. As the car got closer to Silverton, people greeted them (and more importantly their car) every few hundred feet, and many well-wishers ran alongside the car for long distances. Much of the crowd had never seen a car before. When the group reached Silverton City Hall, bells were rung, dynamite was set off, the city band played, and a party was held. Otto Mears, who was living in Silverton at the time, was on hand to help promote improved roads in the San Juans and to make a speech in which he pushed for a Durango to Grand Junction highway that would be passable along the entire route by automobiles. The next day, the Croxton-Keeton made it (with help again) over Red Mountain Pass to Ouray.

Shortly afterwards another car became the first to make it *up* to Ironton from Ouray. That honor went to L. G. Crosby, a Ouray doctor, who with several friends made it in his Model T to Ironton Park on a house call. The Montrose paper wrote "It was a trip that few believed could ever be accomplished. It was one of the most exhilarating, thrilling, unusual, and stirring automobile trips that could be made or imagined." That same year, the State Highway Commission designated the "road" from Ouray to Silverton as State Highway 13, even though to call it an "automobile road" was a gross overstatement. It was 1911 before a car made it to the top of Red Mountain Pass totally under its own power.

By 1910, the D&RG Railroad was beginning to see a decline in passengers as automobiles gained favor; and, in 1911, the D&RG route from Durango to Silverton almost disappeared forever. Miles and miles of D&RG track was torn out by the torrential waters of an Animas River flood. Most Silverton merchants didn't have their winter supplies of food and coal yet, and there was no decent wagon road to bring supplies into town. This event made Silverton residents realize what a dangerous situation they were in when the train provided the only access from Durango. Otto Mears called in every favor he had coming and rounded up every available piece of equipment and every piece of coal he needed to run the engines. He even closed the Silverton, Gladstone and Northerly Railroad so he could bring its men and equipment to help replace the D&RG tracks. Work was

Chapter 5: CHANGING TIMES　　　　　　　　　　　　　　❋ 115

On June 22, 1911, the first automobile made it to the top of Red Mountain Pass, but it is hard to tell where the road (if any) is in this scene.

Author's Collection.

---

pushed hard, the railroad line was reopened by December (luckily winter came late that year), and the town was saved.

A 1912 tour guide, *Highways of Colorado: Official Guide and Tour Book*, by the Clawson Map Company, gives a good view of the "highway" at the time:

> The road between Ouray and Silverton is a windy, steep road, rather narrow, often on solid ledges with some pretty steep grades. It is used more or less by automobiles. Built by Otto Mears in 1883, and considered a wonderful piece of engineering. Can hardly be recommended at present for automobiles.... Some of the greatest scenic wonders known to man can be viewed on the road from Ouray to Silverton and in the region thereabouts. Mountains on all sides rear their peaks far into the

> *region of perpetual snows. Ouray and Silverton are the center of a great mining district.... Tourists who do not care to undergo the "scenic highway" by automobile can stop in Ouray and go by stage to the various mining camps. Days can be spent here viewing the great works of nature.*

Once it got limited funding, one of the first items on the agenda for the Colorado Highway Commission was to identify roads that were important enough and in good enough shape to be brought immediately into the State of Colorado road system. Surprisingly, the Montrose to Durango highway was one of the first to be accepted. Perhaps this showed just how bad the roads were in the state at that time, but more likely it showed the critical importance of a north-south road through the San Juans. The commission's acceptance only meant the Montrose to Durango road was accessible and not that it was a good automobile highway.

The Colorado Highway Commission sent men throughout the state to physically inspect the roads that had been suggested for acceptance into the state system. Some stretches of road were not only found to be bad – they were found to not even exist. An example was a twenty-five mile stretch of road that was supposed to go over Wolf Creek Pass that never was found by the commissioners.

The Colorado Highway Commission also set standards for roads, road construction, and eventually signage for highways. This was a time when roads were still being built with mule teams, and the highway department had to set some standards that seem pretty obvious today, such as fill dirt had to be compacted and proper drainage away and under the road was necessary. Before these regulations were instituted, roads were usually built in whatever way was the easiest – usually with no engineering and often by local farmers and ranchers who just graded a road across their land with their own plow and a team of mules.

Another problem faced by the Colorado Highway Commissioners was the purchase of rights-of-way. Many counties did not own or have a legal easement across the land on which the county roads had been built, and the State of Colorado had never owned rights-of-way before this time. Therefore there might be no legal right to go across the land until the right-of-way was purchased or given to the state by landowners. The Million Dollar Highway had the advantage of passing through public land for most of its length.

With the flood of new automobiles into Colorado, there continued to be a real push to construct good automobile roads. Otto Mears wasn't just dreaming again when he made his speech in Silverton for a road from Durango to Grand Junction. By 1910, serious thought was being given by many elected officials concerning an automobile road that would run all the way from Durango to Denver. Two routes were being considered – one by way of Wolf Creek Pass and Alamosa and another by way of Montrose and Grand Junction. According to the law at the time, two-thirds of the construction money had to come from the counties in which the road was being built. La Plata, San Juan, and Ouray Counties all quickly agreed to pay for their share of the costs.

It was 1913 before a new highway law provided any serious amount of construction money from the state of Colorado. By that time there was an immediate demand for roads, and the Colorado legislature was in a position of playing catch-up. The state allocated $461,000 for road construction that year. The amount that the state of Colorado designated then rose quickly – for example, $3,896,000 in 1920 and $6,735,882 in 1922. Combined with federal, county, and Forest Service money, the construction of good roads in Colorado could now move full steam ahead.

It is an interesting side-light that during this time the Silverton Commercial Club, which supported good roads, emphasized that priority should be given to another railroad route into Silverton from the south so as to break the monopoly of the D&RG Railroad. There evidently had been many complaints about the high freight rates between Durango and Silverton, and most citizens still looked to the railroad for the transport of their freight, as trucks of the time could not yet carry any substantial amount of weight.

Even in 1913, the Circle Route Tour was still carrying tourists by stage along the Million Dollar Highway. For several decades the stage had run from Ouray to Ironton, where passengers got on the Silverton Railroad. The length of the stage route, however, now needed to be extended from Ouray all the way to Silverton, as the Silverton Railroad was no longer running. The D&RG's pamphlet on the Circle Route assured its clients that the train would run again soon, but for now the stage would parallel the railroad tracks from Red Mountain to Silverton.

The D&RG's pamphlet also advertised that tourists could stop any where along the entire Circle Route and stay a while, as long as the route was completed within sixty days. Many of the tourists chose to stay in Ouray or Silverton, which were now actually on a side trip through the Red Mountains, since the main route was via the Rio Grande Southern Railroad (also owned by Otto Mears), built from Ridgway to Durango in 1892. Durango had the advantage of getting tourists from either route. Because the train was the only easy and comfortable way to tour Colorado before the arrival of the automobile and good roads, the Circle Route included special coaches, sleeper cars, and diners. Tourism was beginning to take off big time in the San Juans and throughout Colorado.

As for the stage coach (which the D&RG pamphlet almost twenty years earlier had said would disappear), the pamphlet now declared that "the famous Concord coach is still used – drawn by six clattering horses, the driver picturesque on his seat." Besides the natural scenery (the pamphlet declared "the colors of the cliffs and of the foliage are extra ordinary"), the D&RG pointed out the "local color," such as "likely enough a prospecting outfit, with a pack train of burros, is encountered."

The route from Ouray to Silverton was sometimes called the "Circle Route Highway" during this time. In 1913, John Melton opened the Circle Route Garage in Silverton. It was Silverton's first garage, and one of the first in the San Juans, although an automobile dealership had been opened in Durango in 1908. Milton and I. J. Bradford rented cars for forty cents a mile or four dollars a

Chapter 5: CHANGING TIMES ❖ 119

day (it was hard to log ten miles in a day in a Silverton car in those days). The price included the driver and three passengers.

In 1913, the ratio of state to county funding for road construction changed to fifty-fifty. This was the first year that any serious funding was available from the state of Colorado. The increase in the state of Colorado's part of the funding was due in great part to federal funding being made available for Colorado roads starting in 1912. The extra funding was a great financial incentive to get work underway on automobile roads, and the Wolf Creek Pass road was built at this time.

Silverton attorney W. N. Searcy and Otto Mears both pushed vehemently from 1910 to 1913 for a Durango-Grand Junction-Denver highway. Mears never missed an opportunity to talk about the road to anyone that would listen, and several times he spoke to the state legislature and the county commissioners involved about

The Circle Route Stage was still running until the Million Dollar Highway was upgraded to an automobile road. The stage is in front of John Donald's livery stable in Ouray. There are eight passengers on top of the forerunner of today's jeep tours.

Author's Collection.

Even after the Million Dollar Highway was upgraded to an auto road, it was sometimes necessary to use horses and a sled in the winter. This scene is from the early 1930s.

Ruth and Marvin Gregory Collection.

allocating money for the project. After all the counties along the highway had agreed to put up their one-half share of the cost (believing correctly that it would quickly pay for itself many times over by increased tourist traffic), the state of Colorado agreed to the route through Grand Junction. In this sense Otto Mears may truly be called at least one of the fathers of the entire "extended" Million Dollar Highway, as the present auto road had its birth from the project led by Mears and Searcy.

Since the Stony Pass Road could not be easily upgraded for automobiles, that route was basically abandoned at this time. Work south out of Silverton along the first six miles of highway to Molas Pass was started in 1913 at the same time work was started to the north from Durango. This was the true beginning of the extended Million Dollar Highway. The Forest Service records show that San Juan County had continued to work on the road from 1893 until

Chapter 5: CHANGING TIMES ❋ 121

1913, but it fought a constant battle with repairs caused by floods, avalanches, and landslides. Even with total expenditures of over $30,000, the county "road" was open only to pack animals. During this time, the Forest Service had been asked to help the county, but it had no funding available, until the Federal Road Aid Act of 1916.

The American lifestyle was changing quickly. They were enjoying their newfound freedom and the mobility to travel in their exciting new cars. With the decline in local mining, the tourist business was becoming very important in the San Juans. Many of the tourists were Coloradoans, as the population of the state was growing very rapidly. From 1910 to 1920, automobiles and trucks were fast replacing horses, mules and wagons, and a major dent had been made in railroad passenger traffic. Excursions were being made into the mountains by motorized vehicles, many early day recreational vehicles or camper trailers (both usually homemade) and "auto courts" were beginning to appear along the automobile highways.

By 1914, the towns at the edges of the San Juans (like Creede and Durango) were reporting that tourists were arriving by automobile from as far away as Kansas. On the negative side, it was unfortunately becoming evident that state tourism efforts were singling out the eastern slope and ignoring the San Juans and the Western Slope of Colorado in general. There is no doubt that building roads was a much bigger challenge in the mountains, but the San Juan Mountains were exactly what the tourists were coming to see, if they could find their way -- the lack of direction signs made mountain travel a true adventure.

Progress on upgrading the road to an automobile highway was also started at the north end of the Million Dollar Highway, although work began a little later than on the southern end. During 1916 the state of Colorado and Ouray County spent $8,000 to improve the first two miles of road south out of Ouray. In 1920, the state of Colorado, federal government, and Ouray County spent $75,000 on a 1.15- mile stretch of road that included the tunnel and improvements at Bear Creek Falls. At the time, it was reportedly the highest price for a mile of road construction anywhere in the state – possibly even in the United States. The tunnel was 200 feet long and 17 feet wide. Again, as a cost saving factor, Navajos did part of the work.

An example of the importance of building automobile roads can be seen in the statistics in the rise of automobiles — there were about 15,000 cars in the state of Colorado in 1917, and over 30,000 by 1920! The federal government started to match the counties' construction expenses under the federal "Good Road Bill" of 1916. The Colorado Highway Department (as opposed to the Colorado Highway Commission) was established in 1917 with a mandate to encourage good automobile roads throughout the state of Colorado. The Colorado Highway Department assumed the maintenance of all state and federal highways in the state of Colorado – another great cost-saving factor for the counties. Colorado was very committed to better automobile roads and was one of the first four states to institute a fuel tax (one cent a gallon in 1919) to be used for highway repair and construction.

After World War I ended, there were more frantic efforts to build new roads. Convict labor was even being used in some parts of the state. Surveys were made in the San Juans during 1917, and it was determined that much of the old wagon road between Durango and Silverton could be used if it was repaired and then elevated to the status of an automobile highway. The exception would be the construction of the new Lime Creek road. The January 13, 1917, *Silverton Standard* reported that the road from Durango to Silverton would be fifty-five miles long and cost $190,000 to build. The cost would be split pretty much equally by the state, La Plata and San Juan Counties, and the U. S. Forest Service. The road was to be started in the spring of 1917, and finished by January 1, 1920. The Forest Service would oversee construction of the two-lane road, which would have a maximum grade of six percent. The new road would be State Highway 13 (later changed to 19). The road was to go up the Animas Valley to Hermosa, up the hills past Electra Lake, down the new Lime Creek route (which would require considerable blasting and upon which most of the construction money

Chapter 5: CHANGING TIMES   ❋ 123

would be spent), then up to Molas Pass and down the existing road to Silverton. The 1918 Forest Service report boasted that "there is much of the country traversed by the new road which very few people have ever explored."

In July, 1918, work started on what was now estimated to be a $350,000 upgrade along this section of the Million Dollar Highway (construction estimates rose quickly in those days, too). Progress was slow because of the many steep cliffs and grades. Construction was impeded even further by the 1918 influenza epidemic, which hit the San Juans so hard that 150 people died in one week in Silverton. The Town Hall was turned into a hospital, and the citizens of Silverton wore surgical masks when they went outside their homes. Individual graves couldn't be dug fast enough, so trenches had to be used, one of which eventually contained sixty-two bodies. Ten percent of the population of Silverton died in a three-week period; and even

Construction workers widen the Million Dollar Highway about 1920, when it was upgraded to an automobile road. This task was easier than the original construction but was still hard and dangerous work.
Photo Courtesy of Colorado Historical Society, F 23,852.

worse, most of them were children and young adults. Eventually, 1,298 Silverton residents contracted the flu or had related pneumonia problems. This was the highest percentage of people to contract (or to die) of the flu of any town in the United States.

After the flu epidemic was over, work continued to progress on the north end of the Million Dollar Highway. In 1920, the Federal Aid Project allocated $50,000 to the Colorado Highway Department to use on the road north of Bear Creek Falls. This would have included work on the tunnel, the large concrete pull off at Bear Creek Falls, and the road all the way back to Ouray.

Throughout the early 1920s, the project to turn the Million Dollar Highway into a true automobile highway (for its time) continued its progression, all the way from Durango to Ouray. At the middle of the route, the Lime Creek Burn (which had occurred forty years earlier) was found to be a very hard area to get the highway through. The construction crews hated this section of road because of the many dead trees – some of which had fallen into huge piles like jackstraws, and the men had to climb over and through them to work (remember this was pre-chainsaw days). Other huge trees were still standing but could easily fall and kill a man instantly. Just as if to remind the construction workers, they would hear a dead tree fall almost every day. The whole route from Molas Lake to the top of Coal Bank Pass was in this kind of condition.

The new section of highway that was being built from Silverton to Durango basically followed the 1905 county wagon road (and was close to the same width and grade), except that it skirted Coal Bank Hill around Potato Mountain to the east through Lime Creek Canyon (the stretch of highway now known as the "Old Lime Creek Road"). Bill Compton, Roy Roff, Fred Salfisberg, Bob Lockwood and a few other employees of the Western Colorado Power Company probably made the first complete trip over the new route from Durango to Silverton in October of 1920, although the road wasn't officially opened for several more years. The power company group had to lay planks for bridges over many of the road's ditches and holes, but the group made it!

Chapter 5: CHANGING TIMES

Construction took longer than expected, mainly because of the extra blasting and heavy rockwork that was necessary along the existing road to widen it to two lanes and reduce grades. When the road was finished, cars could make it from Durango to Silverton, although the road was really rough, and it was still frequently closed to public traffic because of further construction work being done during the summer.

The July 4th celebration in Silverton in 1921 included a dedication of the Durango-Silverton portion of the road, which was now almost finished, but a year and a half after the original estimate. The route was designated State Highway 19. The July 9, 1921 *Silverton Standard* indicated that the cost of the new highway had risen to a half million dollars, but "the view must be seen to understand and be appreciated. It will make even the old-timers gasp in astonishment and realize that changes of Rocky Mountain panoramas are as endless as they are infinite.... Every automobile owner in the San Juan Basin should make a trip over the new highway."

Almost everyone who had a car at the 1921 celebration was driving Henry Ford's new invention. The Model T Ford had made the automobile accessible to many people who could not have possibly afforded an automobile before the Model T arrived on the scene. Henry Ford's little car was available for as little as $300, but that price was for a roadster with no top, windshield, or spare tire. With all of the accessories included, the price of the car was pushed up to almost $600. One of the car's greatest attributes was that it was light and could go almost anywhere, including travel over Colorado's mountain roads, and through mud and snow.

In the early 1920s, the San Juan towns started publishing tourist brochures to attract some of these new travelers. The U. S. Forest Service report for the San Juans for 1918 mentioned that the Durango to Silverton link would be the last piece of the new "Thousand Mile Circle Route" – this time the tourists would be traveling in their cars instead of the train. Durango was especially proud to advertise its wonderful climate and the many nearby attractions. Color postcards became available and were sent home by the tourists, thereby exposing the wonders of the San Juans to more potential travelers. Road maps were created for the first time, and local road information was usually easily available.

The San Juan communities desperately needed the tourist business, as mining production had peaked about 1920. Approximately three and a half million dollars in ore was shipped from Silverton that year, but it would be a record that would never be broken. The D&RG Railroad was in financial trouble and reorganized into the Denver and Rio Grande Western Railroad in 1920. Several major floods occurred along the Durango-Silverton route between 1900 and 1920, causing the D&RG to spend large sums of money for reconstruction. Much of the San Juan freight and ore was now being hauled by trucks, and with the reduced freight traffic, the rail route from Durango to Silverton was losing money.

The United States government took over the D&RGW Railroad during World War I and ran it from 1917 to 1920. A large amount of capital was infused into the line, since the United States government wanted to be sure it could transport base metals (copper, zinc, lead, fluorspar, magnesium, etc.) that were badly needed for the war effort. The railroad would probably have closed at this time without federal help. Most Silverton citizens said later that they wished the government had run the railroad from that point on, but the railroad went back to the D&RGW in 1920.

Back on the north end of the Million Dollar Highway, the July, 1922, *Colorado Highways* magazine announced that work was to begin immediately on a $100,000 upgrade on the original Million Dollar Highway between Ironton and Ouray. This stretch of road was closed on August 15, 1922, to make it easier and faster to do blasting in the canyon, much to the chagrin of the citizens and merchants in Ouray and Silverton, who were worried that the road would not be reopened by the summer of 1923. Extensive work was being done along the high shelf from Bear Creek Falls to the Riverside Slide to widen the road into a narrow two-lane highway.

The new road was getting its fair share of publicity – some good and some bad. An article in the *Kansas City Star* called both

Chapter 5: CHANGING TIMES ❈ 127

This close-up shows some of the incredible rock work (the barriers and the shoring on the side of the road) along the Ruby Cliffs. This was a lot more substantial than the logs that were originally used.

Photo Courtesy of Colorado Historical Society, F 42,577.

the D&RG train and the road from Silverton to Durango "as dangerous as any in the state." A *Saturday Evening Post* article called the route from Ouray to Silverton "the sportiest of all the main roads in Colorado." The *Colorado Highways* magazine of May, 1923, announced that "motor traffic over the wonderful Durango-Silverton-Ouray Highway will be open about July 15, according to road officials. The 'million dollar highway' is one of the outstanding achievements of the Colorado Highway Department, federal Bureau of Roads, and the U. S. Forest Service." This was probably the first use of the road's new name in writing.

The Silverton Railroad (which ran from Silverton to Red Mountain) was shut down several times in the early twentieth century. It was closed for good on June 17, 1922, and its tracks were torn up shortly thereafter. The Silverton Railroad right-of-way went basically to the county of San Juan, but in Ouray County the adjoining private property owners (usually mines) got the right-of-way, or otherwise the land went to the county.

At about the same time, the road was moved from the west to the center of Ironton Park, and that portion of the highway from the south end of Ironton Park to the top of Red Mountain Pass was moved from the east to the west side of Red Mountain Creek. The Silverton Railroad and the original road had both run down the east side of the creek, but the change was made in great part because the Treasury Tunnel (which eventually became the Idarado Mine) was being worked with substantial mill production on the west side. They needed a good road to ship their production since the railroad was now gone. The change in location also meant the road could be widened and straightened somewhat. On the other side of Red Mountain Pass, the abandoned Silverton Railroad bed was used or closely followed to bring the new automobile highway down the steep southern slope from Red Mountain into Chattanooga Valley. A new road route was constructed close to, but not on, the old roadbed bed for much of the way from Chattanooga to Silverton.

The last part of the upgrade, the twelve miles from Ouray to the top of Red Mountain Pass, was finished in 1924. This portion

Chapter 5: CHANGING TIMES ❊ 129

A 1921 highway survey party is working at Red Mountain Pass. The rails of the Silverton Railway are still in place, but they will soon be removed and replaced by the new automobile highway.

J. D. Sears Photo, U. S. Geological Survey.

A crowd of dignitaries gather at the dedication of the Million Dollar Highway in 1924. It was still difficult for two cars to pass each other in some spots.

Photo Courtesy of Colorado Historical Society, F40483.

of the Million Dollar Highway had been graveled for the first time. The entire extended Million Dollar Highway from Durango to Ouray was dedicated in a short ceremony held between the Treasury Tunnel and the top of Red Mountain Pass on July 4, 1924. The road was referred to as "The Million Dollar Highway" at that ceremony, although it was also referred to as the D.S.O. (Durango/Silverton/Ouray) Highway. Several federal officials from the East attended the ceremony, and all of them remarked on the impressive natural scenery along the road. At the time, the highway was not totally finished,

Cars are lined up near the Treasury Tunnel at the dedication of the Million Dollar (Automobile) Highway on July 4, 1924. The route from Silverton to Durango had already been open for several years.

Author's Collection.

but was "rapidly approaching the point of final completion," according to the July 5, 1924, *Silverton Standard*.

The Million Dollar Highway became the lifeline for the cars, buses, and trucks that brought tourists and freight into the San Juan Mountains and hauled the mines' ore out. The north-south road (to this day there is no east-west automobile road through the heart of the San Juans) was still dirt or gravel, and there were no standard highway markers (until 1925). A real effort was made to make the road passable to two cars in all places, but this was not always possible. Regardless, it was immeasurably better than the wagon road of the past. The really steep grades were eliminated, usually by rerouting the road for a short distance. For example, the tunnel that was built by Lars Pilkar near Ouray made a less steep grade possible (six percent vs. the old twenty percent). In most of the places where there are now switchbacks, the road originally went straight up the grade. In fact, in many places along the Million Dollar Highway, the old wagon route is still visible if one looks closely. It was the plan to keep the highway open in the winter, but even though the State of Colorado Highway Department took over maintenance of the road (because it was now a state highway) there were still periods in the winter when the road would be closed for a month or more at a time.

One lesson learned from the original winter operation was that the stone guardrails, which had been so carefully placed along sections of road with steep drop-offs, kept the snowplows from being able to push snow over the edge of the road; so, most of the large stone barriers were removed (some still exist on the old Lime Creek part of the road – a fascinating trip back into time to see what the road was like a hundred years ago). Even today many tourists wonder why there are no guardrails in many places along the Million Dollar Highway, and snow removal is the reason. But don't worry, for as crazy as it sounds, the road is usually less dangerous in the winter. If a car does go over the edge (which seldom actually happens), it is usually cushioned by the snow and slowly comes to a stop due to the snow that piles up ahead of the car.

In addition to the stories already mentioned on how the Million Dollar Highway was named, another tale was that the cost of the highway would be a million dollars a mile to build today. However, there are some mile-long stretches that today would cost much more than a million dollars. A more recent claim is that Otto Mears found a million dollars in ore along the route; but, in fact, no ore was found during the construction that was worth enough to be economically mined (actually the definition of ore is rock that contains enough mineral to be economically mined).

The truth about the highway's name is pretty tame. During the upgrade to an automobile road in the early 1920s, the three contractors (representing the governmental agencies of the State of Colorado, the federal government, and the U.S. Forest Service) that were involved in the upgrading of the road from Ouray to Silverton got together and realized that the total cost of their three projects was almost exactly one million dollars. One of them exclaimed, "Well, I guess we have ourselves a million dollar highway." A few days later a sign appeared in Ironton Park that proclaimed the road as "the million dollar highway" – not really a name, but more like a designation of how much it cost to do the upgrade.

In May, 1923, there was an article in *Colorado Highways*, the magazine of the Colorado Highway Department, which proclaimed "This 'Million Dollar Highway' is one of the outstanding achievements of the Colorado Highway Department, the Federal Bureau of Roads, and the U. S. Forest Service, all three government agencies having expended thousands of dollars on improvements to the road." *The Silverton Standard*, in an article entitled "The Dusty Pages of the Past Revealed in the History of the Million Dollar Highway," also confirmed that the total cost of upgrading the road from Ouray to Silverton in the early 1920s gave the Million Dollar Highway its name.

Before the new automobile highway was built, it would sometimes be the Fourth of July before the road was opened because of a lack of modern day equipment like bulldozers, snowplows and backhoes. A century ago a crew of men would shovel by hand

Chapter 5: CHANGING TIMES ❋ 133

from each end of a drift or slide to clear the way. The Riverside Slide was a particularly bad spot. Even after the upgrade and the use of modern (1920s) equipment, matters were not much better. In the winter of 1929-30 there were ten tractors and five dump trucks allocated for snow removal on the highway, but the highway department still failed to keep the Million Dollar Highway open.

Although Ouray and Silverton demanded that the new Million Dollar Highway *must* be kept open in the winter, it was impossible to do so in the 1920s. The road was usually shut down sometime around Thanksgiving and reopened in late April or early May. Both state highway and county crews would work join in plowing the road, although it was officially the state of Colorado's job.

By 1930, the Million Dollar Highway had some sections that were gravel and some that were asphalt. The road was upgraded almost every year, which continues right up to the present. For example, a steel bridge replaced the old wooden bridge just south out of Silverton over Cement Creek in 1930. The part of the road from Silverton to Molas was greatly widened and surfaced in 1936. Five and two-tenths miles of road around Cascade were upgraded in 1953-54. The tunnel near Ouray was widened to twenty-seven feet across, and then was reworked again in the 1990s to keep water and ice from forming during the winter. Other recent upgrades include the large, lower curve at Chattanooga, the avalanche shed at the Riverside Slide, and the four-lanes for most of the grade from the Animas Valley up to the Durango Mountain ski area. Some major work is done somewhere along the route almost every year.

The constant running of the slides along the highway (and especially the long and frequent Mother Cline Slide and the dangerous Riverside Slide near Ouray) was the main reason for winter closures. In the fall of 1930-31, Ouray and San Juan Counties continued to furiously press the Colorado Highway Department to keep the road open year round, or at a minimum until after the first of the year. However by late January 1931, the road was closed again. In 1932, it took until May 20 for the Durango and Silverton snow removal teams to meet at Molas Pass. The Ouray and Silverton teams met at Red Mountain Pass on May 9 of that year. Some additional federal help was gained when the Million Dollar Highway became U. S. 550 during the 1930s. By 1935, the road was considered to be open in the winter, but even today there are a few days every year when the highway has to be closed for safety reason or to clear slides.

Today it is the quick and deadly rush of the avalanche that brings the greatest danger to the Million Dollar Highway in the winter. Ouray County has suffered many avalanche deaths along the road (most at the Riverside Slide). San Juan County (in good part because people were riding the Durango-Silverton train and the building of the Million Dollar Highway in San Juan County

This view at the Ruby Cliffs shows the road to be wide enough for two cars, especially with the stone guardrails. After the road was kept open in the winter, the stone barriers had to be removed for snowplowing.
Photo Courtesy of San Juan County Historical Society.

was delayed until the 1920s) has only suffered a few avalanche deaths on the highway. However, hundreds were killed over the years in both San Juan and Ouray Counties by avalanches in the nearby mountains – 117 of those buried in the Silverton cemetery died in snow slides, and many more bodies were shipped out of the San Juans for burial. There are no lethal avalanche paths across the Million Dollar Highway in La Plata County.

As the importance of tourism increased, so did attempts to cash in on the reputation of the Million Dollar Highway and the San Juan Mountains. In early 1929 the City of Montrose (thirty-four miles to the north of Ouray) pushed the state and the federal government to change the name of the Million Dollar Highway to the "Chief Ouray Highway" and to extend its length to Montrose, where Chief Ouray's old homestead was located and his wife Chipeta is buried. Neither the state nor the federal government actually had an official name for the highway at that time, other than State Highway 19. The idea of changing the nickname of the highway was fought bitterly by the people of Ouray, Silverton, and Durango. When the Denver and Rio Grande Railroad started using the name "Chief Ouray Highway" in the brochures it produced for the Circle Route, the San Juan Women's Club of Silverton put tremendous political pressure on the railroad to use the name "DSO Million Dollar Highway." The pressure worked. By late 1929, the railroad wrote the Women's Club to notify them that they would not use the "Chief Ouray" name in the future. The federal and state governments also refused to act on Montrose's request, although Montrose did not give up its fight to change the name for several more years. On present day maps "U.S. Highway 550" is usually the only designation. "The Million Dollar Highway" does the road much more justice.

In the 1940s, the state of Colorado rebuilt the old Coal Bank wagon road, and the Lime Creek Road was abandoned. This shortened the route from Durango to Silverton by four miles and made the route along the highway basically the same as it is today. During World War II, uranium was shipped over the Million Dollar

Highway to be milled in Grand Junction for use in the first atomic bomb. As a result, sixty snowplows were constantly on the highway to keep it open (there aren't even six snowplows on the highway at the same time today). The extended Million Dollar Highway was completely paved with asphalt between 1953 and 1955.

In 1962, local historian Josie Crum proposed yet another name for the Million Dollar Highway. Because of all he had done in its original construction and for his contributions to transportation as a whole in the San Juans, she proposed that the road be named "The Mears Highway" in Otto Mears' honor. But after the previous controversies over using the name "Chief Ouray Highway," the movement did not go anywhere, and the name Million Dollar Highway stuck. As has been said, everyone wants to be a part of the Million Dollar Highway, and it is easy to see why.

Even in the 1950s, sheep were often on the road along the Million Dollar Highway. In this postcard view they are near Red Mountain Pass. Travelers just had to wait until they got off the road.

Author's Collection.

Chapter 6

NARROW GAUGE RAILS INTO SILVERTON

THE DENVER AND RIO GRANDE was the logical railroad to conquer the San Juans, as it had already been the first to push into a dozen other Colorado mining districts. Men like General William Jackson Palmer of the D&RG Railroad felt that railroads were called for by Manifest Destiny. To quote Palmer – "Colorado without railroads is relatively worthless." When the D&RG Railroad started over La Veta Pass and continued west towards the San Juans, it seemed a certainty that it would go to Alamosa, Del Norte, Wagon Wheel Gap, and up the Rio Grande River to Cunningham or Stony Pass. Silverton lay 110 miles to the west of Del Norte, but the route that the railroad actually chose to use in 1879 was much longer by way of Chama, New Mexico and up the Animas River – a 245 mile circular route. The survey for the tracks to Silverton was then continued up Mineral Creek to determine if a loop could be made over the Red Mountains to Ouray and Montrose, where the route would tie back in with D&RG

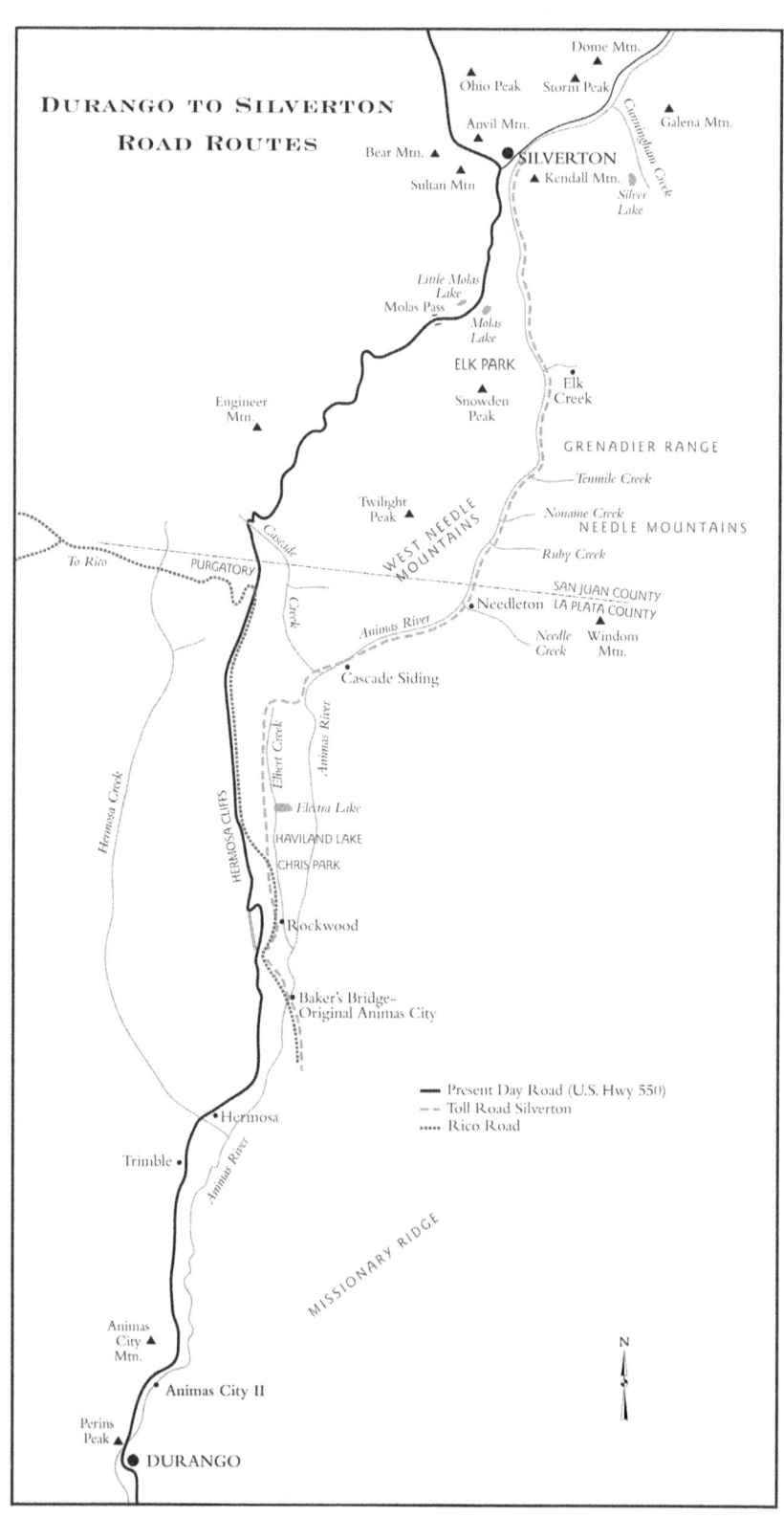

Chapter 6: Narrow Gauge Rails into Silverton

track. The surveyors reported that the construction could be done, although the last potion of the route through the Uncompahgre Canyon would be extremely difficult.

Why the D&RG made the decision for the longer route is still unclear. The route through Chama slowed railroad construction down considerably and probably cost much more money. There were some very difficult sections along the route, so it was not much easier to build the loop to the south. In fact, it eventually took the D&RG two years longer than originally planned to get to Silverton. Perhaps the officials of the D&RG Railroad were looking at where the railroad might expand after Silverton. A route to Durango left all kinds of possibilities for future expansion to the south and west of that city, and a branch could be run to Silverton. However, as it turned out, the D&RG did no other construction out of Durango besides the line to Silverton.

In December 1879, the Animas Canyon Toll Road was purchased by the D&RG Railroad from James L. Wightman, who had

The D&RG Railroad depot in Durango looks pretty much the same today, except in the summer it is a lot busier than shown in this photo from 1910 or 1920. In the 1880s and 1890s it was open twenty-four hours a day and filled day and night with passengers.

Photo Courtesy of Colorado Historical Society, F44096

surveyed and checked out the Animas Canyon thoroughly for his wagon toll road. After he sold his toll road, Wightman became a consultant to the D&RG on the best railroad route through the Animas Canyon. The D&RG was in a hurry and up to 850 men were working at one time on the Durango line. The portion of the Wightman toll road that was actually in the Animas Canyon would become the new roadbed for the railroad.

Heavy winter snows stopped D&RG track laying on December 11 at a spot just slightly into the Animas Canyon above Rockwood. Not only was the winter severe, but there was also a shortage of rail availability. Some work continued in the canyon, but no rail was laid. Most of that winter's efforts were concentrated on blasting what came to be called "The High Line" into the Animas Canyon's steep west side and building the first bridge over the Animas River, which was located just past where the High Line route reached the river at the bottom of the canyon. There would be three more bridges needed before the railroad reached Silverton. Only the fabulous riches that potentially lay in the San Juans kept the D&RG focused on its goal to reach Silverton.

The D&RG Railroad made it to Silverton on July 13, 1882. The importance of the event cannot be overstated. *The San Juan Herald* proclaimed that Silverton was now the "Gem City of the Mountains, the most prosperous and promising city in the San Juans." Freight rates fell from an average of thirty dollars a ton to twelve dollars a ton overnight. A corresponding savings occurred on freight being shipped into Silverton. Now even relatively low grade ore could be shipped to the smelters at a profit.

Most Silverton locals did not mind that the railroad would eliminate the wagon road to Durango, as they would be able to use the easier, quicker, and less expensive train. If they really needed the use of their wagon, buggy, or later their car, they would load them on the train and take them off at their destination. So, because of the railroad, for almost forty years the Million Dollar Highway from Ouray ended at Silverton, or, put another way, the train was, in effect, the southern portion of the Million Dollar Highway.

Chapter 6: NARROW GAUGE RAILS INTO SILVERTON ※ 141

It was often necessary to dig snow tunnels for the trains running through the Animas Canyon when multiple slides piled up snow to almost 100 feet deep. The inside of the tunnel is black because of the soot from the locomotives.

Author's Collection.

The Durango-Silverton train did its job well – for decades the little narrow gauge (three feet between the rails as opposed to four feet eight and one-half inches on a standard gauge) railroad carried millions of pounds of ore out of the San Juans and brought millions of pounds of provisions back in on the return trip. Eventually, $300 million in ore (billions of dollars at today's rates) was brought out of the San Juans by the D&RG. When the pack trails were closed due to deep snows in the winter, the railroad was often the only link that Silverton had with the outside world. Unfortunately, there were times when even the train could not get through the larger avalanches along its route that often brought down tons of snow and debris – sometimes to a depth of thirty feet or more.

Because the avalanches often carried a considerable amount of timber and rocks, the railroad could not always use mechanized means, like rotary snow plows, to clear the track. There were times when 300 men or more, all armed with snow shovels, would be needed to manually clear the rails. There were also times when the men had to resort to tunnels, especially when multiple slides would pile the snow up to a hundred feet deep (think of trying to shovel the long way through a ten story building). Occasionally, the tracks were blocked for months, and mail and emergency supplies were taken into Silverton from the end of the open track by mule, toboggans, snow sleds pulled by dogs, or on the backs of men on "snowshoes" (today's skis). Sometimes packers even resorted to fitting their animals with "snowshoes." They would attach short boards imbedded with cleats to the mules' or horses' hooves.

Although at a much lower elevation and not subject to slides, Durango was also blockaded by the deep snows at times. The period of the blockade was usually shorter, and occasionally a train or two might reach town; but, for example, during Durango's snow blockade between February 5 and April 24 of 1884, the town only had a couple of trains that were able to get through. That same snowstorm obstructed the D&RG line to Silverton completely from February 4 to April 17, a period of seventy-three days. For thirty of these days even the pack animals could not get through from Needleton.

Chapter 6: NARROW GAUGE RAILS INTO SILVERTON ❖ 143

In February 1886, the train was again stopped by avalanches. Slides had run all along the line. At one point several of the slides were 100 feet deep. By the first part of March, all fresh food in Silverton was gone – only flour was left in any quantity, so residents ate mainly bread. Food for both animals and humans had made it as far as Needleton, but the train could go no further. There were times when 400 to 500 men were shoveling snow in the canyon. The men who shoveled the track were paid $1.50 per day for their hazardous and backbreaking work. A relief pack train of mules and a few horses (fifty-two animals in all) would go down the Animas Canyon one day, spend the night at Needleton,

An early-day snow slide shoveling crew could consist of as many as 300 to 400 men. This drawing depicts a cut in a slide that has hit one of the trains in the Animas Canyon.
Author's Collection.

and then come back with supplies the next day. There was a constant danger of avalanches in the canyon, but the relief pack train kept going for weeks. The fifty-one day closure ended on April 11. During this time the Silverton Railroad was also blockaded, and there were an additional 125 men working on clearing the route up to Red Mountain.

When the railroad was closed due to snow for fifty-one days in the winter of 1890-91, Silverton merchants came very close to running out of supplies, and the entire population of the town was facing starvation until the situation was finally relieved. The telegraph was down (telephone service didn't exist in Silverton yet). Milk cows were killed for beef. The newspaper was printed on wrapping paper and later on wallpaper for lack of newsprint. Rescue packers carried freight at a great risk because of the almost continuous avalanches. On April 27, 1897, twenty-three year old burro puncher, Frank Blackmore, and five of his burros were killed by a snow slide in the Animas Canyon.

In the winter of 1926-1927, when the town was again snowed in, the *Denver Post* became very concerned about the situation and brought "relief" to the beleaguered city by hiring an airplane to drop bundles of its latest edition, so that locals could keep up to date with the events in the rest of the world! The few supplies that came in were sent over the Million Dollar Highway from Ouray, but by mules and burros, as the road was closed to automobile traffic. By March 1927, the feed for Silverton's animals was running low, and the local doctor was running out of medicine.

There were 100,000 pounds of mail packed the fourteen miles from Needleton to Silverton during that blockade. One of the reasons for so much mail was Silverton residents ordered everything from food to clothing sent by parcel post, as they knew the mail would somehow get through. One desperate dairyman resorted to sending a ton of hay by parcel post! Regular freight could not make it, but the U. S. Mail got through. The total cost for shipping a ton of hay, repackaged into small bundles that would meet postal regulations, was fourteen dollars at a time when the government was paying the pack train owner fifty cents a pound to carry the mail. The postal service lost eighty-six dollars on this one transaction.

In 1936, a snow slide closed the rails from Needleton for a month. More than 10,000 pounds of black powder were used to shoot the slides to loosen them up before the railroad steam shovel arrived. During the 1930s, the Million Dollar Highway was often closed to automobiles during these periods, but packers could usually make it to or from Ouray or through the Animas Canyon during the blockades. The longest closure of the railroad (but not the most complete because of the construction of the Million Dollar Highway) was an eighty-eight day period between December 26, 1951 and March 24, 1952.

On one occasion, a mixed train (part freight and part passengers) was stopped by a large snow slide. The crew decided to back the train out of the canyon but had gone only a short distance before another avalanche blocked the route behind them. It was obvious that the train would be trapped for several days. So the crew banked the fire in the engine to conserve fuel, and coal was transferred from the engine tender to the small pot-bellied stoves in the passenger cars. That kept everyone toasty warm. A full load of eggs was found in one of the freight cars, so the passengers and crew ate eggs for the duration of their ordeal.

Even after the automobile road was opened to Durango in 1924, many Silverton residents preferred to send their cars to Durango on the train, rather than risk the hazards of the new road; but slowly, highway traffic became dominate. The train's existence was in jeopardy from the 1920s to the mid-1940s; however each time it seemed the branch was doomed, something always happened to prolong its life. During World War II the U.S. government made sure the railroad stayed operating so that badly needed scrap metal could be shipped out for the war effort. Tourists eventually rediscovered the railroad in the early 1950s. During the period that followed, mile for mile, the Durango to Silverton train produced more revenue for the D&RG than any other part of their system. Nevertheless the company was constantly seeking permission to

Snow slides were not the only problem on the D&RG route to Silverton. After winters with heavy snows there were also the dangers of floods. These men are rebuilding the railroad grade where it has washed out and formed a small lake.

Photo Courtesy of Denver Public Library, F40124.

abandon the line, because the official attitude was that "they hauled freight and not tourists." In the 1950s and 1960s, the train was used in many motion pictures, including "Around the World in Eighty Days." As passenger traffic improved in the 1960s, the train ran a daily summer schedule for the first time since the 1930s.

The D&RG abandoned its tracks from Antonito to Durango in the 1960s, thereby isolating the forty-five mile stretch from Durango into Silverton from the rest of the D&RG system. In 1981, the Durango to Silverton route was sold to Charles Bradshaw, and the Durango and Silverton Narrow Gauge Railroad was formed. The Durango-Silverton Railroad not only survives, but now thrives at a time when the D&RG Railroad no longer exists.

Chapter 6: NARROW GAUGE RAILS INTO SILVERTON   ❧ 147

In February 1989, the roundhouse in Durango burned down. Many of the engines were damaged but were later repaired. The roundhouse itself was an almost total loss, but it was rebuilt using what materials could be saved. The railroad depot is the original – built in 1882. The 150-ton locomotive usually pulls fourteen passenger cars carrying about 600 passengers when fully loaded. The locomotives were built by the Baldwin Locomotive Works in 1925 or the American Locomotive Works in 1923. The older coaches are generally from the 1880s. Some of these restored coaches might be on the train, but most of the coaches are faithful reproductions.

The trip takes about nine hours (3 ½ hours up, 2 hours in Silverton, and 3 ½ hours back) and runs May through October. There are water stops at Tank Creek and Needleton, where about 5,000 gallons of water are taken on. Elegant parlor cars can be reserved for a group if desired. West of the Durango depot are the

Steam locomotive #499 and a U.S. Army diesel locomotive have stopped near the Durango turntable in 1955. The steam engine has a snow plow attached to its front. The roundhouse was later destroyed by fire.
Photo Courtesy of Denver Public Library, X-17733.

watering and service areas – the car shop, turntable, fifteen-stall roundhouse, and machine shop. More people (the railroad estimates about 250,000 in 2009) now ride the train in a year than used to ride it in a decade. Enjoy the coal smell, the whistle, the swaying of the train, and the clickety-clack of the wheels on the rail. Hundreds of thousand of visitors each year find the railroad's "Trip to Yesteryear" to be a delightful, breath-taking experience.

If you take the train ride to Silverton you are in for a real treat. Each of the coal-fired steam locomotives heads north out of the Durango yard in the early morning with a load of tourists, crosses the city's main street, uses the trestle over the Animas River, and, at 32nd Street, passes through what used to be the second Animas City. The rail bed starts at 6,500 feet in Durango and rises to 9,300 feet in Silverton. The forty-five mile, historic railroad closely parallels the Million Dollar Highway for the first eleven miles to the north out of Durango, traveling straight up the broad and beautiful Animas Valley, always green and fertile in the summer because of Animas River water. (Much of this part of the route is described in Chapter 7.) The hills are at first generally rounded, but every now and then the bluffs of red sandstone are sharply inclined to the north — the beds were lifted up by the formation of the San Juan Dome. The reds in the sandstone can be absolutely dazzling, especially after a rain. Ridges, one behind the other, rise back from the valley up to the horizon.

Cedar, scrub oak, sagebrush and pinion lend their greenish color to the red landscape. Soon the walls of sandstone are topped with caprock, and we move into the grey colors of volcanic tuff. The train passes Waterfall Ranch with the Fall Creek Anasazi site above and then Trimble Hot Springs. The red cliffs are up to 2,500 feet thick at this point. Their color comes from iron bearing minerals. The track crosses the Million Dollar Highway at Hermosa and starts climbing into the hills. In the valley, the train averages about eighteen miles an hour, but the train will be chugging a little harder now because the grade changes from 1% up the valley to 2 $\frac{1}{2}$% from Hermosa to Rockwood. The rail yard and water tower at Hermosa might be considered to be the center of the settlement, which is quite spread out. A little further up the hill, at the point where the track goes under U.S. 550, the train and the highway part. Just north of this point was the former Bell Siding, where John Bell mined limestone for use as a flux in the Durango smelters.

Although now separated, the rails and the highway both begin to twist out of the valley floor as they approach Rockwood. The railroad will enter the Animas Gorge and will eventually pass between the Needles and West Needles Mountains, while the highway passes between Engineer Mountain and the West Needles. In the winter, the train (if running) usually ends its run at Rockwood and returns to Durango, as the path through the Animas Canyon to Silverton is still avalanche prone.

Rockwood is located at an elevation of 7,367 feet in a lovely little park just south of where the railroad enters the shelf road on the Animas Canyon. A post office was established at Rockwood in 1878, and after the toll road to Rico was established, passengers bound for that town could meet the stage at Rockwood six days a week. Rockwood was the terminus for H.A.W. Tabor's Pioneer Stage and Express line, which ran from Rockwood to Rico, Ophir, and Telluride until the arrival of the Rio Grande Southern Railroad in those towns in 1891. Rockwood was also an area where many of the ties were cut for use by the railroad through the Animas Canyon to Silverton.

In the winter of 1881-1882, the town of Rockwood became the primary work camp for the D&RG Railroad as it pushed its way into the Animas Canyon. A wye, depot, and siding still exist at the small settlement and are used to turn the train around for winter trips. The town was named for Thomas Rockwood, who ran the Central (also known as the Centennial) Hotel in Silverton before moving to Rockwood. Tom Rockwood married into the hotel business in Silverton, then moved to Rockwood in 1879 after his wife's death and built the first hotel in town. The stages, lodging, logging, and freight businesses were the original mainstay of the local economy, supplemented greatly by the arrival of the railroad.

By 1882, the settlement of Rockwood had a cemetery, school, sawmill, saloon, and several hotels among other businesses. During the early 1880s, there was so much traffic through the town that a blacksmith's shop reportedly stayed open twenty-four hours a day shoeing mules, oxen, and horses. But even after the Rio Grande Southern Railroad reached Rico and Telluride in 1891, and the Pioneer Stage Line route was abandoned, Rockwood never became a ghost town because of the area's rock and lime quarries, railroad, and large timber activities. One of the largest contiguous stands of yellow pine in Colorado runs all along the southern edge of the San Juans, but Rockwood's lumber jacks also harvested local fir and spruce. All together it is estimated that more than one billion board feet of lumber was shipped from Rockwood between 1900 and 1925. Rockwood still had a population of about fifty in 1900, and is slightly larger than that today.

A few well-dressed passengers wait for the train at Rockwood about 1885, while the burros evidently realize they won't be put to work this day. A little of the town is in the background.

Photo Courtesy of Denver Public Library, X-13194.

Chapter 6: NARROW GAUGE RAILS INTO SILVERTON ❖ 151

The Rico House was established just north of Rockwood in April, 1880. It served as a hotel and consignment area for freighters. At this point, the wagon road forked into two routes, the western going to Rico and the northern to Silverton. The Rico road passed through the present-day Glacier Club (Tamarron), followed the line of the Million Dollar Highway north for about nine miles to the small town of Murnane (near the present-day ski area), and then went west for nine miles to a small settlement named Meserola in the upper end of Hermosa Park. Then the toll road went over Scotch Creek Pass for seventeen more miles into Rico. Wightman's Silverton toll road went down Little Cascade and Cascade Creeks into the Animas Canyon. The Wightman toll road was short-lived, as the D&RG Railroad soon arrived at Rockwood and took over much of its right of way.

It was impossible to construct the D&RG tracks through the extreme southern part of the Animas Canyon around Rockwood or to follow the steep grades that the Million Dollar Highway now takes, so it was necessary to enter the Animas Canyon at a spot other than at the river's mouth. In 1885, George Crofutt described the "impossible" first five miles of the Animas Canyon in his tourist guide, *Crofutt's Gripsack Guide to Colorado*, as "apparently impassible for a hummingbird," but the railroad made it into the canyon by blasting into the massive, sheer, red granite cliffs from Rockwood. The shelf road still ranks as one of the greatest engineering feats in railroad history. The train almost doubles back on itself as it creeps along the eight-foot wide ledge, sometimes as much as 400 feet above the Animas River on 600 or 700-foot cliffs. Because of the tight curve, there are permanent orders that the train is to go no faster than five miles per hour through this section, and the squealing and groaning of the wheels makes the ride even more exciting.

Surveyors were let down on ropes from the top of the cliffs to put paint on the rocks to show the construction crews the route that the rails would follow. After the track goes through the Rockwood cut for about 900 feet, it slowly descends toward the bottom of the canyon over the next three miles, where the route

The famous "High Line" is just north of Rockwood. It was the most spectacular spot on the route to Silverton, made necessary by the impassible Animas Canyon to the south. The Needle Mountains are in the background.

Author's Collection.

then follows alongside the boiling river. The railroad chose to cross the river immediately after reaching the bottom of the canyon, and it generally stays on the east side of the river for the remainder of the trip. However, the train crosses the river three times in the canyon. The railroad forges into the remote Needles Wilderness Area, which is a part of the two million acre San Juan National Forest. Most of the country from Rockwood to Baker's Park is accessible only on foot, by horseback, or on the railroad; and it is likely that the railroad will remain the only easy access into this extremely large, rugged region of natural wilderness, which straddles the Continental Divide.

After the train reaches the Animas River, it passes through the Needle Mountains, which were the center of the great San Juan

Dome of millions of years ago. The mountain range spreads out like a giant pinwheel of 13,000 and 14,000-foot peaks. The name of the range comes from the many extremely steep spires and horns that make up the tops of the mountains, which includes the sub-range of the Needles proper, the West Needles, and the Grenadiers. In 1874, Franklin Rhoda of the Hayden Survey was inspired to write: "In some places the number of the pinnacles massed behind one another presented the appearance of church spires, only built of a much grander style of architecture than our modern edifices." Some idea of the ruggedness of the area is suggested by the names of a few peaks – The Guardian, Knife Point, and Storm King, for example. Windom Peak is 14,,047 feet – just one foot lower than neighboring Mount Eolus, which is named for Aeolus, the God of the Winds. Windom was not named for the wind, but rather for a member of the 1904 U. S. Geologic Survey that surveyed in the Needles Mountains. Sunlight Peak has the rounded dome, and is the tallest and fills out the group of fourteeners at 14,059 feet. There are also eleven other peaks in the Needles Range that are over 13,000 feet.

About two miles after the track reaches river level lies Tacoma (elevation 7,313 feet), a hydroelectric generating plant that was built in 1905, driven by a giant Pelton Wheel and powered by the force of water that comes from Electra Lake, which is 1,071 feet higher in elevation. There used to be a small settlement (about eight houses in 1908) at Tacoma, a true company town, which was named by an electric company employee who came from Washington State. The early-day company employees and their families made up the entire population of the little settlement. After September 25, 1906, a post office was located in the little town, which did not close until 1954. The railroad was the only access to the spot, so if an emergency arose and no train was available, it was necessary to walk the tracks for three miles to Rockwood, to access the highway to Durango.

Aspen trees now grow in profusion along this part of the railroad route, but something is killing the trees in Colorado. No one knows exactly what the problem is, but about 15% of all Colorado aspens have died in the last few years (2003-2008), and experts predict that all but the very strongest of aspen growing at this elevation may die in the next decade. Silver Falls comes down to the east (right) side of the canyon at this point.

One half mile further is Cascade Tank where the train fills with water. Tall Timber Resort (called Ah! Wilderness Resort from 1952 to 1985) is another half-mile further. Many movies have been filmed in this small park. Small "towns" have even been built for the movies. Vacationers and hikers who wish to temporarily live in

After the train passes the High Line going north, the track follows the Animas River for the rest of the trip to Silverton. This particular train was a special, carrying W. H. Jackson, who took the photograph.
Photo Courtesy of Denver Public Library, McClure 2010.

Chapter 6: NARROW GAUGE RAILS INTO SILVERTON ❋ 155

a very secluded and wild area come to the area. The highly rated Tall Timbers Resort also includes Tree Top Adventures, where you can soar through the trees, rappel down from the tree tops, and picnic in the wilderness. The company bills itself as the "highest, safest, and largest all day extreme adventure."

Three miles further north is Teft Spur (also called "Teft Siding"). This is the spot where a mile of the old Wightman Wagon Toll Road went up the mountain via three large switchbacks to conquer the steep grades around Cascade Creek and then followed Little Cascade Creek for the rest of the climb. The small settlement of Cascade (elevation 7,712 feet) started out as a stage stop and post office at the top of Cascade Hill. When the railroad was built in 1881, the town at the top of the hill was mostly abandoned; a section house was built near the railroad; and a small settlement with the same name of "Cascade" was built at the bottom of the hill.

The lower settlement of Cascade had a post office from 1882 to 1889. Crofutt was so enamored with old Cascade that he gave it more space in his *Grip-Sack Guide of Colorado* than Durango. In part, he wrote that it "consisted of a stage station, a post office, a hotel, all in one little lone cabin at the summit of Cascade Hill, 22 miles south from Silverton, 26 miles north from Durango, and 15 miles east by trail from Rico. 'Oh it was a dandy, we here got our "sow-belly" straight, and a "shake-down" on the ground floor." Small sections of the toll road can be seen alongside the track from lower Cascade to Silverton, although most of the road is now directly under the railroad bed. Cascade Siding was about a mile north of Teft. Just after Cascade Siding, the Bitter Root Mine is visible to the north (left) of the track.

The next stop on the railroad (about four and a half more miles) is Needleton (elevation 8,135 feet). A post office was established on May 26, 1882, discontinued for short periods in 1892 and 1896, and closed permanently in 1910. Needleton was originally "a jumping off" point for prospectors in the Needle Mountains, which surround the little stop. Jim Marshall started a saloon in Needleton and had a piano brought in by freight wagon, since the train wasn't in operation yet. Needleton's big excitement came in 1882-83 when the railroad opened up the possibility of transportation. Most of the nearby veins were short, not deep, and pinched out, because the upper part of the vein had already eroded away. Low grade veins still cover the Needle Mountains, but the ore would be too costly to mine and ship out from the remote and rugged terrain, much of which is now in the Weminuche Wilderness Area (at 459,804 acres, it is the largest wilderness area in Colorado). An official Wilderness Area does not allows mines, roads, or motorized transportation. A little over $200,000 in ore (worth perhaps $5 million today) was shipped from Needleton, but the mining district was basically abandoned by 1905.

The original town of Needleton was located about two miles south of today's Needleton siding because a flood in 1927 washed out the old siding and the D&RG moved the track. The common practice of moving the line rather than repairing it creates what is called "shoofly" track. The snow slide at Needleton was the most southern of the stretch of slides along the next twelve miles, which often closed the railroad. The old wagon road to the Needles' major mining district in Chicago Basin goes up Needleton Creek. Some of the mines that took gold from Chicago Basin include the Mastadon, Sheridan, List, and Waterfall.

The train stops seven and a half miles further at Elk Park for hikers, fishermen, and hunters. It is also a favorite spot for backpackers to start their trip into the Weminuche Wilderness Area. Elk Park (elevation 8,883 feet) was a mining, timber, and cattle camp during the 1880s and 1890s. A wye (now removed) and siding allowed the train to turn around and return to Durango or Silverton from this point. It was especially handy in the winter if avalanches had closed the route ahead, and burros and mules were being used to take freight and mail from this point to Silverton. There are some beautiful waterfalls in the area and magnificent Garfield Peak dominates the countryside to the northeast (it is in the southwestern end of the Grenadier subrange of the Needles).

Chapter 6: NARROW GAUGE RAILS INTO SILVERTON ❖ 157

About two miles north of Elk Park, the old toll road can easily be seen across the river. The twisted rails in the river were actually left from one of the big floods. The remains of a snow shed can be seen to the east. Two slides come down from opposite sides of the canyon at this point. The 150-foot long snow shed worked, yet was partially torn down in the 1940s. From this point into Silverton (about four miles), valuable mineralization begins, and the remains of quite a few old mines can be seen along the route. The Detroit,

Ernest Ingersoll was an Eastern travel writer who wrote many books on Colorado. This drawing comes from The Crest of the Continent *and only slightly exaggerates the steepness and ruggedness of the Needle Mountains. Note the train near the bottom of the drawing.*
Author's Collection.

Famous train photographer, Otto Perry, shot this scene of the D&RG train coming into Baker's Park about 1950. The Animas River twists and turns through this area.

Photo Courtesy of Denver Public Library OP-8245.

Champion, Empire Tunnel, and Montezuma are a few of the many cuts and tunnels.

The Denver and Rio Grande Railroad found the terrain in the canyon to be relatively easy to conquer north of Elk Park into Silverton, although there continued to be avalanches along the way. The track travels up an ever-widening valley into Baker's Park. True to form, the D&RG originally planned to build its depot about one and a half miles south of Silverton, just where the track entered Baker's Park. It was another chance to make money through real estate development, but there was such an outcry from Silverton businesses that the railroad moved the depot site to within three blocks of Silverton's business district. Silverton was in a better position to bargain with the railroad than Animas City, as there really was not enough room for another town in the swampy southern Baker's Park. So the D&RG Railroad trip ends at Silverton, and this is where you might have lunch, do some shopping, and then return to Durango by train or by bus.

Chapter 6: NARROW GAUGE RAILS INTO SILVERTON ❊ 159

There used to be three other railroad lines, running even higher into the mountains, out of Silverton. Although the D&RG Railroad could have built past the town of Silverton, it didn't. Four narrow gauge trains (including the D&RG) in one small mountain town made Silverton a true transportation hub and still makes it the focus of many narrow gauge railroad fans today. The Silverton Railroad (Silverton to Red Mountain) will be discussed at length in Chapter 8, since its roadbed is now a part of the Million Dollar Highway. Mears also built the Silverton Northern Railroad up the Animas River from Silverton to Animas Forks and leased (and for five years owned) the Silverton, Gladstone, and Northerly Railroad, which went north up Cement Creek to the town of Gladstone and the Gold King Mine.

When Otto Mears built the Silverton Northern Railroad, he followed the basic route of his Lake City toll road to Animas Forks for thirteen miles north out of Silverton. This was also the same road to Animas Forks he later upgraded for the county. Although the railroad cost $600,000 to build, the large mines along the way picked up most of the costs. For example, the cost of the first two miles out of Silverton was paid by the Edward Stoiber family to get the railroad to the Silver Lake Mill and their electric plant, which needed coal from Durango. In exchange, they received very cheap freight rates along the line. A branch at Howardsville was built for one and a half miles up Cunningham Gulch in 1905 and was paid for by the mines located there, basically the Old One Hundred Mine and Mill and the Greene Mountain Mill (which was concentrating ore for several other mines in the gulch.)

Mears had conceived the idea of building a railroad to Eureka as early as 1888, and he had Charles Gibbs survey the route in 1889 and 1890. At first the route was considered to be a part of the Silverton Railroad. Grading began in 1892, but was interrupted by the Silver Panic of 1893. The Silverton Northern Railroad was not officially organized until 1895, when the rails were extended six and a half more miles to Howardsville, and the short spur was constructed up Cunningham Gulch. In 1904-5, the railroad was extended even further to the Gold Prince Mill at Animas Forks.

At this time the little railroad was at its peak and had three locomotives, two combines, and twenty freight cars. The Gold Prince Mine in Animas Forks and the Sunnyside Mine in Eureka paid a large part of the cost of their extensions. The last part of the route, from Eureka to Animas Forks, was so steep a grade (7%) that only two loaded cars could be pulled up, and only three loaded cars could be used on the downgrade (which was still extremely dangerous because of braking problems). The train was limited to a speed of four miles an hour because of the steep grade, but it initially ran three passenger trains each day from Silverton to Animas Forks, except for Sundays when there were two trains.

The little narrow gauge engine had to push cars up the route from Eureka because the couplings between the cars could come undone on the 7% grade and hand brakes would not have held the cars on that steep of grade. Both the Silverton, Gladstone and Northerly and the Silverton Northerly had plans to eventually cross through the range to the D&RG track at Lake City, as it would have cut 153 miles and fourteen hours off the trip to Denver. In 1909, Mears even made a survey as far as Mineral Point to get ready for the extension of his line. Not only did that not happen, but service was discontinued to Animas Forks in 1916.

Mears used the exclusive dining and club car that he named *Animas Forks* on his Silverton Northern Railroad; but one of that route's most unusual sights was a "railroad bicycle" built by Mears out of two standard bicycles for Mrs. Edward Stoiber of the Silver Lake Mine and Mill. The contraption was called "Judy." The bicycle car could operate at a speed of eight to ten miles an hour. The Silverton Northerly on occasion ran a "columbine special" to Animas Forks. Passengers once bragged of picking 25,000 of the Colorado state flower for a party in Denver. This was obviously in the days when there were no ecological concerns, and to this day there are very few columbines in the Animas Forks area. The Eureka to Animas Forks track was torn up in 1923, at the same time as the removal of the track on the Silverton Railroad. The route operated the shorter distance from Silverton to Eureka until

Chapter 6: NARROW GAUGE RAILS INTO SILVERTON ❈ 161

These proud gentlemen show the results of a day picking Columbines around the upper Silverton Northern Railroad tracks. Unfortunately, they picked 25,000 Columbines, the Colorado State flower, to ship to the Eastern Slope.

Photo Courtesy of Denver Public Library, F26360.

1939, when the Sunnyside Mill closed. The closure of the railroad at that time also spelled the end of Howardsville, Eureka, and the other little settlements along the line.

Otto Mears didn't build the Silverton, Gladstone and Northerly Railroad (rather the Gold King Mine in Gladstone built the short seven-mile line in 1899), but Mears, his son-in-law James Pitcher, and Jack Slattery of the Hub Saloon in Silverton leased it and the Gold King Mine in 1910. They later bought the railroad in a foreclosure sale in 1915. The little seven and a half mile line cost about $250,000 to build and provided a vital link between the rich Gold King Mine in Gladstone and the D&RG Railroad at Silverton. The railroad's equipment included three locomotives, twenty freight cars, and two passenger coaches.

Excursion trains were occasionally sent from Silverton to Gladstone for picnics, gathering flowers, or a chance for Silverton residents to simply get out of town and just enjoy the scenery.

Originally the Gold King Mine ran the train twice a day, but it was later changed to an "as needed" basis. In 1915 ownership of the line was transferred to the Silverton Northern Railroad. In 1917 Mears, Pitcher and Slattery gave up their lease on the Gold King Mine, and Mears left for California and retirement. The Gold King Mine bought back the railroad in 1920 and owned the line until it was officially abandoned in 1934 (although it had not been used since 1924). When the railroad was abandoned, its equipment went to the Silverton Northern Railroad. Today, the dirt road up Cement Creek follows the railroad grade closely, but a few sections of grade, bridges, or abutments can still be seen.

With so many railroads leading into town, Silverton became not only a supply and transportation center but an important milling center. The ore could be crushed and separated in or near Silverton to reduce transportation and smelting costs. The value of the ore mined locally eventually exceeded 200 million dollars (worth several billion dollars today). To date, almost 100 tons of

Bob Richardson took this photo of the D&RG freight train at the depot in Silverton in 1953. There are plenty of other freight cars waiting for use.
Photo Courtesy of Denver Public Library, RR-1888.

Chapter 6: NARROW GAUGE RAILS INTO SILVERTON ❋ 163

The snow can (and did) get pretty deep in Silverton, even covering the windows in this photo from about 1900. With this much snow, it is doubtful that the train was running, but the depot is open.

Photo Courtesy of Colorado Historical Society, F-44094.

gold and 2,000 tons of silver have been extracted from San Juan County alone. As the fortune of the local mines rose and fell, so did the economy and number of railroads in Silverton. But, by the late 1920s and the opening of the Million Dollar Highway for truck traffic, the ore went out by road instead of by rail. The last days of significant mining in the San Juans were in the 1970s and 1980s, although small mines still operate to this day. The last big mine (the Sunnyside) worked until 1991.

Today, there is just one railroad in Silverton, and both the D&RG Railroad and the town's economies are both based on tourism. To put the Silverton to Durango train into perspective today, one needs only look at its passenger traffic. In 1947, about 3,500 people rode the train. This increased to 12,000 in 1953, then 100,000 by 1962, and 177,000 in 1986. The railroad estimates that a quarter of a million people will ride on its tracks each year by 2010.

However, many new challenges face the railroad. As the towns of Durango and Silverton become less economically dependent on the train, they have made extra demands. Silverton asked the train to move its terminus to a spot near the downtown district. This gave passengers more time to shop and eat lunch. After being threatened with a lawsuit by the U. S. Forest Service, the train sends cars after each train to look for forest fires that may have been started by hot cinders. Efforts are being made to keep down the smoke and noise pollution in Durango. Nevertheless, the railroad still operates "The Train to Yesteryear."

Today's train allows you to really get the feel of a narrow gauge railroad from the 1880s. You can ride (for an extra charge) in a vintage car, the locomotive, a maintenance car, or almost any other equipment they have on the line. Be sure to stop at the railroad museum at the rail yard. There is no charge for those who purchase a ticket on the train, and it is usually open all year, except for some times in November. There is also a museum at the Silverton freight yard that is open in the summer. The winter train only goes part of the way to Silverton and is closed November through February, except at Christmas when the "Polar Express" runs. Train tickets can be combined with soaring, rafting, jeeping, hiking, or fishing. Do not hesitate to take the train back to Durango. There is an entirely different view going south. The Durango-Silverton train has served Durango and Silverton well for over 125 years. All indications are that it will continue to do so for many years into the future.

Chapter 7

THE TOWN OF DURANGO AND A TRIP TO SILVERTON

DURANGO AND SILVERTON have always been in competition in some way or another, but they have also always needed each other, and therefore have worked closely together for many reasons. The train, the Animas River, and the Million Dollar Highway obviously pass through or connect the two towns. The Silverton area originally had the ore, and Durango furnished the shipping and processing. Silverton's wealthier residents often traveled to Durango to spend the winter (and some still do). Many Durango residents now summer in Silverton. And the list of ties goes on. Historian Duane Smith called Durango (elevation 6,512 feet), the "quintessential Western town," so it is worth exploring a little of its history to help understand what it is today. This is also where we will start our trip along the Million Dollar Highway.

Durango now incorporates its predecessor settlement of Animas City (the second Animas City and not to be confused with the settlement of the same name at the north end of the Animas Valley) into its boundary of about two square miles, so it is important to give some of the later town's history. The need for a town at or near this spot was immediately obvious. Lots were being put on the market as soon as the Utes sold the San Juans in 1874, but the town of Animas City was not surveyed until August of 1876. A post office was opened May 24, 1877. The 1880 census showed 286 residents and a small business community. A guidebook to the San Juans in 1877 mentioned that "the Animas City area is being rapidly settled by a highly intelligent and industrious class of people." It also declared "every fertile farm or ranch in this area is as rich a possession as a mine." It was a very true and astute observation.

Most of the farmers and ranchers moved to the valleys around Animas City in the mid-1870s for the expressed purpose of growing hay, grains, and vegetables for the miners, prospectors, and store owners in the San Juan Mountains, where their commodities drew a very high price. Farming was not even attempted in the mountainous areas of the San Juans. *The Silverton Weekly Miner* put it pretty well, "God never made this country for farming purposes, and we never attempted to set aside the will of the Almighty." By the beginning of 1881, Animas City reportedly had a population of 451.

The City of Durango was founded as the result of the decision by the Denver and Rio Grande Railroad (D&RG) to build from Alamosa in the San Luis Valley through Chama, New Mexico, and into Silverton. Animas City was an obvious spot for an extensive railroad facility to be built before the route entered the San Juans Mountains, but the town's trustees evidently did not cooperate with the railroad. When it was first reported that the D&RG would build a new town instead of locating in Animas City, the Animas City *Southwest* newspaper of May 1, 1880, made fun of the situation:

> *The Bank of the San Juan has issued a circular in which it is stated that a branch office will be opened at the new town of Durango on Rio Animas! Where the new town of Durango is to be, or not to be, God and the D&RG only know. If they are in cahoots, we ask for special dispensation.*

In the hindsight of many years, it seems the railroad probably never wanted to build into Animas City. The Durango Trust, which

Chapter 7: THE TOWN OF DURANGO AND A TRIP TO SILVERTON   ❈ 167

The second Animas City (the first was ten miles north near Baker's Bridge) had a small business district; but it included a drug store, post office, coal company, and general merchandise shop. This photo was taken about 1880 at the height of the town's prosperity.

Photo Courtesy Denver Public Library, X-6608.

was formed in 1879, had evidently planned a new town since the decision of the D&RG that year to extend its tracks to Silverton. The Durango Trust was a group of investors, most of whom were tied to the D&RG Railroad in some way or another, that planned to control the new town, a smelter, and local coal and timber, as well as the transportation on the railroad. The enterprises would all connect, giving haulage to the railroad and cheaper rates for the Durango Trust's or its owners' business interests.

The name picked for the railroad's new town was "Durango," as the terrain was similar to Durango, Mexico, which had recently been visited by Colorado Governor Hunt, one of the members of the Durango Trust. The Mexican town, in turn, got its name from the Basque "Urango," which appropriately meant "water hole" or a place for travelers to stop and rest before continuing their trip. "Durango" is also said to have the meaning of a "valley with a river running through it."

Durango was surveyed by Charles M. Perin on September 13, 1880 (the mountain to the west of town bears his name). Perrin designated Main Avenue as the wholesale district, 2nd Avenue as the business district, and 3rd Avenue as the residential area. The new town of Durango boomed from the very start. When the first Durango lots were offered in September, 1880, they sold for $250 to $500 each, much higher than the going rate in other nearby towns. By the end of September, a brickyard and sawmill had been established, which provided the raw materials for substantial new construction. By December, the town had a newspaper, *The Durango Record*.

John Porter, another member of the Durango Trust, announced soon after the founding of Durango that he was moving the Greene Smelter from Silverton to just outside Durango. In October, 1880, Porter began construction across the river, and by mid-November, 1882, the smelter was operating. It was originally the San Juan and New York Smelter, then later the Durango Smelting Co., and finally the San Juan Smelting and Mining Co.

John A. Porter was an interesting man. He helped lay out and plan the details of Durango along with General William Palmer of the D&RG and Dr. W. A. Bell, another member of the Durango Trust. Porter trained in metallurgy in England and in the United States and had been asked to supervise the treatment process of Silverton's Greene Smelter, owned by Judge George Greene. Porter came to the San Juans in 1875 with his assay equipment and two large bags of coal, which he needed for his assays. When he saw the good coal deposits in the Durango area, he supposedly threw away the heavy fifty-pound bags of coal in disgust. Once Porter moved the smelter to the present Durango area, construction of the railroad was pushed with even more fervor.

Porter started the Porter Fuel Company to mine coal around Durango, and extended its operations to the mines alongside the Rio Grande Southern tracks. The coal was used for heat in local homes, for power-generating plants, at the smelter, and for the railroad's locomotives. Porter eventually bought the rich Smuggler

Chapter 7: THE TOWN OF DURANGO AND A TRIP TO SILVERTON ❈ 169

Mine near Telluride and also became very involved with Otto Mears' Silverton Railroad that ran to the Red Mountain Mining District. The Smuggler produced over $20 million in ore by 1900. The mine had a wide vein and, therefore, had little waste rock involved with production. Its ore ran a very rich 100 to 300 ounces of silver and one to six ounces of gold per ton. The Durango Trust's Aspen Mine near Silverton was also very successful. The mine's three to eight-foot silver vein had ore averaging about $200 per ton. It was the perfect combination of business interests, since the Durango Trust or its members owned the ore from the mine, the railroad the ore was shipped over, the smelter where the ore was refined, and the coal needed for the smelting and locomotives.

On the first of November, 1880, there were an estimated 2,000 people in Durango, but many of them were either from the railroad construction crew or the gamblers, saloon keepers, and prostitutes who always followed them. By mid-November, 1880, the Durango business district had seven hotels, several restaurants, two bakeries, two blacksmiths, eleven saloons and dance halls, and many other businesses. At the end of 1880, it was reported that Durango had twenty-five saloons and two "theatres" for the railroad workers, cowboys, prospectors, and gamblers who flocked into town with the coming of winter and the approach of the railroad. Durango's red light district and high crime area was north and west along the river, mainly between 10th and 11th Streets.

Some of Durango's houses of prostitution were named after their owners – Bessie's', Nellie's, Jennifer's, and Mattie's for example. Nellie supposedly sang well and dipped snuff. Bessie had her sister Jessie and six other girls working at her place. There were reported to be as many as four girls at Jennifer's place. Jennifer's brother was a well-to-do businessman and respected member of Denver society, who evidently did not know of her occupation. Mattie also had four girls working for her. There were also the Variety Theatre, which was one of the few "vice" establishments on Main Avenue, the Silver Bell, the Hanging Garden of Babylon (a black establishment), and the 550, which was the first dance hall

In the rush to get their businesses in operation, many Durango businessmen built their buildings on D&RG land and later had to move them to another location, as shown in this photo.

Photo Courtesy of Denver Public Library, X-17762.

in town. The Hanging Garden of Babylon burned to the ground in 1900. The rumor was that a disgruntled lover set off a stick of dynamite under the building.

By January 1, 1881, over a thousand people lived permanently in Durango, even though it wasn't until July 27, 1881, that the D&RG's first construction train entered the town. The first passenger train arrived just four days later. The population of Animas City continued to dwindle, while almost 2,000 people lived permanently in Durango by January 1, 1882. By the 1885 census, Animas City had only eighty-three residents, while Durango boasted 2,254. By 1885, George Crofutt wrote that Durango "has lost almost entirely that character of the usual frontier town and fairly won the position of a residential center. Durango is the commercial hub of the entire San Juan country and a portion of New Mexico."

In response to all the violence in the new town, a lynching occurred in 1881. One early traveler who came upon the lynched man's body in April, still hanging from a tree, said there was a note pinned to him that read, "Who cuts me down takes my place." A year later, George Wood was hung in the only legal hanging in Durango.

Parson Hogue, an Episcopal minister, started the first church in Durango by soliciting money from the men at the saloons and dancing halls. Parson Hogue was reported to walk in with his gun belt and six-shooter strapped to the outside of his cassock, and yell out, "Let us pray." The prospectors loved him, and a box was kept on the wall of several saloons labeled "The Parson's Box." Big winners were asked to put a percentage of their winnings into the box, and the money was used to help build Hogue's church.

On July 1, 1889, a tragedy struck Durango, which could have spelled doom for the fledgling town. A fire started in a small,

Within just a few years of its founding, Durango was already very prosperous. The smoke coming from the smelter was in those days a sign of prosperity, not pollution. The Harper's Weekly *artist put the frontiersmen in the foreground to indicate how quickly things had changed.*

Author's Collection.

downtown fruit stand and rapidly destroyed seven residential and business blocks in the center of the city. Durango's citizens proved to be a resilient group. No one moved away, and the residents immediately began rebuilding; and this time, instead of the hastily erected frame buildings of the original town, the reconstruction was mainly done in brick and stone. Instead of a calamity, the fire and subsequent construction gave Durango even more momentum, and the added benefit of an air of permanence.

Durango and Silverton continued their fine working relationship. For example, in 1881 the U.S. Land Office was moved from Lake City to Durango, which meant that San Juan prospectors now needed to go to Durango to register their claims. *The Durango Daily Record* wrote that "all the wealth of the San Juans will

By 1889 Durango's pollution was getting bad. Smoke came from several smelters and the train, and the river was polluted by toxins from mills located as far upstream as Silverton. Nevertheless, it was also a major tourist area.

Harper's Weekly, July 13, 1889, Author's Collection.

Chapter 7: THE TOWN OF DURANGO AND A TRIP TO SILVERTON ❖ 173

percolate through Silverton to Durango. By 1890, Durango's population was 2,700, and one year later, in December, 1891, Otto Mears' Rio Grande Southern Railroad arrived in town. It connected Durango to the north up the Dolores River via Lizard Head Pass, with the towns of Rico, Ophir, Telluride, and then on to Ridgway, Colorado, where it connected with the D&RG Railroad.

But there was more than mining wealth "percolating." Tension rose between Silverton and Durango about 1890, because Silverton was badly polluting the Animas River with both human waste and industrial toxins. The Animas River couldn't filter it all, and the residents of Durango were trying to use the river for drinking water. Silverton partially cleaned up their pollution, but its smelters and mills still poured toxic waste into the river. Durango did the neighborly thing – it found a new source of drinking water.

By the early 1900s, Durango had definitely taken on an air of respectability and prominence. Fine homes had been built on the Boulevard (now called Third Street), and classy hotels were constructed on Main Avenue. A trolley line ran between Durango and Animas City. Durango became known as a good place to spend the winter, or a spot where wealthy men might leave their families in safety while they ventured into the mountains. A lot of respectable women were living in the town. Churches, the opera, choirs, and other forms of civilization came with them.

By the late 1890s, the smelter process had become much more efficient (and costly). By 1900, no one in the San Juans could compete with the Durango smelter. With gold being found in the San Juans, there was a true resurgence in mining, and as a consequence, Durango now had another smelter. (There were four large smelter towns in Colorado – Leadville, Denver, Pueblo, and Durango. All had large supplies of coal nearby.)

However, at the same time that Durango was gaining its respectability and permanence, it still had its rowdier side. To quote the *Solid Muldoon*, "When the sun is tired of shining on the busy hive of Durango, and the moon peeps over the mighty hilltop, the hour is nigh in which our nightly carnival takes place." The rowdiness of the carnival was evident from another *Muldoon* article, "There is not a man in Durango who does not carry on his person a double action six-shooting revolver." Saloons and brothelsl flourished. The area between the river and the railroad tracks continued as the town's red light district, and the west side of Main Avenue, between 9th and 10th Streets, also boasted many saloons and gambling halls.

The air and noise pollution of the smelters and the trains competed with the otherwise tranquil setting enjoyed by the tourists, who were now showing up in large numbers in Durango. The city became a stopping point on the "Narrow Gauge Circle Route," which was an extensive tourist excursion through Colorado's mountains. Durango's area attractions eventually included nearby Mesa Verde National Park (established in June of 1906 by President Theodore Roosevelt) and the Ute Indian reservation. The Utes were a good source of revenue, both as a tourist attraction and when they came to town to spend their allotment money. Later the "Galloping Goose" also became an attraction coming into town on the Rio Grande Southern tracks. There were actually seven of them over the years — a freight car mated to a Cadillac or Pierce Arrow automobile with flanged wheels, augmented compressed air brakes, and one operator. They were noisy and they waddled down the track like a goose, as they economically transported passengers and freight in the 1930s and 1940s. The Goose often left the tracks, but only a few accidents were serious.

Durango's period of rapid growth leveled off near the end of the late nineteenth century, when the San Juan mining boom cooled after the Silver Panic of 1893. The decrease in mining also meant a decrease in timber and coal shipments; and the railroads went into a decline. The Rio Grande Southern Railroad even went into receivership. Farming and tourism remained viable, however, and helped the local population struggle through these hard times. By the early 1900s mining had rebounded. At this time, the mines produced substantial amounts of gold, and silver was basically only a

Chapter 7: THE TOWN OF DURANGO AND A TRIP TO SILVERTON ✣ 175

Durango had a fine residential district called "The Boulevard" which is shown in the foreground of this photo. The street also includes many beautiful churches that were built early in the town's history. But there still was that pollution – or rather "prosperity."

Photo Courtesy of Colorado Historical Society, F44091.

byproduct of their mining activity. Both Prohibition and the Great Depression hit Durango hard, but everyone hung on. In World War II, the local smelters turned to processing uranium. The building of Purgatory Ski Area (now called Durango Mountain) in 1965 also helped the area continue to grow. All sorts of winter attractions were added to the summer activities.

What was left of Animas City (which was located at about 32nd Street and U. S. 550) was incorporated into Durango in 1947. In the middle of the twentieth century, oil and natural gas fields to the south and southwest were added to the list of the Durango area's plentiful natural resources. There was also a uranium boom in the Four Corners area in the 1950s. The old smelter closed for good in 1964, and the resulting tailings were removed in the 1980s; but the smokestack still stands as a reminder of another age. During the 1940s and 1950s, Durango and the narrow gauge train became a mecca for western movie directors who produced such films as *Naked Spur, Across the Great Missouri,* and *Ticket to Tomahawk.* The establishment of Ft. Lewis College in 1956 made Durango a college town and brought many cultural benefits.

Present-day Durango, although not large in population, is still perhaps the major city in southwest Colorado (only the town of Montrose, 100 miles to the north, comes close). The town of over 15,000 people (perhaps double that amount including the nearby towns, suburbs, and the students) straddles the Animas River and boasts an abundant wealth of climate, location, sporting opportunities, and natural resources.

The totally paved highway between Durango and Silverton became a reality in 1955. Trucks and automobiles immediately became the common mode of transportation between the two towns. Today, traveling north from Durango on the extended Million Dollar Highway, the road starts out by hugging the base of Animas City Mountain (elevation 8,170 feet) until it enters the broad, gentle Animas Valley, which was scoured out during the Late Wisconsin glacier period. A U-shaped canyon is very typical of a glaciated canyon, but the Animas Canyon does not particularly look U-shaped because the Animas River has brought down huge amounts of silt that have filled the valley floor. In fact, 15,000 years ago, it was a lake, now called "Lake Durango" by geologists.

Many of the little hills and mesas near Durango are actually terminal moraines, where the glaciers stopped moving and dropped the rocks and gravel they had picked up along the route. The Animas River constantly twists and turns back on itself throughout the almost level Animas Valley, forming ox-bows and new channels, as it meanders for over ten miles; but the river did little to erode the area compared to the sculpting done by the glaciers. The Animas River can be a raging torrent or a peaceful stream. It runs as low as 400 cfs (cubic feet of water per second) in the fall to a roaring 5,000 cfs during the peak of the spring runoff (the big flood of 1911 occurred when the river hit 25,000 cfs and flooded the entire valley, taking out bridges and changing the course of the river in several places). The river and the ancient lake made the valley a rich and fertile place for farmers and ranchers, but now residential communities

Chapter 7: THE TOWN OF DURANGO AND A TRIP TO SILVERTON ❖ 177

The Animas River twists and turns as it flows slowly through the almost level Animas Valley, which was the site of an ancient lake (Lake Durango) that filled with silt and later drained leaving what we see today.
Photo Courtesy Denver Public Library, F40125

The little creeks that run in the Upper Animas Valley were crossed by going over log bridges, like the one shown in this photograph from about 1929.
Author's Collection.

take up most of the space. The present highway goes almost straight as an arrow through the middle of the valley (parallel to the railroad in most places). The extended Million Dollar Highway was moved to the center of the valley in 1950. Originally the highway ran down the extreme west side (now County Road 203).

One sight not seen from the highway is "Hidden Valley," which lies behind the long north-south ridges on the west side of the road. Hermosa Creek probably formed Hidden Valley during the last ice age when a huge 1,500-foot high glacier filled the valley about 18,000 years ago. Hermosa Creek had no where to go when it hit the ice, so it turned south. The Fall Creek archeological site was in the southern end of this valley. Among other discoveries made in 1937 was a cave that yielded quite a few mummies, one of whom was called "Esther" and was displayed at Mesa Verde National Park for many years. Native Americans were not happy about this situation, so Esther is no longer on display. There were eighteen whole or partial mummies found in the caves that are 1500 to 1600 years old. Signs of human habitation in the Fall Creek area go back to the Basketmaker period in 300 B.C.

"The Basketmaker" was an early Anasazi period in which the people had no bows and arrows and used baskets instead of pottery. They hunted with spears, atlatyls, and throwing sticks. They were an earlier phase of the same culture as Mesa Verde, but they lived in the valleys of the Four Corners area before the Anasazi had to retreat into the cliffs and on to steep-sided mesas. Later American farmers, clearing or plowing their fields in the Animas Valley, found Anasazi and Basketmaker relics for decades. Today, Hidden Valley is a public use area with good hiking trails and many delights for nature lovers – it is also a favorite winter grazing area for elk. Access can be gained by going west on 25th (Junction) Street out of Durango for about three miles, then turn on CR 205.

On the west, and a mile and a half into the Animas Valley, is Waterfall Ranch, obviously named after the beautiful waterfall created by Fall Creek, as it cascades down the steep side of the valley. The ranch was originally homesteaded by Hugh Lambert and then bought by Thomas Wigglesworth, who was the construction superintendent for the D&RG Railroad when the company built its branch line into Silverton. Wigglesworth was totally enchanted by the spot. A hiking trail up to Hidden Valley is near the ranch.

About six miles north of Durango, Trimble Lane leads west from the stoplight, going about 100 yards to Trimble Springs. Anasazi and Ute Indians were undoubtedly the first to use the hot springs, but the springs were named for Frank Trimble, who settled on the spot in 1874. He used the water for his rheumatism and to heal wounds that he had received in the Indian War in Oregon; and he reported a miraculous recovery. He also claimed that the water cured his corns! Eventually, two springs were developed that furnished 150 to 200 gallons of hot water a minute, varying in temperature from 96 degrees to 126 degrees. A small hotel was built at the site. Trimble advertised that the waters had "a pronounced curative value, including the healing of rheumatism and kidney complaints as well as the eradication of the tobacco habits...." The spot was especially popular with the local miners, who used it to help combat pneumonia and other hazards associated with mining in the high mountain areas.

Tom Burns and his family took control of the hot springs in 1882. They ran Trimble for almost forty years. They built a 6,000 square-foot two-story frame hotel that included fourteen guest rooms, a parlor, and a dining facility. Regular D&RG excursion trains were run to the siding at Trimble Hot Springs. A small community developed around Trimble, which included a little school, a doctor's office, and a post office, which opened in January 1883. Trimble's old bathhouse was 100 feet long by 32 feet wide, and was equipped with a variety of baths. In those days, bathhouses had bath tubs for use as needed! The *Durango Herald* of December 13, 1883, called Trimble "the favorite health and pleasure resort in the San Juans." It also declared "the curative powers of the springs are unsurpassed." Trimble was a big part of the D&RG's "Circle Route" marketing, which heavily emphasized all the health resorts along their route.

The Hermosa House at Trimble Hot Springs was a large, imposing structure with beautifully landscaped grounds. Unfortunately it burned, but there are plans to recreate the building. The pool has stayed in the original location.

Author's Collection

Evidently the curative powers of the water worked well, at least in those days. Fossett, in 1885, wrote "men have been brought here unable to walk; in a week's time they have jumped upon the (railroad) car to return home, completely cured." He further wrote that the spot was "well patronized by the residents... never missed by the tourists." Father J. J. Gibbons wrote "Hither throng, year after year, multitudes of tourists, the sick, the decrepit and rheumatic, all taking the medicine waters that boil up from solid rock...." But he also mentioned "pneumonia is much feared at the mines and when the first symptoms of the dread disease appear, the sick miner at once seeks a low altitude and enters the sister's hospital in Durango." The Burns' original frame hotel burned in 1892 and was replaced four years later with a beautiful three-story, forty-room, brick building called "Hermosa House." Eventually, riding stables, a saloon, a bowling alley, a gym, and a large dance hall were all built around the spring. Tennis, golf, and croquet were offered, as well as hunting, fishing, hiking, and a nine-mile bicycle route to Durango.

Dave Day's wife, Victoria, leased the springs for five years (1906-1911). Starting in 1923, a bus ran from Durango to Trimble five times a day bringing scores of visitors. In the 1920s, Trimble advertised its waters as a "positive cure for rheumatism, also for skin diseases of every nature, liver, kidney, bronchitis, and more." Then on July 30, 1931, another fire destroyed the Hermosa House. The resort was again rebuilt, but not to its former glory. In 1938, the large bathhouse burned, but by that time Trimble was mainly a dancehall and nightclub. The old dance hall was moved to the Hermosa House foundation and a new building was also built. Dance bands and rodeos were popular in and near Trimble at the time. Clark Gable and Marilyn Monroe were a few of the notables who visited Trimble. In 1957, another fire destroyed the main building, and for a long while the hot springs sat closed and basically abandoned. In the mid-1980s, the spa reopened, and it has been a very popular spot ever since. The present owners are in the midst of a project to bring Trimble Springs back to its former glory. There are even plans to recreate the fabulous Hermosa House.

Continuing north for about a mile and a half to the point where the highway crosses the railroad tracks, one comes to a railroad and stagecoach stop called "Hermosa" (elevation 6,640 feet and meaning "beautiful" in Spanish). The area was first settled in 1873, and by July 27, 1876, a post office was established. The 1877 population of seventy expanded to about 200 in 1880. Hermosa was used as a large construction camp when the D&RG Railroad was built through the valley. In 1882, Ernest Ingersoll wrote "a few cabins constitute Hermosa," and he was prone to exaggerate; so it is obvious the census takers were also counting the nearby farmers and ranchers, who got their supplies at Hermosa. At one time, Hermosa was a full section camp for the railroad with a wye, depot, section house, bunkhouse, water tower, and coal storage.

Hermosa was a stop on the D&RG route for many years. The little station served the area farmers and ranchers. This photo was taken about 1940.

Photo Courtesy of Denver Public Library, X-8951.

The Silverton-Durango train still has supplies and equipment stored there.

Hermosa Creek flows through the valley to the west of Hermosa. It is an 85,000-acre drainage through timber-lined canyons that is managed by the San Juan National Forest as a roadless area. It is therefore a paradise of wonders to the backpacker and hiker. County Road #203 winds to the west and then north about four miles into the Hermosa Creek drainage and connects with the Colorado Trail. At the end of the road, the Hermosa Creek Trail goes north almost to Cascade Creek near Durango Mountain. At one time the D&RG considered Hermosa Creek for a rail route to Rico but eventually gave up on the idea.

A couple of miles north of where the D&RG tracks cross the highway at Hermosa, there is an old logging road (Animas Springs Road/FR 682) that heads east and can be seen creating switchbacks up Missionary Ridge, which was named by an army unit stationed in the Animas Valley during the 1879 Ute scare. It

Chapter 7: THE TOWN OF DURANGO AND A TRIP TO SILVERTON   ❊ 183

reminded them of the hills by the same name near Chattanooga, Tennessee. The road winds for miles up into the backcountry and could make an interesting day's trip in itself.

The highway and the train lose sight of each other about three miles north of Hermosa. The Animas River moves to the far eastern side of the valley, where it comes out of the impassible part of the Animas Canyon, a section that man has never conquered. Pinkerton Hot Springs is located directly alongside the Million Dollar Highway and a half a mile south of Baker's Bridge. The spring was named for James H. Pinkerton, who arrived in 1875 and was one of the first settlers to settle in the valley. Pinkerton and his sons came to Silverton over Stony Pass in 1875 and brought with them thirty dairy cows, so the trip from Del Norte took twenty-two days. By late summer, Pinkerton felt he should move to a lower elevation and came to the Animas Valley, where he homesteaded 160 acres of land that included the hot springs. He sent for

Pinkerton Hot Springs still bubbles up along the Million Dollar Highway. Its flow has been reduced but its colors are dazzling, and there is a good interpretive sign at the sight.

Jan Smith Photo.

the rest of his family and was elected the La Plata County Judge in October 1877. He left the area in September, 1881.

One of his sons, Charles Pinkerton, recalled that the first Animas City was on their ranch, but it was deserted when they arrived. The family used some of the logs from the Animas City cabins for their home and other buildings on the ranch. One entire cabin was moved and used as a school. There were no roofs on any of the cabins, so Charles assumed that the roofs were made of canvas; however, he did find a big pile of unused shingles that had been split at the site and were ready for use. He counted about twenty-five cabins in the deserted town and saw another six or eight cabins up Elbert Creek (could it have been Camp Pleasant?). He encountered several graves in the area, giving stark testimony to the dangers that faced the original Baker party.

When the Hayden Survey party reached Pinkerton in 1874, the men were close to starving. The valley around Pinkerton was abandoned because of an Indian scare, but crops had been planted and were ready for harvest. The Hayden group ate corn, melons, tomatoes, carrots and other vegetables until they were almost sick, and then filled their pockets with everything they could carry with them. They did not say if they left money to cover their feast.

A later owner promoted the springs and named them after Pinkerton. At that time there were no accommodations at the spot. The springs are not as hot as Trimble, with a temperature usually in the 90s, but they can produce a lot of fog in the winter. Ouray, the famous Ute chief, stopped at Pinkerton Springs just days before his death in 1880 and tried to get some relief from Bright's disease. In the 1920s and '30s, Pinkerton Hot Springs did have lodging available, when tourism was being pushed along the new Million Dollar Highway. It was called "Pinkerton-in-the-Pines Swimming Pool" at the time. Evidently, water wells dug in the Animas Valley have significantly lowered the water pressures of both Trimble and Pinkerton springs.

At the very north end of the valley, a half-mile east from Highway 550 on County Road 250, is the site of Baker's Bridge.

A bronze marker that was erected by the Colorado Historical Society in 1961 commemorates the spot where Charles Baker or his followers built the first bridge in Southwestern Colorado. The bridge itself was directly north of the marker. It was used for fifty years, but is no longer standing, although the site is obvious.

There is an unlikely legend that, when Charles Baker left in 1861 to join the Confederate Army, he buried gold a short distance above Baker's Bridge. He supposedly marked the spot with blazes on several nearby trees, and each man in his group was given a map showing how the burial site was marked. When Baker came back after the Civil War, the trees had been cut and no one could find a single blaze. There are problems with this legend. As far as is known, Baker only found a very small amount of gold that year and had no reason to not take it with him. Some people claim that Baker took the gold when he returned in 1868 and then left for Arizona. It is fact, not legend that Paul Newman and Robert Redford leapt from the spot of Baker Bridge into the Animas River during a scene from the movie "Butch Cassidy and the Sundance Kid." Beyond the bridge, the road leads back south to Durango along the east side of the Animas Valley, or on up into the wilds of Missionary Ridge.

Back on the Million Dollar Highway, U. S. 550 winds uphill for about a mile through the aspen and pine forests and crosses the large bridge over the Silverton Railroad's tracks (the large parking area is a good place to take pictures of the train). Ingersoll wrote that "once in the hills (between Hermosa and Rockwood) the road becomes very rough, but magnificent yellow pine surround us on every side, and we continually passed by piles of (railroad) ties."

A mile and a half later, County Road 75 descends about a mile east into the lovely little park that contains the town of Rockwood, which is located seventeen miles north of Durango at an elevation of 7,367 feet. Rockwood was one of the terminuses for the Rico Toll Road, which went thirty-five miles west over Scotch Creek Pass to Rico and was also a stop on the Durango-Silverton train. The U. S. Forest Service has recognized the importance of the Rico route by erecting a marker in Chris Park Campground between Haviland Lake and Glacier Club (Tamarron), and the road was named a National Historic Landmark. Traces of the early road can easily be seen there, and it now functions as a cross country ski trail in the winter.

Rockwood was a transfer station for the stage passengers and wagon freight, because it sat at a fork in the roads – one way going to Rico on the Dolores River and one going to Silverton on the Animas River. The town had several large warehouses, hotels, saloons, a dance hall, the railroad station, a blacksmith shop (open 24 hours) and a cluster of houses. Today, the train still maintains a station and wye at Rockwood.

The toll road builders were following trails established by the Anasazi, the Utes, and later by fur traders traveling between the Dolores River and Animas River drainages. The toll road was finished to Rico the last week of August, 1881, but Rockwood was

The old school still stands at Rockwood, right next to the D&RG tracks, station and wye. It sits in a beautiful little park.

Jan Smith Photo.

Chapter 7: THE TOWN OF DURANGO AND A TRIP TO SILVERTON ❊ 187

already getting plenty of business from the new Durango-Silverton Toll Road and the construction crews of the railroad. The new toll road to Rico was a much shorter route than that of today, which goes from Durango to Cortez to Dolores and then Rico. Several different companies worked on the old toll route before it was finished. The Rockwood to Rico stage ran to Murane near the present-day ski area, then west nine miles to Meserole, then seventeen more miles to Rico for a thirty-five mile total trip.

The first attempt at building a Rico toll road was the ambitious sounding Animas Valley and San Juan Mine and Turnpike Company, which was incorporated January 21, 1875. That road was evidently never started. On May 25, 1875, the Silverton and Hermosa Turnpike Company was formed. It evidently got only as far as the settlement of Hermosa in 1877, when locals asked that the road from Animas City to Hermosa be declared a public road. On August 11, 1879, the Rockwood to Dolores Wagon Road Company was incorporated. Prospectors in Rico had made some large silver discoveries and access to the new town was important. James Pinkerton and one of his son-in-laws incorporated this road, which, like the others, was never finished. In fact, no one is even sure where it was, although the "Pinkerton Trail" was said to cost $10,000. On July 3, 1879, the Hermosa Creek Toll Road Company was incorporated. (Hermosa Creek's headwaters are near the Durango Mountain ski area and evidently the road was to go up Hermosa Creek from the town of Hermosa, and then on to Rico.) This road was also never built, although the D&RG did consider it as a possible railroad route to Rico.

On July 20, 1880, Pinkerton's road was approved for toll after a representative of the company made the claim that eight miles had been finished. This was the easiest part of the route where a wagon could travel even without a road. By 1881, the Rico mines were doing well enough that they needed to send ore to the smelter in Durango, so the Rico and Durango Toll Road was incorporated. On May 14, 1881, three carloads of equipment for a smelter were unloaded at Rockwood to make the trip over this road to Rico, so the road was evidently passable, if not finished. On June 18, 1881, a burro train with 3,529 pounds of ore arrived in Durango from Rico. By July, a mail route had been established over the road, and more ore came out in August, even though the road was not officially finished until September. By October, complaints were already being received about the road's condition. The Reverend J. J. Gibbons did not have too many nice words to say about the Rico stage: "Sometimes you traveled in a wagon, at other times in a sleigh, and sometimes you were forced to walk. It was the last straw on the camel's back — to have to pay seven dollars for the privilege of riding on the stage." The Rico Toll Road was pretty well abandoned after the Rio Grande Southern Railroad arrived in Rico in 1891.

Just a half-mile north of Glacier Club is the Goulding Creek Trail. It leads west from the highway to the top of the Hermosa Cliffs and to a secluded valley beyond. Various points along the highway north of Glacier Club offer outstanding views of the peaks to the north. The road to the east (CR 671), near the top of the long uphill grade, leads to Haviland Lake, a National Forest Service Campground with forty-five camp sites — a beautiful place for camping or a picnic. The rock around Haviland Lake is some of the very oldest Precambrian exposed in the San Juans, at least 1.8 billion years old. This area is sometimes called the "Upper Animas Valley," and it contains many small lakes that were scooped out by "recent" glacial activity, as well as many camping spots and hiking trails.

Two miles north of Haviland Lake is private Electra Lake, which stores the water used at the Tacoma power plant in the Animas Canyon. Electra Lake was originally much smaller and called "Ignacio Lake." H. T. Henderson, one of the electric company engineers on the project, renamed it. There was a small community on its shores for a while called "Bishop." The lake is not open to the public, but from the road, this is a good place to get a great view of the mountains you will be going through (or rather around). From west to east are Engineer Mountain (elevation 12,968 feet), Potato Hill (which looks much higher that its 11,871 foot elevation), and the

Chapter 7: THE TOWN OF DURANGO AND A TRIP TO SILVERTON ❋ 189

southern end of the West Needle Mountains. About five miles further at The Needles, a small community located at the point where Elbert Creek crosses Highway 550, you can obtain one of the few unobstructed views of the Needle Range proper. Pigeon (13,972 feet) and Turret (13,835 feet) Peaks are the two sharpest mountains, rising almost 6,000 feet straight up. These mountains were never covered by the glaciers and rose like islands in a sea of ice, even though the ice was 2,500 to 3,000 feet thick at this point.

The Durango Mountain ski area is two and a half miles north of The Needles and twenty-five miles north of Durango. It was previously called "Purgatory." Chet Anderson, Forest Service weather expert, and Ray Duncan opened the ski area in 1960. They knew the area got almost 300 inches of snow a year. It now includes over thirty-five miles and 630 acres of ski trails; and it has eighty-five runs at the main ski area. In addition to good downhill skiing, there are several kilometers of established cross-country ski track, thousands of additional acres for unimproved or virgin cross country skiing, and many snowmobile trails. The elevation of the ski area ranges from 8,800 feet at the base to 10,800 feet at the summit. It is known as one of the best family-oriented ski areas in Colorado. The Durango Mountain ski area has several festivals in the summer as well as a system of bike trails for summer use. "Purgatory" (besides being a part of the Animas River's full name) got its name for the small, open area below and across the road from the ski area, which was named "Purgatory Park" many years before the ski area arrived.

The original stagecoach road from Rockwood to Rico can be seen along the base of the ski area, before it turns west and heads into the mountains. County Road #593, just beyond the ski area, leads to a National Forest campground. The Hermosa Valley can be accessed from FR#578. There is a Forest Service Campground six miles off U. S. 550. The old toll road becomes four-wheel drive after about eight miles and has two branches – one goes over Bolam Pass and the other over Scotch Creek Pass. Both come out of the mountains near Rico.

There was a small stage stop called "Cascade" downstream near Purgatory Park on Little Cascade Creek." The "town had a peak population of only fifteen, but it had a couple of cabins and several barns at one time. It had a post office from 1880 until 1882, when the train started running to Silverton and the wagon toll road was abandoned. Croffutt described the two miles of zigzagging road coming out of the canyon past a chain of five "cliff lakes" as marshy and contained no fish. He also observed a family cutting the plentiful grass from around the lakes to sell in Silverton. They said they were making a very good profit doing so.

Shortly after Durango Mountain is the San Juan County line. One mile further at the sharp curve at Cascade Creek, there is a short National Forest road to the west that leads to some unimproved campsites and some beautiful little waterfalls. You can drive up the creek for several miles, and then continue on a hiking trail. This was one of the early routes into Silverton and Baker's Park, used first by Utes and then by prospectors. The entire route runs up Cascade Creek, around Bear Mountain, and down Bear Creek or South Mineral Creek to Baker's Park.

A very interesting, but challenging, summer automobile trip is on the other (inside) side of the Cascade curve. The eleven mile Old Lime Creek Road (U. S. Forest Service [FR] No. 591), is basically that part of the old Million Dollar Highway which skirted Potato Mountain to the east and followed the course of Lime Creek. It now ties back into the route of present U. S. 550 at the lower northern end of Coal Bank Pass. The awesome little road travels through thick forests, open meadows, and small ponds (Scout Lake, three miles down, is full of lily pads). Ducks, geese, and beaver may be seen along the way, as well as many varieties of big game.

The Lime Creek Road was built when the Million Dollar Highway automobile highway was built in the early 1920s. The present route for the Million Dollar Highway over Coal Bank was built in the late 1940s, the relocation project being finished in 1948. The Lime Creek road is still passable by automobile, although you might want to use a four-wheel drive or high clearance vehicle. The road adds an hour to an hour and a half to the trip, but has good fishing, primitive campsites, and spectacular views along the route. The road was originally an Indian trail, then a part of the Durango-Silverton wagon toll road in 1910, then part of the auto road, and then abandoned as part of the automobile upgrade. Three miles from the Cascade Creek curve is the "Spud Mountain" hiking trail to Potato Lake and a primitive camp ground. Most of the Lime Creek road is not plowed in the winter, which makes for some good cross country skiing.

Back on the extended Million Dollar Highway, U. S. 550 begins to climb steeply at Cascade Creek, heading onto the lower slopes of Engineer Mountain (12,968 feet) and Grizzly Peak (13,738 feet), which are visible to the left. Engineer (there are three Engineer Mountains in the San Juans, so it gets a little confusing at times)

There are many beautiful little lakes along the Lime Creek Road, which attract all kinds of wildlife. Durango Mountain ski area can be seen in the background. Lime Creek is a very special place.

Jan Smith Photo.

is the conspicuous, pyramid-shaped mountain that dominates the view along this stretch of highway. There are several strenuous hiking trails to the summit of Engineer. One starts at Cascade Creek, one begins about a mile past Cascade Creek, and another is at the summit of Coal Bank Pass, which is about five miles up the highway from Cascade Creek. The trail from Cascade Creek to Engineer is steep and four and a half miles roundtrip. The trail from the top of Coal Bank is shorter, but even steeper. Pass Creek Trail can be accessed from the summit of Coal Bank, to climb to the top of Engineer or access the ski trail called "Power Line," which goes from the top of Coal Bank Pass down to Durango Mountain ski area.

At the top of Coal Bank Pass (elevation 10,640 feet and originally known as Cascade Divide) are rest rooms, large interpretive signs, and a rest area. Coal Bank is actually misnamed because what was taken to be coal is actually shale. You have now reached the part of the road where the highway gets exciting. You are also entering avalanche country, so be careful to look for avalanche signs if traveling the road in the winter and don't stop in these areas. There is a trail up Coal Creek just on the other side of the pass near mile marker 52. In the upper reaches of Coal Creek is the location of a lost gold mine (or in this case, a lost gold vein) called the "Baker Brothers Seam."

Sull and Charlie Baker were brothers who were both sheepherders who lived in Aztec, New Mexico, but came to the San Juan Mountains around Silverton every summer to graze their sheep. In the summer of 1932, during the worst of the Great Depression, times were tough, and it was suggested to them that they might work an abandoned mine to make some extra money (a lot of men in the San Juans successfully worked small mines during the Depression). They were told that there was a mine near the headwaters of West Lime Creek or Coal Creek, where they might find something. The prospector who had worked the mine was dead and had never received legal title to the mine.

Sull and Charlie started their search for the mine up Coal Bank Creek. Near the top of the mountain, they broke out of the timber into a high meadow. They never found the mine they were looking for, but they remembered later that they sat down to rest right where the lower part of the high meadow became a steep slope, near a creek (we assume Coal Bank), and with a waterfall only a short distance below. Some sod had slipped down the steep slope exposing a seam of ore. They took samples, but it was some time later that a friend told them the ore might be gold. It assayed at $44,000 a ton at $16 an ounce for gold! It was a harsh winter, so they could not return until the spring of 1933. Evidently, more sod had slid over the seam and hidden the vein. They came back many times to where they knew they had discovered the seam, but with no luck. Many people have found rich float (broken off pieces of ore) in the upper reaches of Coal Creek, but no one can find the source. The float is a brown, rusty color with large amounts of free (100%) gold in it. The vein is evidently still waiting to be found on a high bluff about twenty feet above a waterfall and on the edge of a meadow.

Just shortly after Coal Bank Pass is a pull-off to view 13,158 foot Twilight Peak across the Lime Creek Canyon. Twilight Peak is a prominent part of the West Needle Mountain range, which lies between Lime Creek on the west side and the Animas River on the east side. Twilight Peak is the site of another lost gold mine. Levi Carson discovered a very rich vein in the 1890s. It was a type of gold ore that had not been seen before in the areas around Silverton. Two hundred pounds of the rock yielded $2,400. He brought the ore to Silverton, where it was assayed and purchased. The assayer tried to buy Carson's mine on the spot, but the prospector refused. Then several men tried to follow him back to his mine. They could tell he was headed toward the West Needles and Lime Creek, but the men lost him in the tangle of dead trees in the rugged Lime Creek Burn and West Needles area.

The next year, Carson was spotted by cattlemen coming out of the West Needles. He went back several more times but eventually had a heart attack and died on Molas Pass. Travelers found his body, and he had evidently been heading back to his mine in the

West Needles. It was then discovered that Carson had told a relative about his mine. He had only said it was on Twilight Peak at the far northern end of the West Needles. He said he hadn't done any real mining; he was just picking ore out of a rich outcrop. He also mentioned that he couldn't bring his burros to the spot, as it was too steep. Several treasure hunters began looking for his camp, and they found several places where it looked like he had stayed for a while. The biggest and most heavily used camp was at the head of Twilight Creek.

Because of all the dead timber in the Lime Creek Burn, it used to take days to get to this spot before one could even start looking for the mine. But the new Lime Creek Road opened up the area. John Edwards, a treasure hunter, found float of the same type of ore that Carson had brought to Silverton in Twilight Creek. He also found abandoned dynamite and drill steel. In 1922, Juan Quintana, a Mexican sheepherder, saw what seemed to be the beginning of a mine on the slopes of Twilight Peak, but didn't know the story and wasn't looking for ore. He did, however, take an interesting piece of rock back with him, which turned out to be the same rich, Carson ore. Quintana (perhaps wisely) assumed he might be killed or tortured if anyone found out about the mine, so he covered it up. Later he related the story to a trusted friend, whom he told he would take to the mine the next summer. Unfortunately, Quintana died that winter, and no one else has seen any sign of the Lost Carson Mine.

About three miles north of Coal Bank Pass, the Lime Creek Road ties back into the existing Million Dollar Highway. To the north, the old, abandoned road can be seen below and ahead of the present highway in many places. The Lime Creek Burn is quite evident. An enormous forest fire burned 26,000 acres in forty days in 1879, consuming 150 million board feet of lumber. It started near the present-day ski area, then burned north up Lime Creek and eventually came within two miles of Silverton. Because of strained relations with the Ute Indians, the whites blamed the Utes for intentionally setting the fire, but it is much more likely that lightning was the cause.

Chapter 7: THE TOWN OF DURANGO AND A TRIP TO SILVERTON   195

The stone barriers still look much like they did ninety years ago on the Lime Creek portion of the Million Dollar Highway. It is like taking a trip back to yesterday, when many of the spots along the road had the same type barriers.
Jan Smith Photo.

The Lime Creek Burn is very evident in this view from about 1929, but the area has pretty much healed today. Although narrow, there's room for cars to pass — in most places.
Photo Courtesy of Ft. Lewis College, Center for Southwest Studies.

The snowplows were still trying to open the Million Dollar Highway through the Lime Creek Burn when this photo was taken in the 1930s. A few trees are starting to grow after the reforestation project, but it still looks mighty bare.
              Photo Courtesy of Ft.Lewis College, Center for Southwest Studies.

Because of the high altitude and rough winters, the area would probably still be barren if the Forest Service, Boy Scouts, and Colorado Federation of Women's Clubs hadn't joined together in 1911 and started a huge reforestation campaign. Lodgepole pine seeds were planted over seventy-five acres in 1911, but had a hard time growing in the high altitude and cold. Different types of seedlings were tried between 1924 and 1936, and those did much better. In 1936 lodgepole and spruce seedlings were used in earnest. Unfortunately, the program was dropped, even though thousands of acres still need to be replanted.

Yet another lost gold vein is possibly located up West Lime Creek. It can be accessed from where the creek goes under the big curve in the Million Dollar Highway at the bottom of Molas Pass on the south side. The tale could be just another version of the Coal Creek story; or if true, it could even be an extension of the

Chapter 7: THE TOWN OF DURANGO AND A TRIP TO SILVERTON ❦ 197

same vein that the Baker Brother's supposedly found. This story takes place at the beginning of the twentieth century when huge herds of sheep grazed in the San Juans in the summer. (Now the Forest Service allows only a few small bands.) Silverton even had a Sheepherders Celebration about the first of September each year when the sheep were coming out of the high mountains. Not only was there good grazing in the mountains, but the cold nights made the sheep's wool thick.

The Lost Sheepherder's Lode was discovered in the upper reaches of West Lime Creek Basin in 1909. The shepherd found pure gold nuggets lying alongside the vein. Up to that time, a few rich gold pebbles had been found along upper Lime Creek, but the vein had never been located. Like Coal Bank Creek, the problem was that the basin has a lot of dirt on top of the rock, which makes it a good place for sheep but not for prospectors. A group of lambs were

Sheep roamed the area around the Million Dollar Highway until the 1960s. There was no way to go through them, you had to let them go around you.

Postcard from Author's Collection.

playing and kicked up the dirt, exposing the vein. Unfortunately, the sheepherder covered it back up, fearing someone else might find it while he was off confirming that what he found was gold. After finding out that he had found almost pure gold, he went back to the spot, but he could not find it because the sheep had smashed down the ground. Someday the dirt will be washed away and some very lucky person might find the vein again.

As you pass through the Lime Creek curve and travel up Molas Pass (it is about five miles to the top) the old highway is often visible below the road. About a half-mile before the summit is the Andrews Lake road, which leaves to the east. The lake has fish, there are some good campsites and restrooms, and you will enjoy wonderful views. There is an easy, but long, trail from Andrews Lake to Crater Lake.

Molas Pass attains an elevation of 10,910 feet. The name is Spanish for "moles," many of which still dig in the soft dirt surrounding Molas Lake. The top of Molas Pass was given the official designation of the cleanest air in the United States. There is a good observation point with vast and breathtaking views. A new overlook (which has nice restrooms) provides a wonderful view of the Grenadier Range (the northernmost part of the Needle Mountains) to the northeast. Grand Turk (13,087 feet), with its twin summits is to the west, and 13,361-foot Sultan Mountain is straight ahead. The deep canyon to the east is the Animas Canyon, finally coming back into sight along the highway. The mountains behind it make up part of the Continental Divide. The scarcity of trees comes from the Lime Creek Burn, but this leaves plenty of sun for a profusion of wildflowers to grow in the wet soil in the summer. The road to Little Molas Lake is just on the other side of the pass. Little Molas has good fishing and a few unimproved campsites. Just north of the summit, the highway intersects the 470-mile Colorado Trail.

Three quarters of a mile further is the Molas Lake Recreation Area, which includes a campground and store. It is owned by the Town of Silverton, but is usually leased to private individuals. The

Chapter 7: THE TOWN OF DURANGO AND A TRIP TO SILVERTON ❋ 199

Molas Lake sits in one of the most scenic areas in all of the United States. The Town of Silverton owns the lake, but usually leases it out. Campers, hikers, and fishermen are welcome. The Needle Mountains are in the background.

Jan Smith Photo.

lake lies in a shallow basin dug out by glacial action. In fact, the entire Molas area has been smoothed and scoured by glaciers; and the scratches the glaciers made on the hard rock (called "glacial striate") can be seen in many places around the lake. The Snowflake Hiking Trail starts at Molas Lake and goes down to the river and Elk Park. The Molas Trail leads into the Weminuche Wilderness.

Shortly beyond the flat area around Molas Lake, Kendall Mountain (13,451 feet) becomes prominent to the north across the Animas Canyon. It is the site of a most unusual footrace. The runners leave Silverton and climb more than 3,700 feet in elevation before reaching the top of the mountain, and then they must return to town. It is said that the idea for the race came from a local miner who made a bet in a saloon that he could climb the mountain and return to the saloon in less than two hours. He evidently did!

After Molas, the Million Dollar Highway makes a steep, narrow, and twisting five-mile dive into Baker's Park. This is one of the steepest and highest drop offs along the entire highway and one of the narrowest parts of the road. One mile down the steep stretch is a pull off and nice waterfall at Deadwood Gulch. The highway passes near and sometimes immediately over some of the area's old mines, including the Champion, Lodore, and North Star, and a dozen or so lesser prospects. Soon the town of Silverton is visible thousands of feet below – so far below that most travelers begin to wish they were already in Silverton. So massive are the mountains surrounding the town that Silverton looks like a toy town nestled in the narrow valley.

Silverton is dramatically situated at an elevation of 9,320 feet in the south end of the hourglass-shaped Baker's Park, which was formed by glacial scouring and then filled with gravel deposits as the glaciers receded and water, gravel and debris flowed into the park from three large rivers. A comment often heard is that Baker's Park has no trees. It is due to the naturally boggy ground in the park and the cold temperatures at night. This condition drastically shortens the growing season on the floor of the park. Cold air sinks, so it is often warmer up in the mountains than it is down in the town.

As the highway goes down, it is easy to note the avalanche chutes that come near to Silverton. Both the Kendall Mountain Slide and the Idaho Gulch Slide run periodically in the winter and, at times, have come very close to hitting the town. The Champion Slide runs across the Million Dollar Highway itself shortly before the big switchback down to Baker's Park. A few years ago it swept an entire Greyhound passenger bus down the mountain, but luckily no one was badly injured.

Silverton will forever be a mining town. Over the years, the town has been called "The Silver Queen of Colorado" and "The Treasure Chest of the San Juans." In 1893, the Sherman Silver Purchase Act was repealed, which ended the government purchase of silver, and, for a while, it looked as if Silverton would become

Chapter 7: THE TOWN OF DURANGO AND A TRIP TO SILVERTON ❖ 201

The Town of Silverton is nestled in Baker's Park like a toy city on a railroad model maker's table. On the far right above the town is the Hillside Cemetery.

Bill Fries III Photo.

a ghost town. Fortunately, large deposits of gold were found soon after. More recently, lower metal prices and government regulations forced most of the mines in the area to shut down, but with the high price of metals at the time this book is being written, some of the mines are already making plans to reopen.

Silverton is one of the access points to the four-wheel drive Alpine Loop – another federal scenic designation. The other access points from the Million Dollar Highway are at Poughkeepsie Gulch or the Engineer Pass road near Ouray. The Alpine Loop is a seventy-three mile road that travels through the heart of the high country of the San Juans. Most of it must be traveled in a four-wheel drive vehicle. From Silverton it goes up to the ghost town of Animas Forks, over 12,600 foot Cinnamon Pass, then through the ghost towns of Whitecross, Burrows Park, and Sherman, and on to Lake City. The loop then goes back over 12,800 foot Engineer Pass to Mineral Point and Ouray. The "loop" is completed on the Million Dollar Highway from Ouray to Silverton – the only section of paved highway in the "loop" except for a small stretch of road near Lake City. The route is usually only open along its entire length from June through September. It passes numerous mines, mills, and ghost towns along the way. Marmots, elk, mountain sheep, pika, deer, lynx, and bear can often be seen on the route.

The Million Dollar Highway descends into Baker's Park, but before it passes into the Silverton town limits, the road goes over Mineral Creek and then forks and forms a triangle. The right fork leads to Silverton and the left fork goes on to Ouray via the

The Silverton Visitor's Center sits right next to the parking for the train at the southwest edge of town. It is well worth stopping here to orient yourself to all the things to do in the area.

Jan Smith Photo.

Million Dollar Highway. The Silverton Visitor's Center is the large Victorian building on the right fork and is well worth a stop. While you are there, check out what events are going on in town (there is always something in the summer). This is also the spot where the trains park while their passengers are having lunch and doing some shopping in Silverton. You will probably want to do the same.

Chapter 8

THE TOWN OF SILVERTON AND THE RAINBOW ROUTE

THE TOWN OF SILVERTON (elevation 9,305 feet and with a year-round population of about 600 people) is a fascinating place to visit, because it still retains the flavor of a booming nineteenth century mining town. As a true piece of Americana, Silverton has gone through many trials to earn its nickname – "The Mining Camp That Never Quit." One of the town's attractions is the existence of many ornate commercial buildings from the late 1800s and early 1900s, which still stand on Greene Street (Silverton's Main Street). Another favorite place to visit is the two block long section of Blair Street, which at one time contained a good part of the town's forty saloons and some of the most notorious gambling houses, opium dens, and houses of prostitution in the State of Colorado. In the summer, the air is filled with the noise and smells of the narrow gauge train, coming from and leaving for Durango.

Frances M. Snowden built the first cabin within the future town limits of Silverton in 1872, but there was no town at the time.

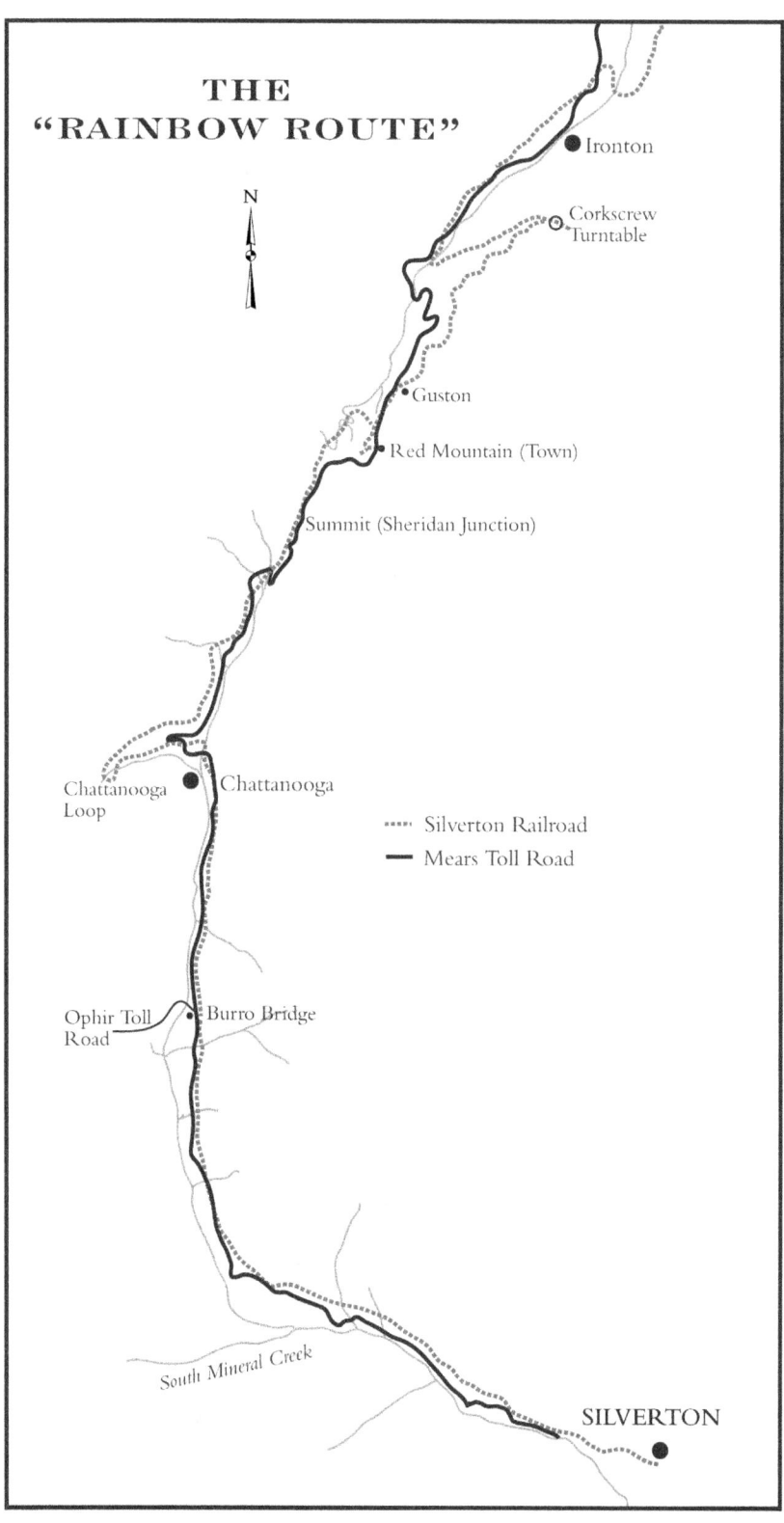

His cabin was very small, but Snowden liked a good party, and it was said that many late-night dances were held there in the 1870s. Dempsey Reese, Tom Blair, and William Kearn officially laid out the Town of Silverton in 1874 in the part of Baker's Park where Cement Creek and Mineral Creek join with the Animas River. Reese took on the job of selling lots in the town, which had several names over its first year of existence. Originally, it used the name "Quito," then "Reeseville," and then "Greeneville," before the name "Silverton" was finally agreed to by all. Legend has it that the town's name came from a prospector who said, "We may not have gold, but we have silver by the ton," but most likely it is simply a contraction of the words "silver town."

Early on, Howardsville was the largest town in Baker's Park even though it had only a dozen cabins. It was, located near the narrow "neck" of the hourglass. On February 10, 1874, La Plata County was carved out of Lake and Conejos Counties by the Colorado legislature, and Howardsville was made the county seat. In early 1874, a sawmill was brought into the park piece by piece over Stony Pass and set up on Mineral Creek by a Mr. Tower and his wife, the first female in Baker's Park. Enough freight to fill five to ten wagons was reported to be coming or going over Stony Pass every day that summer, although none of the wagons themselves made it without a lot of help (usually they were slid in without wheels or with the wheels locked). Most of the wagons were unpacked on the east side of Stony Pass, and the freight was taken into Baker's Park by mules or burros. By late summer, Silverton was made the new county seat.

This move was brought about so quickly because Silverton's founders were extremely aggressive in their promotion of the southern part of Baker's Park. Lots were often given away, especially to merchants or other people who could help the town grow. The only catch was that the new owners had to build "respectable" buildings as quickly as possible. Reese convinced John Porter to take over Judge George Greene's smelter near Silverton. Greene also operated a sawmill in connection with the smelter. The sawmill and the smelter did much to secure the future of the new town. The Greene Smelter's bricks and components were hauled by wagon from Colorado Springs to Del Norte and then by burros over Stony Pass in 1874 at a reported freight rate of twenty-five cents a pound.

Judge Greene also owned the biggest store in Silverton, but he knew little about metallurgy. Greene made one run on Arrastra Gulch gold in late 1874, but the smelter's process did not work at all. It was reworked by Porter and ran again from August to November of 1875. Unfortunately, its expenses ($33,000) outstripped its revenues ($25,000) during this time, so it ran only periodically until it was purchased in 1879 by the New York and San Juan Smelter and Milling Company and moved to Durango. The Greene Smelter was the first smelter in southwest Colorado. Because its bullion contained a lot of lead, it was heavy (one-third to one-half the weight of the original ore), the owners had to have a railroad nearby to keep their shipping costs down.

L.L. Ulford and about fifty other men and eight women, stayed in Baker's Park during the winter of 1874-75. His cabin served as the courthouse and unofficial post office. The local prospectors who were leaving the valley for the winter began to give him their excess whiskey with instructions to sell it during the winter. So, in effect, Ulford's cabin became the first saloon in Silverton. Drinking water was delivered to the residents during the first few years by dog sled in the winter and by wagons pulled by dogs in the summer. Pete Schneider ran the operation, getting the water from a spring near town and having two large dogs draw the sixty-gallon barrels (weighing almost 500 pounds when full) on a sled around town. Pete also had the dogs haul lumber from Greene's sawmill. Word was that Pete rewarded his dogs with a shot of whiskey for a good day's work.

As opposed to Durango, Silverton went through all the phases of a typical Colorado mining town and took about twenty-five years to grow from adolescence to full maturity. The population of Silverton rose from about fifty in 1874, to around a hundred in early 1875. The first "post office" opened February 1, 1875, but for several weeks the postmaster had to keep the mail in his pocket as he roamed about the town, because there was no actual building available for his operation. The mail came over Stony Pass on the backs of men on snowshoes. The town's first newspaper, *The La Plata Miner*, was opened on July 10, 1875, by John R. Curry. By the early summer of 1875, the town was booming. The Rough and Ready smelter was opened within the town limits that summer. A school (although it did not meet a full nine months a year), a church (although it had no building), and a very cramped hotel were all open.

By the summer of 1876, Silverton's population soared to over 500. San Juan County was carved out of La Plata County in January 1876, and Silverton remained the county seat. That year the town had ten saloons, and prostitutes showed up for the first time. The Fourth of July celebration (the centennial of the United States) went on for days. Although the summer activity was immense, and about a hundred houses and other buildings had been built, the town only had about 250 residents who remained during the winter of 1876-1877.

By the end of 1877, there were nearly 300 buildings in Silverton. Enough businesses had moved to the town in 1877 that a business district began to develop on Greene Street between Thirteenth and Fourteenth Streets. Silverton's first shootout occurred in October, 1878. More shootings took place in 1879, resulting in a vigilante hanging. Shootings again occurred in 1880. A volunteer fire department was formed in 1878 and new fire equipment arrived to great excitement in 1879. Silverton residents began the new decade of the '80s with the knowledge that the D&RG Railroad was building toward their town. The Bank of Silverton (a Thatcher Brother's Bank) opened in 1880, and the First National Bank soon followed. When this was coupled with the discovery of large amounts of ore at Red Mountain in 1882, it helped Silverton progress to the status of a city by the end of the decade.

Chapter 8: THE TOWN OF SILVERTON AND THE RAINBOW ROUTE ✣ 209

This drawing of Silverton in 1877 is actually labeled and numbered to show many of the locations of the local mines and smelters. It gives a very accurate representation of the town at that time.
Photo Courtesy of Denver Public Library, Western History Department, X-11384.

As the D&RG Railroad approached, crime went up in both Durango and Silverton. In August 1881, the Clint Stockton gang was pushed out of Durango and decided to rendezvous in Silverton. The night marshal, Clayton Osgood, was killed when he responded to help the La Plata County Sheriff arrest the men on Blair Street. After the killing, the gang split up and disappeared. Vigilantes lynched a possibly innocent black man called "the Black Kid," then tracked down the leader of the gang and, after a quick trial, legally hung him two days after the shooting (that is quick justice). The coroner's jury supposedly reported that the gang leader "came to his death from hanging around." A third member of the gang was shot to death in Durango a few days later. When the train arrived in Silverton on July 8, 1882, the rowdiness picked up even more.

Horse racing and boxing were early Silverton sports. Chief Ouray would often stop in Silverton to race his ponies. Ouray had a standard bet of five dollars and usually won. Later, Silverton built a racetrack and held all kinds of races in the 1880s. It was a half-mile track surrounded by an eight-foot fence and had both judges and grandstands. The Silverton Jockey Club ran the operation. The grandstand held 1,200 people and often was full. The track was dragged, sprinkled, and rolled. Ponies, burros, mules, and trotters all raced, as well as the town's firemen (hose cart and hook and ladder competitions were very popular in those days).

The shootings and fights continued. In 1883, Wyatt Earp and Bat Masterson were both in town, gambling or helping to run gambling establishments. Doc Holliday visited them in May of 1883, but only for a short period of time. George Brower, who owned

This postcard shows the highway and the site of the early-day race track, which had been turned into a baseball field. The spectacular Needle Mountains are in the background.

Photo Courtesy of Ft. Lewis College, Center for Southwest Studies.

Chapter 8: THE TOWN OF SILVERTON AND THE RAINBOW ROUTE ❉ 211

Silverton's Arlington Saloon, hired Wyatt Earp to run his gambling hall. Wyatt had a bad reputation by that time (it was two years since the famous gunfight at the O.K. Corral in Tombstone), and there were even rumors that he was wanted for murder. However, efforts were being made to "clean up" the town.

Ernest Ingersoll, who was trying hard to present Silverton as a civilized town, wrote: "Though these mountains are yet full of men who go about all day with a big six-shooter in their belt; and though the streets of Silverton (like those of other frontier places) contain too many drinking and gambling saloons, yet the town has never passed through such as rough history as most mining camps see, and it is today (1883) the most orderly village in the whole region. This is chiefly due to the quietly determined attitude its best citizens have taken, and their fixed purpose to not let lawlessness rule."

Wyatt Earp did go after those who broke the law, but he made no attempt to close down the raucous Blair Street establishments. He enjoyed the saloons, dance halls, and gambling halls too much

The northern side of Silverton was known as "Quality Hill," as many of the wealthy citizens lived there. They definitely had some large, beautiful Victorian homes.

Photo Courtesy of Colorado Historical Society, CHS X4401.

himself during his off hours. He did a lot more good in restoring law and order by talking to his rowdy friends than by using a gun. Rumors (good and bad) constantly flew around Earp. The May 12, 1883 *Silverton Democrat* reported:

> The Club Rooms of the Arlington are conducted by Wyatt Earp who is a pleasant and affable gentleman, and not mixed up in the Dodge City broils, as the Denver papers would have us believe, and the editorial paragraph in the Denver Republican *of the 16th placing him at the scene of the action and counseling the citizens of Dodge City to take the law into their own hands, is wholly unwarranted, from the fact that Mr. Earp is now, and has for the past three months, been a peaceable and law-abiding citizen of Silverton, and not been in Dodge City for the last four years.*

Masterson, Earp, and Holliday left town just a few days later to participate in the "Dodge City broils." The fuss came about when Luke Short, a good friend and part owner of the Longbranch Saloon in Dodge City, was run out of town after a political battle involving his partner. Short and his partner were prepared to return with the help of a few of their friends. Earp and Holliday were old Dodge City sheriff deputies and added a dash of "legality" to their position. They sent a wire from Durango asking that four of their gunslinger friends meet them in Dodge City. The whole affair was a real melodrama, taking place over a period of months and with lots of posturing; but in the end, Luke Short went back to running his saloon, the new mayor left Dodge City, and no shots were fired.

What absolutely secured Silverton's position as the main settlement in the San Juans was the arrival of the D&RG Railroad on July 8, 1882; and, eventually, three other narrow gauge lines were built out of Silverton. Silverton was undoubtedly the transportation center in the San Juans. It was doing at least as much shipping as Durango, and most of the later town's freight came from or was

Chapter 8: THE TOWN OF SILVERTON AND THE RAINBOW ROUTE ❋ 213

going to Silverton. The first true census was taken in Silverton in 1885, and it showed a population of 1,195 people.

About 1890, Silverton finally became more sophisticated and started "growing up." Its rowdy, adolescent side did not stop, but it was relegated to the background. One example of how the town was caught between two worlds was a most unusual orchestra. Jack Sinclair started the "Original Dodge City Cowboy Band" in the late 1880s. It was one of the stragest bands in Colorado, if not in the entire United States. There was no connection at all to Dodge City, and the band members were not cowboys. Sinclair said he just picked the name on a whim. The band eventually performed at presidential (President Harrison) and gubernatorial inaugurations. They wore ten-gallon hats and cowboy clothing and brought a burro with them – even putting on demonstrations on how packing was done in the mountains. The band played at the Kansas City Cattlemen's Convention without any one evidently knowing their true roots!

A few members of Silverton's famous Dodge City Cowboy Band pose on Greene Street in their cowboy outfits. At this time it seems to have about fifteen members, but at times it had over fifty.
Photo Courtesy of Colorado Historical Society, CHS X 4738.

This photograph of Greene Street (Silverton's Main Street) was taken in the 1880s. The wide street gave plenty of room for the horses and wagons of the day.

Author's Collection.

By the 1890s, the Gold King, Sunnyside, Silver Lake, Old One Hundred, Yankee Girl, Guston, and Gold Prince were only some of the large gold mines in the Silverton area. They and many smaller mines made the 1890s the most successful decade of mining to date in San Juan County. With all the miners coming into town for their recreation, Silverton still had a boomtown flavor, but its population exceeded 6,000 for the first time during the 1890s.

Despite the Silver Panic of 1893, all four narrow gauge railroads were operating, and the town had over one hundred "legitimate" businesses in 1900. A lot of additional gold was discovered near Silverton in the early twentieth century, and mining reached its peak from 1900 to 1912. Silverton's population pushed or exceeded 5,000 all during this time, making it one of the largest Colorado towns of the era, and much bigger than Durango or Ouray. Most of the governmental and many of the substantial business buildings of Silverton were built at this time. *The Silverton Miner* wrote: "There was a time when the word 'gold' was not popular in this section. That was for two reasons. The people did not know that they had it, and they did not know that they needed it. Now they know both."

In 1914, Colorado voted to go dry – four years before the rest of the nation and effective January 1, 1916. Prohibition wasn't popular in the mountain towns of Colorado, which had all voted overwhelmingly against it. San Juan law officers didn't enforce the law, and railroad officials tipped off the locals when state or federal agents were coming in on the train. At one time during Prohibition it was said there were sixty bootleggers working in the alley behind Blair Street. One local commented on the local booze, "It never killed anybody that I know of. Out of here though, I've heard that it blinded some people." Silverton still had its wild side. In 1932, there were thirty-two "licensed" prostitutes in Silverton.

The flu hit Silverton quick and hard. On October 11, 1918, the mail from Durango was fumigated because of the pending influenza epidemic, but there were no known cases at the time. By October 18, there were two cases in Silverton, and public places were closed down. By October 25, forty-two people had died. Part of the Town Hall was being used as a hospital. By the first of November, 128 people were dead. The total death count for San Juan County reached 146. The Spanish flu had killed almost ten percent of the population. Everyone said that with Prohibition and the flu the "good old days were gone forever in Silverton."

Mining started to decline around Silverton in the 1920s, and the Great Depression of the 1930s hit hard. Charles Chase, owner of the Shenandoah-Dives Mine, which was located just a few miles northeast of town, kept his mine running, even though it was sometimes losing money, because the mine and the mill were so important to Silverton's economy. In 1959, the Sunnyside Mine reopened, and Chase's mill was modified in the 1960s by the Sunnyside Mine, which brought its ore out at Gladstone and trucked it to the mill. In 1996, the Sunnyside Gold Company donated the mill to the San Juan Historical Society, and it now serves as a very interesting mining museum.

One amazing and relatively recent event regarding the local mines occurred in 1978 after the Sunnyside Mine had reopened the tunnel from Gladstone to Sunnyside Basin to tap the Sunnyside's workings near Lake Emma. On June 4, 1978, one of the major

After such a big deal was made of the first automobile that came into Silverton in 1910 over Stony Pass, the next year's Fourth of July parade featured "The first Horsemobile over Stony, 1879."

Author's Collection.

Chapter 8: THE TOWN OF SILVERTON AND THE RAINBOW ROUTE ✤ 217

stopes (an area where ore is being excavated) was drilled too close to the bottom of Lake Emma. Miraculously, when the lake broke through, it was a Sunday and there was no one in the mine. As the lake emptied, a torrent of water flooded the tunnels and washed machinery, timbers, and some good gold ore for miles down Cement Creek and into the Animas River. It took two years to clean up the mess and get the mine back into production, but the Sunnyside closed down anyway in 1991.

The entire town of Silverton is a National Historic Landmark. Since Silverton has never had a fire that destroyed more than a few buildings, almost half of Blair Street's original buildings are still standing, as well as the vast majority of Greene Street's commercial buildings. Blair Street is now the northern terminus of the Durango to Silverton Narrow Gauge and contains a number of false-fronted shops, while Greene Street is an easy walk away.

It is truthfully said that, even though Silverton's elevation is 9,305 feet, all of the roads out of Silverton lead up. This was part of the reason that Mears' toll road to Ouray was originally dubbed "The Rainbow Route." Several other interesting trips take you off the Million Dollar Highway, but can be easily done by automobile. One route is north along the abandoned Silverton, Gladstone and Northerly railroad route to Gladstone and another is along the Silverton Northerly route northeast to Animas Forks (which is the most intact ghost town in the San Juans). Remnants of the railroads can be seen on both of these routes, as well as many old mines and mills. The trips are short (about thirty minutes to an hour each way), but they include a million dollars of history and scenery.

The automobile route to Animas Forks goes east, then north out of Silverton and passes through the ghost towns of Howardsville, Middleton, Eureka, and Animas Forks. From there, it is four-wheel drive only up Engineer Pass to Engineer City, Rose's Cabin, Capitol City, Henson, and Lake City. Or you can go over Cinnamon Pass to Whitecross, Burrow's Park, Sherman and Lake City. There are also many interesting four-wheel side trips off these roads that could take days or even weeks to explore fully.

Animas Forks is still a well-preserved ghost town and is well worth a visit. It can be reached by automobile from Silverton in the summer. Don't try it in the winter; the snow could be ten feet deep!
Photo Courtesy of Denver Public Library Western History Department, X6614.

Going back to the Cement Creek road near Silverton, a graveled road follows the old Silverton, Gladstone and Northerly roadbed to Gladstone. There are several mines along the way that are still worked off and on by some of the miners left in Silverton. The Silverton Xtreme Ski Area is located a few miles before Gladstone. Silverton Mountain is rated #1 for steepness and powder. Some call it "Xtreme skiing" and some call it "heli-skiing without the helicopter" (using a chairlift instead). Some of the old structures or their foundations still stand at Gladstone, although a good bit was washed away by the mine's great flood from Lake Emma.

And now, back on the Million Dollar Highway we will head north to the Red Mountain Mining District and Ouray. Much of this portion of the highway is built on or near Otto Mears' toll road and later his little narrow gauge railroad. The Million Dollar

Highway heads up the Mineral Creek Valley toward Red Mountain Pass. Plan on at least an hour for the twenty-six mile trip to Ouray, and that is the travel time without stopping to enjoy the spectacular scenery. At first the mountains are high, steep, and colorful, but not precipitous as they roll back on either side of the valley floor, which in some places is a quarter of a mile wide. The greens of the grass and bushes carpeting the valley, dark greens and blues of the fir and spruce, reds and oranges of the mountains, oranges and yellows of the aspen in the fall, and, of course, the magnificent blue of the Colorado sky, all add additional contrast to the scene. The brilliant reds and oranges of the scree rock to the east side of the road are due to volcanic fluids that percolated up with iron oxides and clay when the Silverton caldera was being formed.

It was only a few years after Mears finished the Million Dollar Highway toll road that he proposed a railroad to Red Mountain. The Silverton Railroad was his first rail line, and it ran only a total of eighteen miles to the Red Mountains. Mears had constructed the Silverton-Red Mountain toll road with the thought in mind that some day it might become a railroad, and he began to examine the details of the profitability of upgrading the toll road into a railroad. He eventually determined that a railroad to the Red Mountain District should carry 170,000 tons of ore, 1,700 tons of freight, and up to 12,000 passengers a year for gross earnings of over ten dollars per day for each mile traveled by the train. This was at a time when railroads were breaking even at two dollars per mile per day. To further enhance his profit, the mileages for the railroad were evidently overstated (no one knows whether this was on purpose), with the result that shippers were charged an inflated freight rate of about ten percent.

The Silverton Railroad was incorporated on July 5, 1887. Many of the local mines made contributions to its construction or subscribed to its stock. The Yankee Girl Mine alone bought $15,000 in stock. Outside investment capital was only $76,000 in 1887, which shows how confident Mears was that he could raise the additional capital. By the time the railroad was finished, almost a million dollars had been invested, if the cost of equipment was also included. Grading on the railroad started with 150 men at work in August 1887, and track was being laid by October, 1887. The construction crew laid track 5.3 miles to Burro Bridge that year.

At Chattanooga at the southern base of Red Mountain Pass, the railroad route split from the old toll road. Here the toll road had gone up a series of switchbacks that were too steep and sharp for a train. In fact, passengers sometimes had to get out and help push the stage up this section.

It was May, 1888 before the railroad construction crew could start work again. By July, regular passenger trains were running to Chattanooga, and the construction train had reached the summit of Red Mountain Pass. The train reached Red Mountain Town in September, 1888. By the time that winter snows shut railroad

The surveyors of the Silverton Railroad were staying at the manager's house at the Yankee Boy Mine when they posed with their gear for the photographer about 1887.

Photo Courtesy of Denver Public Library, F29444.

This letterhead was used before the Silverton Railroad was even completed. The engraving was probably a stock item, because it represents the railroad going the wrong way up Red Mountain.

Author's Collection.

construction down, the tracks were almost to Corkscrew Gulch, which meant that the railroad was serving most of the big Red Mountain mines, although spurs had not been completed in many places.

Track laying again resumed in May, 1889. The biggest challenge ahead was Corkscrew Gulch, where a turntable was eventually installed on the main line. By June, 1889, the turntable was in operation, and soon thereafter regular passenger service was available to Ironton. After only minimal winter use it was obvious that the turntable would have to be covered due to snow and ice buildup.

Mears spent many frustrating years trying to figure out how to extend the railroad from Ironton into Ouray. The problem was that a six percent grade was the absolute maximum for a traditional railroad, and even that grade could not be maintained for a very long time. An electric railroad was considered after Mears' engineers calculated that it could run on a seven per cent grade. A cog railroad was also considered as it could have run on a ten per cent grade. But in this case, Mears' concepts were only dreams, and meanwhile the stagecoach continued to meet passengers at Ironton and bring them down to Ouray.

Mears promoted all his railroads in a number of ingenious ways. The famous early-day Western photographer, William Henry Jackson, was hired to take photographs of the amazing scenery along the routes. Numerous railroad companies issued free passes; however, Mears fabricated his passes from silver, lambskin, buckskin, and even a few were made from gold. The passes were made into watch fobs, lockets, medallions, and even spoons. Mears purchased the luxurious *Animas Forks* (a combination sleeping, dining,

Otto Mears used his ornate passes as advertising for his railroads. Four different types of passes are shown here: From top to bottom, buckskin (issued to HAW Tabor), silver, silver filigree, and a silver medallion or watch fob.
Photo Courtesy of Colorado Historical Society, F3883-A.

and club car) for his railroad, though the entire trip on any of his Silverton lines took only two hours! The *Animas Forks* was originally a standard gauge Pullman car and was therefore much longer than most narrow gauge cars at forty-eight feet. Mears rebuilt it as a kitchen, diner, and sleeping car, but its length was a problem on sharp curves, and it derailed three times.

The *Animas Forks* was often used as a poker parlor on wheels. Mears learned to love playing poker in the army, and it was his main distraction from his work, almost to the point of an obsession. It fit in well with his personality. Word was that there were some great parties and poker games held on the *Animas Forks*, as it sat on various sidings along Mears' routes. One poker game started on the way from Animas Forks to Silverton and was still going when the train reached its destination a few hours later; so the car was parked on a siding, the porter fed the men food, they took occasional naps in the berths, and the game didn't end until three days later.

The Silverton Railroad's profits were $21,000 in 1889, $29,000 in 1890, and $38,500 in 1891. The railroad completely dominated passenger travel and freight shipments in and out of Red Mountain. However by 1892 silver prices were falling sharply, and by 1893 silver was at sixty-three cents an ounce – less than half of what it had been two years earlier. In October, 1893, the Silver Purchase Act was repealed, and silver fell to fifty cents an ounce within minutes. The resulting crash of 1893 hit the San Juans hard, but especially the silver-rich Red Mountain District. Ouray and Silverton were fortunate in that considerable amounts of gold were found near both towns in the early 1890s, but Red Mountain was totally a silver district. Most of the Red Mountain mines cut back and then closed. The railroad slashed its rates, and everyone in Colorado pushed Congress to restore the silver standard. However it gradually became obvious that silver would never rebound. One by one the Red Mountain mines shut down, businesses closed, and people moved away. In 1896 the Silverton Railroad, just a few years earlier the most profitable in Colorado, went into receivership.

The Red Mountain Mining District rebounded slightly about 1900 when the price of silver rose a little. The Silverton Railroad was reorganized in 1903 as the Silverton Railway (instead of "Railroad"). One of the new owners was George Crawford, who had bought the Silverton Railroad at a foreclosure sale. Crawford also owned the Joker Tunnel and saw the railroad as a natural way to lower his transportation costs. Otto Mears and others joined in the new business. The Silverton Railway continued to operate sporadically, but many of its spurs became inoperable, and the north end of the track (in Ironton Park) was abandoned. The operation of the Joker Tunnel and small discoveries of gold caused the railroad to change hands and show some signs of life, but in 1922 the railroad was abandoned. There were less than twenty-five people living along its entire route at the time. This was at the same time that the Million Dollar Highway was being rebuilt into an automobile road, and a lot of the Silverton Railroad's route became part of the highway.

The stage played an important role in the D&RG's "Circle Route," carrying passengers to Silverton or Red Mountain after the Silverton Railroad was built. This scene is between Silverton and Chattanooga.
Photo Courtesy of Colorado Historical Society, F-44097.

Chapter 8: THE TOWN OF SILVERTON AND THE RAINBOW ROUTE ✣ 225

The Silverton Railroad letterhead had changed in 1891. It was now being promoted as the "Rainbow Route." The scene is beautiful but doesn't appear anywhere on the route.

Author's Collection.

As you follow "The Rainbow Route" today out of Silverton, look for signs of the railroad grade just above the road, as the road paralleled, but did not take over the route from Silverton to Chattanooga. Just a few tenths of a mile towards Ouray on the present highway was the Charles Fisher Brewery. It is no longer there, but its history is just too good to pass up. The brewery was started by Charles Fisher in Howardsville, and after moving to Silverton he offered free beer from a spigot and cup he placed outside the brewery building. Fisher made a small lake beside the brewery, from which he cut ice in the winter to use for the summer refrigeration of his beer. He lived in a small house at the brewery, which was as fine and modern as any in Colorado at the time.

One half mile north of the triangle intersection, County Road #6 leads east to the Christ of the Mines Shrine. The statute was carved in Carrera, Italy, weighs twelve tons, and is over twelve feet high. The base and backdrop of the shrine were made of stones taken from the Fisher Brewery. The shrine was built at a time when the local mines were all closing, and it was hoped that it might stimulate the mining industry. A few months after the shrine was dedicated, metal prices rose again, and the American Tunnel was driven into the Sunnyside Mine from Gladstone. Hard rock mining was again alive and well in Silverton – "The Mining Town That Never Quit."

At almost the same spot as the shrine road, but along the Million Dollar Highway, is an area of black, flint-like gravel, which is the residue from the smelting process for refining the silver, gold, copper, and zinc ores. It is the discharge from the furnaces of the Martha Rose Smelter (known later as the Walsh Smelter) — a liquid, white hot, molten rock, which cooled into this form. The Martha Rose Smelter was built in 1882, in just 104 days, but shut down after just three days of operation. It was built mainly to service ore coming in over Ophir Pass from Telluride and Ophir; but it was evidently badly underfinanced. One Silverton resident commented "they were out of money before they started." In 1894, Thomas Walsh bought the smelter. When Walsh was looking for flux for the smelter, he discovered gold in Imogene Basin and developed the great Camp Bird Mine, which ultimately made him one of the richest men in America.

Just outside Silverton, and west across Mineral Creek from the shrine road, are the North Star Mine and Mill. Although in sight of Silverton, the North Star wasn't discovered until March of 1876, and it wasn't until 1882 that its owners realized just how much their property was worth. It has been worked off and on right up to the present, yielding respectable amounts of galena (a silver-lead ore). The Comstock Sampling Works was built below the mine in 1883. When it was sold to the North Star Mine in 1886, it became known as the North Star Mill. The Sultan Mine sits above the ruins of the North Star Mill.

After passing by the old smelter's site and the North Star Mill, the road basically bears west until it reaches the forks of Mineral Creek, and then it slowly curves to the north to reach Red Mountain. The Silverton Railroad gained elevation more quickly than the present road, and its grade can be seen above the present highway for several miles. The South Mineral Creek road leaves to the west and gives good access to the high country along a dirt road that reveals good fishing and several campgrounds. South Mineral Creek was one of the original routes into Silverton from the south, but could only be traveled by pack animals.

Chapter 8: THE TOWN OF SILVERTON AND THE RAINBOW ROUTE ❖ 227

The Walsh Smelter is pouring out plenty of smoke, while the Fisher Brewery offers free beer at its plant in the foreground. The Silverton Railroad tracks (today's Million Dollar Highway) are between the two enterprises.
    Photo Courtesy of Denver Public Library, Western History Department, F21617.

The Circle Route Stage heads toward Silverton with several well-dressed ladies on top. Since the Silverton railroad tracks are in the background, this shot was probably taken in the early 1900s, when the railroad had shut down but the Circle Route Stage still ran.
Photo Courtesy Denver Public Library, Western History Department, F11888.

For the most part, the road is now easily accessible by car. There is a Forest Service Campground four miles up the creek from U. S. 550 with twenty-two sites. A hiking trail leads one and a half miles from the campground to Ice Lake, and there is also a jeep road off the South Mineral Creek Road that goes two miles to Clear Lake. The Bandora Mine is at the end of the main road up Mineral Creek. It produced gold and a small settlement was started near the mine. The gold ore was fairly rich but unfortunately was almost impossible to smelt, making it nearly worthless.

Back on the Million Dollar Highway, there are many avalanche paths visible to the west, but the ones to worry about come in from the east and cannot be easily seen. About three miles north of the South Mineral Creek road, the Ophir Pass road (CR8) leaves the main highway to the west at Burro Bridge. A small settlement was located on the creek near the junction of the Ophir jeep road and the Million Dollar Highway. There were a few cabins at Burro Bridge, some used as dwellings and others used for storage or stables for the burros and mules that worked the route over Ophir Pass. Burro Bridge was a regular stop on the Silverton Railroad, picking up passengers coming from Telluride and Ophir until the Rio Grande Southern Railroad was built to Telluride in 1891. An ad in the *Red Mountain Review* in 1883 read "When on the road from Silverton to Red Mountain, don't forget that William R. Shelton

A buggy heads up the scree slope just outside Silverton on the Million Dollar Highway about 1885. The Silverton Railroad later used this route, which is still visible above the present highway that is now near the bottom of the slope.
 Photo Courtesy of Denver Public Library, Western History Department, F39613).

will set you out a square meal at Burro Bridge for fifty cents." Like many of the San Juan roads, the Ophir Road was first an Indian trail – in fact, one of the most heavily traveled in the San Juans.

The road was used as a pack trail in the 1870s, then upgraded by J. H. Mountain in 1881 to a wagon toll road to allow ore wagons to come from Telluride to Silverton over the pass. The stage, mail carrier, and freighters took advantage of the shortcut to Telluride via Ophir, but in 1883 it was reported that toll receipts were only paying for repairs and the toll keeper's salary. The road is still used as a very scenic four-wheel jeep road between Silverton and Telluride, and it is one of the easier ones in the San Juans. There is a magnificent view of the Wilson Range to the west from the top of Ophir Pass (11,700 feet). From the south to the north are Mt. Wilson, El Diente, and Wilson Peak – all "fourteeners." The part of the road on the west side of the pass that travels through the scree slope is one lane for a very long distance, but you can see all the way down to determine if other vehicles are coming. The road goes through Ophir to New Ophir (at the paved highway), then turns south on Highway 145 to go to Rico or north to go to Telluride.

When Ophir Pass could not be negotiated in the winter by horses, mules, or burros, the mail carriers turned to snowshoes. The carriers were not required to make such a trip during a severe snowstorm, but twenty-five year old Sven Nilsen had the 1883 Christmas mail and money to deliver. Sven failed to arrive in Ophir, and he did not return to Silverton. It was soon suspected that he had been caught in one of the big Ophir avalanches, but some people felt he had absconded with the mail, which probably contained a lot of money at that time of year. When Sven disappeared, his brother Nels came from Sweden to the United States and went out looking every day for months for his brother's body. For two years search parties probed the snow and watched for some sign of Sven's body. Then, two and a half years later, Sven's mail sack melted out of a large slide and was spotted by a stagecoach driver. After a little digging, Sven's body was found — frozen and perfectly preserved. All the mail was dry and in good condition. Sven's

Chapter 8: THE TOWN OF SILVERTON AND THE RAINBOW ROUTE

body was put on the stage and transported to Ophir for burial. True to his trust, Sven's mail did reach Ophir – only thirty months late! When the mail sack was opened, it was found to contain an unopened letter from his wife.

There was another avalanche death near Burro Bridge that year, when on February 2, 1883, Martin Hubner was killed while working outside the Little Burro Mine. Members of the rescue party were almost hit by a later avalanche at the same spot. They saved themselves by climbing a tree and holding on for dear life until the avalanche had passed. Hubner was not found until the snow melted in May.

And still another death was reported from the same storm, this time on the road itself. Robert Roberts (who was a mail carrier), and Robert McNichols (who worked for the Mears Transportation Company) were trying to pack down the road from Silverton to Ouray after five feet of snow fell in the storm. McNichols was only a quarter of a mile past Burro Bridge when an avalanche struck. It took six hours to get to him, and sadly it looked like he had been packed in by snow so tight that he could not move and had suffocated while waiting to be rescued. Twelve of his eighteen pack animals were also killed.

From Burro Bridge to the foot of the Red Mountains many beaver ponds are scattered along the floor of the valley. Beavers live in houses made of twigs and small branches in the middle of their ponds. They enter and leave their houses from the bottom by an underwater route, but sleep above water inside their home. Beaver do a great deal to conserve water and reclaim the land by building their dams. At one time they were basically eliminated from the creeks of the San Juans, but now they are back in abundance.

Only a few remnants of the town of Chattanooga are located at the end of the Mineral Creek Valley, on the last available spot of level ground before the steep climb up Red Mountain Pass. Lookout Mountain is the large peak to the northwest at the end of the valley. At one time the town thrived with burro punchers, muleskinners, and wagon drivers filling Chattanooga to capacity.

Chattanooga reoriented its Main Street after being hit by an avalanche. The Eagle Slide, which demolished the town, can be seen in the background. It is 1910 and only four homes and four businesses remain. Photo Courtesy of Denver Public Library, Western History Department, F646).

Only a few cabins had been built on the spot before the Red Mountain discoveries were made. These were residences for the Silver Crown Mine and a few smaller mines in the area. When the Red Mountain discoveries were made, Chattanooga became a freight transfer and forwarding point. Supplies were brought in from Silverton by wagon and then transferred to mules or burros for the trip up the pass.

The town of Chattanooga was officially founded in March, 1883, and by April 3 had a post office. Chattanooga quickly grew to 350 people, living or working in about seventy-five buildings that included a hotel, restaurants, and saloons. The coming of Mears' toll road in 1884 hurt the town, and the arrival of the railroad in 1887 effectively killed it, as there was no further reason for the town to

Chapter 8: THE TOWN OF SILVERTON AND THE RAINBOW ROUTE ❋ 233

exist. Then a snow slide in 1888 and a fire in 1892 destroyed most of its buildings. In 1898, Rev. J. J. Gibbons recorded that "ruins of roofs and houses were strewn half a mile over the valley and the population of this once flourishing hamlet dwindled to two" (a saloon keeper and a widow in the laundry business).

Some of the remains of the Silver Ledge Mill can still be seen to the north of the highway in Chattanooga. The mill was big enough that it warranted a post office in 1904 and 1905. The Silver Ledge Mine is located up the hill a ways and was connected to the mill by tram. The mill could dump its concentrates directly into the Silverton railroad's freight cars. The mill burned in 1919, and the mine shut down at that time. The old bridge to the east was a part of the Million Dollar Highway until just a few decades ago when the large, built up curve was constructed. Mills in the nineteenth century charged a penalty for zinc, since that metal had very little value and was difficult to separate from the more valuable metals. Zinc was first economically recovered at the Silver

The Silver Ledge Mill was still operating in Chattanooga in 1910. The road above the mill was used by wagons and pack animals, while the railroad tracks can be seen in front of the mill.

Photo Courtesy of San Juan Historical Society.

This view, looking south, shows Chattanooga before it was hit by the avalanche. About 300 people lived there at the time. Bear Mountain is in the background.
From a stereo card in Author's Collection.

Ledge Mill in 1904, and their process was used as a model for other areas of the country.

There are many snow slides in the Chattanooga area, and if you take the time to look around, their paths are obvious. Two large avalanches are just beyond Muleshoe Curve and above Chattanooga. The Muleshoe and the Telescope run often and sometimes at the same time. The Telescope and Muleshoe Slides can, in turn, each cover the road in two spots, since they start above the loop. The Eagle is also a huge slide that runs in from east of Chattanooga. The Brooklyn Slide to the southeast often covers the road. These slides usually stop traffic until snowplows arrive. The Brooklyn is a very wide slide but not too deep (usually only four or five feet). Other slides, however, can cover the road for short distances with twenty or thirty feet of snow. Jack Dolan was killed by a snow slide in Mill Gulch (at the center of the Horseshoe Curve) on December 21, 1883. It was another avalanche death to add to the toll that horrible year.

The Silverton Railroad track basically followed the horseshoe curve that the highway now makes out of the Chattanooga Valley.

Chapter 8: THE TOWN OF SILVERTON AND THE RAINBOW ROUTE ❧ 235

It was a 200-degree turn with a constant five and a half percent grade for one and three-quarter miles – an engineering marvel to build without a loop or a larger curve. Part of the secret was getting a good elevation at the bottom in Mill Creek before heading up. The track just followed the contour of the mountain.

The highway (which today has taken over most of the railroad bed) begins to climb sharply at the Chattanooga Loop. Mill Creek comes down through the large curve. The Hoosier Boy Mine is tucked back into the basin. Gold was found at the Hoosier Boy in 1893, just when silver was declining radically. This sparked a small "gold rush" to the area, and fifty-two new claims were quickly filed. Unfortunately, the gold played out almost as quickly. The Million

The ruins of the Silver Ledge Mine still sit alongside the Million Dollar Highway. The original road to Red Mountain ran up the gulch to the left of the mine.

Photo Courtesy of Denver Public Library, X62196

Dollar Highway is at its narrowest during the three-mile climb to the top of the divide. At several points the grade of the railroad can be seen just slightly above the road. Sometimes a tie or two may give the route away. On the way down this stretch is a good time to see the image of a bear holding a honeycomb (outlined by the trees) on Bear Mountain. Going either way, the driver needs to focus on driving this dangerous section of road.

A little further north, the decaying structures of the Silver Ledge Mine are visible below the highway. The mine was first located in 1883, and produced some very valuable ore. The March 3, 1883, *Red Mountain Pilot* reported that the Silver Ledge had the largest body of ore the editor had ever seen. It was big enough that the mine was worked for years, and there was a good-sized settlement at the mine as well as another small town near the mill in Chattanooga. In late 1891, the shaft house of the mine caught fire, igniting forty pounds of dynamite in the powder house and blowing most of the mine's surface buildings into little bits of kindling. Luckily no one was killed, and the mine's buildings were rebuilt quickly.

At about this spot, a four-wheel drive road leads to the left (west) for about a mile into Porphyry Basin. A little ways up towards Porphyry Basin there is also a cross road that ties in with the Black Bear Road. The Bullion King Mine and Bullion King Lake (actually two lakes) are located in beautiful Porphyry Basin at the end of this jeep road.

We have now progressed far enough along the "Rainbow Route," that we have entered the Red Mountain Mining District – the place where one of Colorado's biggest mining booms occurred and brought about the building of this scenic highway. It is also one of the most beautiful spots in all of Colorado.

Chapter 9

THE RED MOUNTAIN MINING DISTRICT — MOUNTAINS OF SILVER

AT THE SUMMIT OF RED MOUNTAIN PASS there is ample room to park and roam, but you should be careful around the old mines – not only are they private property, but many are dangerous. One hundred and twenty-five years ago you would have been standing in the middle of a railroad yard, alongside the toll road from Red Mountain to Silverton. It would have been a busy place. Several thousand people lived within a mile or two of this spot. The train, ore wagons, mule trains, and herds of burros would have been passing by almost constantly. The local blacksmiths and the explosions of dynamite in the mines would have added to the din.

Today this spot is quiet, but without the Red Mountain Mining District, the Million Dollar Highway might not exist today. The area around Red Mountain was found to have valuable ore as early as 1881, but the first big discoveries were made in the fall of 1882. Excited men prospected all winter, often staking claims in the snow and building cabins without foundations on the ice. By the early spring of 1883, there were already six towns in the Red Mountain District. It was appropriate that the first big discovery, the fabulously rich Yankee Girl Mine, also became the major mine of the Red Mountain District. A torrent of prospectors flocked into the Red Mountains in the spring of 1883. Soon, speculation kept the prices being paid for new mine prospects constantly

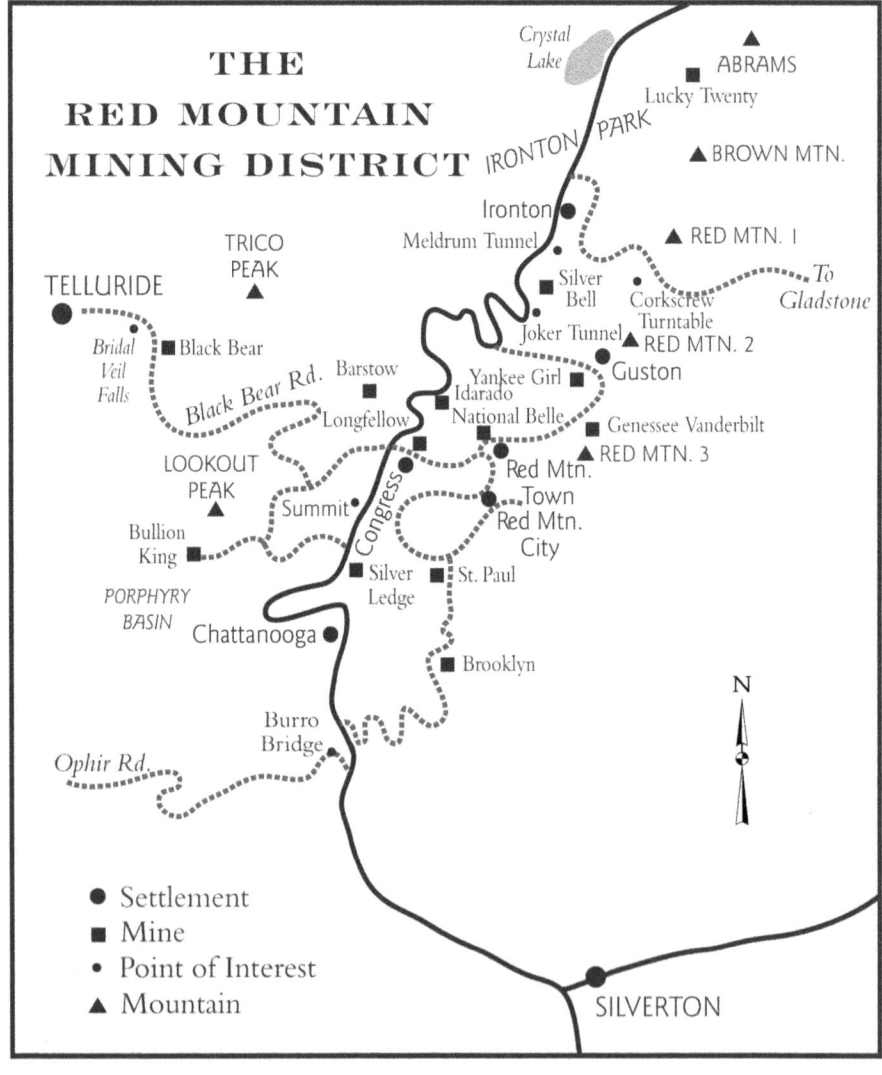

Chapter 9: THE RED MOUNTAIN MINING DISTRCT　　　　❦ 239

rising. Then a "treasure cave" was discovered at the National Belle Mine. No one had ever seen such a sight. The entire mining district appeared to be one huge mountain of silver ore.

At its peak, the Red Mountain Mining District was the premier mining area of Colorado. It was also found to be one of the most unusual, geologically speaking, with its soft ore appearing in "chimneys" that were up to a hundred feet wide and went almost straight down into the earth, instead of the usual hard rock veins that run throughout the San Juan Mountains. Basically, all three Red Mountains was found to be low-grade ore – which would only be worth mining if silver and base metal prices were high or if the ore could be mined by leaching or strip mining. But it was the rich chimneys that the early miners concentrated on.

Today there is no mining at Red Mountain and, because of its historical significance and scenic beauty, there have been extensive efforts over the last decade by the Red Mountain Task Force and the Trust for Public Land to try to preserve the Red Mountain Mining District. The effort started in 1997, when the San Juan Skyway was designating historic sites. In 1999, the groups purchased 11,000 acres in connection with the United States Forest Service. The money to save the Red Mountain District has come from both public and private funds – over $14 million to date.

But let us start at the flat area at the top of the pass, which was the location of "Summit," a place where the Silverton Railroad had a switching track, wye, and a shelter for the locomotives. Summit wasn't really a town, but rather a spot where railroad cars could be kept until a trip was made down to Silverton (only two or three cars could be pulled up the northern slopes of Red Mountain at a time, but ten loaded cars could be taken down at one time). The area was also called Sheridan Pass or Sheridan Junction after Jim Sheridan, who was a saloonkeeper, postmaster, innkeeper and liveryman, who lived at the spot.

The Longfellow Mine is just to the east of the flat spot. A four-wheel drive road leads about a mile east to the sites of Congress Town, the Congress Mine, and Red Mountain City. The first ridge

The Silverton Railroad had a station at the top of Red Mountain Pass called "Summit." It looks like the train was full this day, as it only had one passenger car.
      Photo Courtesy of Denver Public Library, Western History Department, M1532.

to the south of the road was the location of Congress, one of the first towns in the Red Mountains. Congress had a post office by April 2, 1883, but it closed just nine months later. To the south, a half-mile further up the road (past the remote weather station), is the St. Paul Mine, which is now operated as a cross-country ski resort in the winter. The Brooklyn Mine road skirts the St. Paul and runs several miles back south to the Million Dollar Highway. The Congress Mine is only two-tenths of a mile further up the road from the St. Paul. It was one of the first mines discovered on Red Mountain. The Congress Mine continued to be worked over the years and eventually its production totaled a half million dollars. Above Congress was the site of Red Mountain City (not to be confused with Red Mountain Town), which thrived for a few months and then was moved, almost in its entirety, to Red Mountain Town. Red Mountain City was founded in

Chapter 9: THE RED MOUNTAIN MINING DISTRCT ✣ 241

January, 1883, with the foundations of its buildings being laid directly on three feet of packed snow. When spring came the buildings tilted in every direction. It was close enough to the Congress Mine that there was a constant battle between the two settlements over who should have the post office. Red Mountain City was located in San Juan County, but only a few hundred feet south of Ouray County.

By March there were twenty-five cabins at Red Mountain City. Its businesses included butchers, hardware stores, hotels, a doctor and a drugstore, a barber, and four or five saloons. However, Red Mountain City faltered as fast as it had originally grown. By April the town's merchants realized they were going to be quite a ways from the main route being used over Red Mountain Pass (the route used later by the Million Dollar Highway). By May, most of the town's merchants were moving to other settlements. Many of their buildings were literally jacked up and moved by mules to their new locations, and others were salvaged and the lumber reused. By

Congress was one of the first towns on Red Mountain. It was located at the top of Mineral Creek about 100 yards to the east of the present road. It had totally disappeared a few years after this photo was taken.
Photo Courtesy Denver Public Library, Western History Department, C102.

the end of the year, Red Mountain City was down to just a few cabins (several of which are still there). Red Mountain City had boomed and busted in less than a year! The road is blocked near the site of Red Mountain City.

Altogether there were five or six towns (depending on what you would call a town) within a mile of each other, near the top of the pass. The editors of the Silverton and Ouray papers were always extolling the wonders of their towns and mines and running down the mines and towns located in the other county. Red Mountain Town finally won out as the major town of the district when Otto Mears toll road passed through it and the Congress Mine's production started falling.

Back on the Million Dollar Highway, another four-wheel drive road leads to the west of the flat spot at the top of Red Mountain Pass. This is the spectacular Black Bear Road that goes over Ingram Pass at 12,840 feet and then down past the Black Bear Mine to a series of sharp and steep switchbacks that lead to Telluride. The road is so steep that it is the San Juans' most difficult and dangerous jeep road. There used to be a sign at the start of the road that read, "You don't have to be crazy to drive this road, but it helps." That sentiment very adequately sums up the situation. The road is two-way from the summit of Red Mountain to the summit of Black Bear Pass, but it is one-way going down from the summit. The road is extreme. It seems someone is seriously injured or killed on the switchbacks every few years, but there are some beautiful sights like Bridal Veil Falls, and it is a real thrill for the adventurer. People who want to drive the road from Telluride usually go up Ophir Pass or Imogene Pass and then come down the correct way.

The official summit of Red Mountain Pass is at the north end of the flat area and is also the dividing line between (to the south) the San Juan National Forest (more that 1.9 million acres) and to the north the Uncompahgre National Forest (more than one million acres). Teddy Roosevelt established both national forests in 1905. The Bureau of Land Management also controls four million

Chapter 9: THE RED MOUNTAIN MINING DISTRCT

This modern-day jeep is at the top of Black Bear Road overlooking Telluride. The most dangerous part of the road — the steep, talus slope switchbacks—is still ahead.

Bill Fries III Photo.

acres of land in the San Juans. Red Mountain Pass is the watershed for the Animas and Uncompahgre Rivers, and also the dividing line between Ouray and San Juan Counties.

Just north of the summit, Mears' toll road no longer followed the route of the present highway, but rather ran northeast to Red Mountain Town and down the eastern side of the canyon to Ironton Park. This was the original route of the Million Dollar Highway, passing the big mines of the Red Mountain Mining District, until the auto road was built in the 1920s. The present road goes down the west side of the canyon, where there is a good view of some of the mines that made the San Juans great.

The Red Mountains (also called "The Scarlet Peaks" in the early days) are red because of massive iron pyrite deposits in all three mountains (numbered 1, 2, and 3 from north to south) that make up what is commonly called just "Red Mountain" today. Basically rust make the mountains red, especially after a rain. A side effect of decomposing iron pyrite is sulphuric acid, which was a constant problem in the local mines. Shaft cables would snap, ladder rungs would fall off when the nails dissolved, mine rails broke in half, and even the human body was often affected if protective clothing was not worn.

The Red Mountains were covered with "towns" because of town site speculation, which became as rampant as the speculation in mining properties. In the three years after the initial discoveries, the settlements of Chattanooga, Congress, Liverpool, Guston, Red Mountain City, Rogersville, Summit, Ironton (also called "Copper Glen"), Red Mountain Town, Burro Bridge, Del Mino, Sweetville, and Butte City were all laid out — their newly surveyed lots awaiting potential purchasers. However, only Guston, Red Mountain Town, and Ironton reached any great size or lasted for very long.

Just three-tenths of a mile north of Red Mountain Pass, a short, but somewhat rough road leads beyond a small lake (a short distance to the east) to the site of Red Mountain Town – the premier town of the Red Mountains. The road (which is still public) then continues on through the Red Mountain mines (four wheel drive recommended), following basically the same route as the Otto Mears' toll road during Red Mountain's heyday. At the north end of what little remains of Red Mountain Town, the walls of its jail still stand because they were made of 2 x 6 inch lumber laid flat and fastened with six inch cut nails. The jail had two cells and could be quite uncomfortable because it had neither heat nor glass in the windows. The railroad bed, with its wye for turning the train, is still roughly discernable near the jail. The Red Mountain depot was built in the center of the wye and astride the creek because space was so limited.

Rogersville was a small town just north and east of Red Mountain Town, and located a little earlier. In fact, it was probably the first "town" on Red Mountain. It was named for Jack Rogers, who had a cabin nearby that was used as a post office from

Chapter 9: THE RED MOUNTAIN MINING DISTRCT   245

March to June 1883, as the settlement itself was also very short-lived. Although not in Red Mountain Town's city limits, it was close enough that there was no further reason for it to exist after Red Mountain Town thrived.

Both Red Mountain City and Red Mountain Town were moved to this site from their original locations. Red Mountain Town was originally located in the flat but swampy spot (in the summer) above the small cliffs, about a quarter of a mile to the south of the eventual site. The reasons for the move was to get the buildings out of the swampy area and to relocate it directly on the

This view of Red Mountain Town is looking north with the National Belle Mine towering above the town. The school is in the center of the cluster of buildings near the center of the photo.

Photo Courtesy of Main Street Photography.

Otto Mears toll road. Red Mountain City was originally located at the top of the steep climb coming out of the Chattanooga Valley above the Congress Mine but very close to the top of the pass going over Red Mountain to the Hudson Mine. Most of its buildings were also moved into Red Mountain City in order to be on the toll road.

Red Mountain Town was a typical rowdy mining camp. The local paper, *The Red Mountain Review* of April 14, 1883, pointed out that there were "only six saloons in town and three restaurants. Verily, bread is not the staff of life in the mountains." The miners were ready for women to arrive in town early on, but not the civilizing type. Even the paper reported on their arrival, "The female divines, Long Annie of Silverton, Molly Folly and Lizzie Galore of Durango were among the distinguished arrivals this morning." The editor also pointed out in the same article that Deaf Mat from Silverton was on her way to Red Mountain, but the lady later tried to kill him for listing her with the prostitutes.

By May 1883, Red Mountain Town already had a domestic water system, fire hydrants, city ordinances, a mayor, and a marshal. It also had saloons and prostitutes, the number of which always increased substantially in the summer. The July 24, 1885, *Solid Muldoon* announced that in Red Mountain Town "the rainy season is here. A profusion of flowers and soiled doves are hereabouts." By that year, the town had a population of 598, telephone service, two newspapers, a school, a post office, and many more saloons.

Life was a mixture of the harsh realities and the awesome beauty of the Red Mountain area. A man might easily be killed by an avalanche, falling rocks, freezing temperatures, deep snows, or a hundred other hazards in the mines; but the gambling establishments, saloons, and dance halls were reported to run night and day. There were several killings in Red Mountain because of all the drunkenness; but as much as we think of miners and prospectors as men who like to "raise hell," the small jail at Red Mountain Town testifies to just how little trouble there actually was. Music and dramatic groups often visited the city (usually performing in the saloons), and debates and lectures were popular.

Everyone in the Red Mountain District realized that they lived in one of the most strikingly beautiful places in the world. The tourists who thronged to Red Mountain knew it too. Red Mountain's residents would often send reports to Ouray or Silverton when the wildflowers were blooming or a big horn sheep had been spotted. Some residents wrote poetry about the beauty surrounding them. Recreation in Red Mountain included hiking and picnics in the summer and skiing in the winter. Races and boxing matches were popular, as well as hunting and fishing. Christmas was a wonderful time of year, with many special activities and lots of snow. The other big day of the year was the Fourth of July, but it was usually celebrated in Silverton or Ouray. Numerous books, newspapers, and magazines also arrived daily.

The hill to the immediate west of the town site is known as "The Knob," and on its slopes are the remains of the National Belle Mine. The shaft house is the tall structure still standing. The mine was opened in January, 1883, and at first produced easily-mined and valuable soft carbonates, galena, and grey copper. The ore was so soft and rich that it was merely shoveled into bags for shipment.

The fabulous National Belle Mine was actually located within the city limits of Red Mountain Town. The truly remarkable discovery came when workmen broke into a cavern. A miner took a candle and crawled in to find himself in an immense natural chamber with streaks of silver and galena glittering in the roof, and masses of crystals, soft carbonates, chlorides, and pure white talc throughout the cavern. It was so rich, unusual, and beautiful that all mining stopped for a few days so that the locals could come and see it. The local paper modestly called it "The Greatest Discovery in the World." There were also many smaller chambers off the main chamber, showing the same rich and colorful minerals. The reporter for the newspaper wrote, "it would seem as though nature had gathered her choice treasures from her inexhaustible storehouse, and wrought these tunnels, natural stopping places and chambers studded with glittering crystals and bright minerals to dazzle the eyes of man in after ages, and lure him on to other treasures hidden deeper in the bowels of the earth." Eventually the mine was developed to a depth of 450 feet and became one of the largest and best-known mines in the country, reportedly producing over two million dollars in ore before it closed in 1897.

Red Mountain Town eventually grew to a population of about 600. It had a post office from 1883 to 1913. The town was laid out with named-and-numbered streets and a two-block long main street featuring a full compliment of the necessary enterprises – gambling houses, saloons, real estate offices, houses of prostitution, lawyers' offices, hotels, and stores of all types. There were also several fraternal lodges and a miner's union, known as the "Sky City Union." To the east of Main Street, on a little hill, was a well-developed residential area.

The stage has just arrived at the depot and post office at Red Mountain. Once again, everyone is on top to see the views.
Photo Courtesy of Denver Public Library, Western History Department
X-21826.

Rev. J. J. Gibbons wrote, "The lights never went out in the camp, unless when coal oil failed or a stray cowboy shot up the town. The men worked night and day, shift and shift about, and the people were happy. The gambling halls were never closed; the restaurants did a profitable business; and no one could lay his weary bones on a bed for less than a dollar. Whiskey was as plentiful as the limpid water that gushed from the hills behind the town, sparkling in the sunlight."

Like most Western boom towns, Red Mountain Town was hurriedly built of rough green lumber, and devastating fires were common. In spite of the fire hydrants and its finely organized volunteer fire department, the town burned on August 20, 1892, and again on June 13, 1895. Both fires destroyed over half of the town's buildings. The Silver Panic of 1893 forced most of the silver mining in the state to shut down, so very little of the town was rebuilt after the second fire. By 1900, Red Mountain Town's year-round population had dwindled to only thirty hardy souls. That portion of the town that was rebuilt after the second fire was almost entirely destroyed by a forest fire in 1939, but no one lived in the once booming Red Mountain Town at the time.

Much of the reason for Red Mountain's boom and bust cycles could be laid on the local newspapers. A newspaper in those days was the town's main contact with the outside world. Most editors were like today's chamber of commerce organizations, and they were expected by the local citizens to make bold proclamations of the booming economies of their town and its nearby mines. In fact, they would often flat out lie about the boom in their area. The grass always looked greener where the newspapers sprouted. *The Red Mountain Pilot* was located at Red Mountain City and the *Red Mountain Review* was at Red Mountain Town. Both papers made some totally outrageous claims. To add to the confusion, there were also newspapers at Ironton (Ouray County) and Chattanooga (San Juan County). Silverton had *The La Plata Miner* and *The San Juan Herald* to boast about the mines and towns on its side of the pass, and Ouray had *The Ouray Times* and *The Solid Muldoon* to exaggerate the

The railroad came into Red Mountain from the north, after making a loop around the Knob and National Belle Mine. The jail (the small structure above the train) still stands.
                Photo Courtesy of Denver Public Library, Western History Department, F16681.

---

worth of the towns and mines in Ouray County. All of this "puffing" made it hard sometimes to know what was really going on. The only facts you could count on were if a paper said something good about a neighboring area that also had a paper.

    North of Red Mountain Town and across the valley from today's Million Dollar Highway, are many of the ore dumps from the big mines of the Red Mountain District. The old road passes immediately through this area, but it is now a four-wheel drive road with many confusing side trails (many are actually sidings to the various mines for the Silverton Railroad). However, most of the buildings and the Silverton Railroad right of way are visible from the Million Dollar Highway, so we will describe the mines from that vantage point.

Chapter 9: THE RED MOUNTAIN MINING DISTRCT ✤ 251

While looking at the Red Mountain District from across the valley, it is obvious that even at this altitude and relatively flat area there were often snow slides. In 1883, thirty year old Thomas Brennan and ten mules were killed in a slide between the Yankee Girl and what would become known as Red Mountain Town. His companion Jim Barr was found alive by rescuers. Three years later, another avalanche hit in the same area. Nine men were swept down the mountain, but only five were saved. Warren Goldsmith also died of a heart attack after shoveling snow all night looking for survivors. Another man, Barney McGinney, was helping transport the bodies to Ouray and stopped at the tollhouse at Bear Creek for a drink on the way down. It was a mistake that cost him his life, as the alcohol aggravated his being out in the cold weather and caused him to freeze to death when walking to Ouray later.

At the top (south end) of the row of mines seen across the valley is the Genesee-Vanderbilt Mine. It still has several steel clad buildings standing, since it was operated relatively recently (during World War II) and some exploration work was done into the 1990s. It produced about a million dollars in ore and was worked to 700 feet. The Genesee and Vanderbilt were originally discovered in 1882. They were worked separately until 1888, when it was recognized that they were both working the same vein. The two mines eventually joined together, instead of paying lawyers, and produced over a million dollars in basically low-grade ore. Most of the mine's production came between 1891 and 1896, although some work was done almost into modern times. The Genesee-Vanderbilt is a good example of a mine that probably would not have been worked if it had not been located on the tracks off the railroad.

To the north of the Genesee-Vanderbilt is the tower-like shaft house of the Yankee Girl Mine. It is a tall, slender building, standing alone because the other structures around it have collapsed. The Yankee Girl was the pride of the Red Mountain Mining District – a very rich mine developed to over 1,000 feet in depth. Ores as rich as 15,000 ounces of silver per ton (almost 50% silver) were taken from this mine as well as the adjoining Robinson Mine, which bottomed out at 700 feet. One ten-ton carload of Yankee Girl ore sold for $75,000 (about a million dollars today). The Yankee Girl eventually produced over eight million dollars (some estimates are as high as twenty million dollars). It was staked in August, 1882, when John Robinson was resting while hunting and picked up a rock, which he realized was very heavy for its size. Upon further examination it turned out to be very rich galena, and its source was soon located nearby. The Yankee Girl Mine paid a dividend of 45%

The Yankee Girl was the greatest of all the Red Mountain mines. This early photo shows burros loaded with its rich ore in the background.

Author's Collection.

Chapter 9: THE RED MOUNTAIN MINING DISTRCT ✤ 253

to its stockholders (one of whom was Otto Mears) in 1890. Not one Colorado mine in ten paid any dividend at all.

The Yankee Girl was the mine by which all the other Red Mountain mines were measured. The editor of the *La Plata Miner* in Silverton called it "the biggest mine ever discovered in Colorado" shortly after its discovery. The Yankee Girl was written of favorably by the Silverton papers, even though it was in Ouray County, because many of the owners of the mine lived in Silverton. Fossett wrote in 1885, "The Yankee Girl, for its age, is one of the most profitable mines in the world.... The ore averages a full $8,000 per ton. Now there are a great number of 'bald heads' that would like to hug a Yankee girl of this character." So much "low-grade" ore was left on its dump that the waste that had been discarded was milled in the 1920s and 30s at a very good profit.

The Guston Mine is located slightly further to the north of the Yankee Girl. A small settlement grew up around the mine even though it was only a mile from Red Mountain Town. Guston grew

A small town around 300 surrounded the Guston Mine about 1888. The Silverton Railroad ran directly above the mine, which is near the back of the cluster of buildings.
William H. Jackson Photo No. 2906. Courtesy of Colorado Historical Society.

to a population of 332 by 1890; and a post office, a church, and stores were located there from 1892 to 1898. The mine itself is in the jumble of buildings at the north end of town. The Guston Mine was located in August, 1881, and developed slowly at first. Total production of the Guston has been figured as low as three

The stage, being pulled by six horses, is arriving at the little settlement of Guston about 1890. Did the woman prefer to ride behind instead of being with the men up top?

Author's Collection.

and as high as seven million dollars. The Guston – one of the first Red Mountain mines – was mined initially in 1881, before the big discoveries at Red Mountain. It was mainly worked at that time for its lead, which was needed as a flux in the local smelters. When the Silverton Railroad arrived in 1888, the Guston became a large producer, eventually reaching a depth of 1,300 feet. Some of the mine's handpicked ore averaged $5,000 in silver and three ounces of gold per ton. The mine's profits were so good in 1890 that it paid an 80% dividend to its stockholders.

Back on the Million Dollar Highway, a mile and a half north of Red Mountain summit, the highway winds past the surface buildings of the Idarado Mine (originally called the Hammond Tunnel and then the Treasury Tunnel). The tunnel has always been meant to access the good gold ore that was left in the mines near Telluride. It was not mining ore that was actually in the Red Mountain Mining District. It was started in 1896 at the very time that many of the Red Mountain mines were shutting down. A 2,000-foot railroad spur was run to the tunnel from the Yankee Girl Mine siding off the Silverton Railroad on the other side of the valley (it is still visible). The mine was worked for over ten years without much success; but after that time good ore was struck, and the mine eventually developed or incorporated over eighty miles of tunnels. By 1937, the Treasury Tunnel had a large boarding house, a big mill, and several offices. The little houses around the mine were hauled in from Eureka after the Sunnyside Mine closed, and they were used by some of the Idarado workers until the mine closed in 1979.

A good four-acre interpretive site has been built at the Idarado Mine, which is a fine vantage point for checking out the big Red Mountain mines. During World War II and for thirty-two years thereafter, the Idarado Mine was one of the largest mining operations in Colorado, producing over thirty million dollars of copper, lead, silver, and gold. The name "Idarado" comes from a combination of "Idaho" and "Colorado." The company was formed in 1939 as a further consolidation of many smaller mines around Telluride. The mine produced some good gold ore, but during World War II the federal government sponsored and subsidized the boring of non-productive tunnels, to access several additional mines in the area. The government had the mine skip over large areas of silver and gold, as they were in need of copper and lead. After the war, those areas were then worked and extensions were made into good gold ore at the Pandora, Black Bear, Smuggler, and Tomboy Mines near Telluride. It was then possible to go through the mine all the way to Telluride, but it was not all on one level. The Idarado closed in 1979, but still contains valuable ore and has a skeleton crew keeping up the mine.

The jumble of big mine buildings across the valley from the Idarado belong to the Guston Mine on the left and the Yankee Girl on the right. Both were very big operations.

Photo Author's Collection.

Chapter 9: THE RED MOUNTAIN MINING DISTRCT　　　※ 257

To the west of (above) the Idarado was the Barstow Mine, located in Commodore Gulch. It followed a small but very rich vein of gold and silver and also produced considerable amounts of fluorspar. Some of its assays ran up to 2,000 ounces of silver and twenty-five ounces of gold per ton, but its average ore was much less valuable. There was a large forty-stamp mill on the site, and it had a short tram to the mine; but the Barstow was plagued with avalanches. The mill or the connecting covered tracks to the mine were hit on several occasions. The mine produced almost a million dollars between 1895 and 1913 before closing, but it was also worked later through the Idarado Mine.

At the switchback between the Idarado Mine and Ironton Park, Ouray County Road 31 leads to the other side of the valley. This is the other end of the original Otto Mears road but only four-wheel drive vehicles should travel it. It leads through a maze of dead end roads through the mines already been discussed and can be seen from the present Million Dollar Highway, and then ends back at Red Mountain Town.

The switchbacks are usually a favorite hangout for marmots from March through August (they hibernate in the winter but come out in early spring). Visitors are always asking what the furry brown animal was that they saw alongside the road. The marmot is a rodent, a relation to the groundhog. The yellow-bellied is the local variety, and it is also known as a "Whistle-pig," because of its high-pitched "chirp." Marmots usually inhabit boulder fields, rock outcrops, or talus slopes in the higher elevations of Colorado. They weigh five to ten pounds, have a short, bushy tails and vary in color from light to dark brown. They are vegetarians, but they also love to eat rubber – often eating the tires or radiator hoses off vehicles left in the high country. They usually mate in March and give birth to a litter of three to six, a month later.

At the lower end of the switchbacks, to the east and just beyond Red Mountain Creek, are a few of the old buildings of the Joker Tunnel. The building in the best shape was the boarding house. The Joker Tunnel was not a mine in the real sense of

The Joker Tunnel was not actually a mine, but rather access to the lower levels of many Red Mountain mines. The Million Dollar Highway passes through the middle of the complex.

Author's Collection.

the word, but rather was built as part of a plan to tunnel under the Yankee Boy, Guston, Robinson, and other rich mines in the Red Mountain District. Because the rich Red Mountain ore was found in "chimney" deposits, going straight down into the earth, shafts were usually the means used to follow the silver-lead and silver-copper ore deposits.

At the time the Joker Tunnel was constructed, all the major mines in the Red Mountain District had been closed after reaching great depths, where they were also down to lower grade ore. The cost of hoisting the ore and pumping water out of the shafts had become so expensive that it was no longer profitable to work the mines. The Joker Tunnel was a way to drain the mines of water and take the ore out in ore cars by gravity to a site that was directly alongside the Silverton Railroad. The plan was that this would reduce costs to an absolute minimum and make the lower grade ore profitable to mine. The tunnel was started in 1905 and was eventually 4,800 feet long. It struck the Guston Mine at a depth of 400 feet, the Yankee Girl at 500 feet and the Genesee at 600 feet. Unfortunately, most of the ore that was left in the mines was still well below these levels, so it was still necessary to use shafts (called winzes inside a mine. All of the mines still proved to have only low-grade ore deposits.

The Red Mountain Railroad, Mining and Smelting Company was formed in October, 1902 to reopen, upgrade, and run the Silverton Railroad as a part of the Joker Tunnel operation. The tunnel was started in 1904 and reached the Yankee Girl in 1906 and the Genesee in 1907. That year there were thirty-five men employed at mining through the Joker Tunnel. Originally the Joker Tunnel was to have gone all the way under the Hudson, National Belle, and the Congress Mine, but it never made it. The Joker Tunnel reopened in 1938, and was used to do a small amount of mining off and on until the 1940s.

One can hike northeast from the Joker Tunnel up along the Silverton Railroad right-of-way (it starts right behind the Joker boardinghouse) and access the Corkscrew Turntable. It was an engineering oddity – the only turntable built on the mainline of a railroad – necessary because of the steep, sharp switchback at the gulch. The cover over the turntable has collapsed, but a good portion of the non-removable portion of the turntable itself is still there (the removable parts were taken to Animas Forks to be used at the terminus of Mears' Silverton Northern Railroad). At the Corkscrew turntable, the locomotive uncoupled, turned on the turntable, and went to the lower track. The cars then came through the turntable by gravity, went down to the lower track by gravity, and were hooked back on to the train.

On the hill behind the Joker Tunnel is the shaft house of the Silver Belle Mine, which was a group of mines that included the Silver Belle, American Girl, and several others. A British group bought the mines in 1890, put almost two million dollars into the Silver Belle, and operated profitably until the Silver Panic of 1893. It managed to reopen and make a small profit in the late 1890s because of small pockets of very rich silver ore that were discovered in the mine. The dumps of the Silver Belle Mine are very visible across Red Mountain Creek. The mine was developed on ten levels, but its plentiful but low-grade ore only averaged about twenty ounces of silver per ton.

Just shortly downhill from the Joker Tunnel was the Meldrum Tunnel. Its entrance is now caved in and covered up by the Million Dollar Highway, but the very large tunnel went under the present road at point a few hundred yards north of the Joker Tunnel. It was an attempt by Andrew Meldrum to blast a tunnel large enough

Above (south) the Joker Tunnel, the Million Dollar Highway switches to the east side of Red Mountain Creek and can be seen looping up the mountain. The Silver Belle Mine is to the left and the Paymaster to the upper right.

Photo Courtesy of Colorado Historical Society, WHJ 2907.

Chapter 9: THE RED MOUNTAIN MINING DISTRCT   261

that a narrow gauge train could run all the way to Telluride, where it would tie in with the Rio Grande Southern Railroad. The cost of the railroad, tunnel, and equipment was projected at three million dollars, but promoters hoped to hit valuable ore veins along the way to help offset some, if not all, of the costs. However the project was abandoned in 1900, with only 2.2 miles of the six-mile project built. The cost at that time had run $250,000. Meldrum was one of the original owners of the Yankee Girl Mine, having grubstaked the prospectors who discovered Red Mountain's most valuable mine.

The well-preserved shaft house a little downstream and across Red Mountain Creek is the Colorado Boy Mine, which was never a very big producer, but whose shaft house provides some great photo opportunities. The mine further downhill, across and directly next to the road on the west side is the Larson Brothers Mine (it incorporates the Beaver and Belfast and the Ida L. Mines). Its ore was low-grade galena (silver-lead) and pyrites containing a little gold and silver (yes, "fools gold" can have value). Harry Larson died and the mine was idle by 1948, but Milton Larson lived in the ghost town of Ironton until he died in the mid-1960s. Milton's death made Ironton the last ghost town in the Red Mountains.

The flat and boggy Ironton Park (also called "Red Mountain Park" and "Copper Flats" at times) lies north of the Joker Tunnel and Larson Brother's Mine. A large glacier carved the valley during the successive ice ages. Later, a landslide came down Hendrick Gulch at the north end of what is now the park, partially blocked the canyon and Red Mountain Creek and its tributaries, and a thick bed of silt then built up in what is now called Ironton Park. "Park" is a term used in the Rocky Mountains for a large, open, level valley surrounded by high mountains. Waste rock from the Treasury Tunnel was used for road ballast through the boggy park when the Million Dollar Highway was upgraded in the 1920s. The original road was moved from the far west side of the park, where it can still be seen at this time.

In the fall, Ironton Park is probably the best place along the Million Dollar Highway to observe the aspen changing colors. The gold, yellow, and red colors are always in the leaf, but masked by the green of chlorophyll until the fall. At that time a membrane forms at the base of each leaf, which seals off the stem and prepares the tree for the time when its leaves fall off. When the stem is sealed off, the chlorophyll in the leaf disintegrates, exposing the colors. What causes the color process to start is still a mystery. The colder nighttime temperatures of autumn may be the reason, or it might be the lack of sunlight. Some scientists believe the leaves fall off at a set number of days after the tree buds in the spring, or it might be any combination of these factors, or some altogether different reason.

The south end of Ironton Park was the site of the Town of Ironton, the settlement from which the park gets its present name. In turn it is said that the town got its name from the iron oxides in the nearby mountains that make them red. To reach the ghost town, turn at Ouray County Road 20D at the Corkscrew Gulch cutoff at the north end of the reclamation pond, and follow the creek to the south back up the mountain for about a half mile. There are still a few buildings worth seeing in Ironton, but they cannot be easily seen from the road. The Town of Ironton lies beneath the nearby tailings site.

Just five days after Ironton was founded in 1883, the town supposedly had thirty-two cabins under construction. Just a few weeks later, Dave Day reported in *The Solid Muldoon* "three weeks ago there was not a building to be seen on the spot where Ironton now stands. (Now), over a hundred buildings of various dimensions are under headway, and the inevitable dance hall is in full blast." By June 1, the booming town contained ten saloons, a mile long Main Street (which was basically its only street), and 200 to 300 tents and cabins. Most of these structures must have been temporary or not have been residences, as the 1885 Colorado census showed only 181 inhabitants of the town, and the 1890 federal census reported 323 persons. Ironton had a post office

Chapter 9: THE RED MOUNTAIN MINING DISTRCT ❧ 263

Ironton was said to have a mile long Main Street, and much of it is visible in this scene. The man with the bicycle to the right seems to be a little out of place.

Marvin and Ruth Gregory Collection.

from 1883 to 1920, a pretty long life for a town that no longer exists. The town was incorporated and had a water system and an electric plant.

Although decline set in, Ironton far outlasted the other towns in the district – about seventy people still lived in Ironton in 1900. The last full-time residents were the Larson brothers. When Milton became the sole resident of the town, acquaintances dubbed him "the mayor of Ironton," which led to his being given an all-expense paid trip to New York City, where he was interviewed on national television. There are still a half dozen houses and other buildings on the site.

North of the town site of Ironton, a large, high "hill" fills a good part of the valley. This is the reclaimed tailings pond of the Idarado Mine. Tailings are what is left after giant crushers and ball mills process the rock and chemical processes take out most of the minerals. It is basically fine sand that was mixed with water and transported three miles in a large pipe to the site. Workmen pulled the tailings to the sides to create a dike until the rest of the water settled. The present-day mass was deposited over a span of only about ten years. It has been "reclaimed," but it is easy to tell that it is not natural.

To the southeast of the flats can be seen what looks like a large suspension bridge. Two tightly stretched cables, with cross ties, supported the tailings slurry coming by pipeline from the mill to the pond. It was designed to bow upwards when empty and lie flat when full of tailings, and it is the second longest suspension bridge in Colorado (after the Royal Gorge). As opposed to "tailings," "dumps" are where the waste rock is thrown after being taken out of the mine. Since a tunnel needs to be at least four feet wide and five or six feet tall, the waste rock that results when the vein being followed is smaller than those dimensions.

Just north of the reclaimed tailings pond is a jeep trail that shortly forks. The right fork goes south and then east up Corkscrew Gulch to Gladstone, and the left fork goes north and east up Brown Mountain (a dead end after several miles). The Corkscrew jeep road leads over a steep pass of 12,217 feet, and down the road between the old mining camps of Gladstone and Poughkeepsie Gulch. The road was built in 1882-83 for the purpose of connecting Silverton to the Red Mountain District by way of Gladstone. The Corkscrew Road should not be attempted in or after a heavy rain, as a portion of the road is composed of clay and is very slippery when wet.

An extremely hard and dangerous road also comes from Ouray via Poughkeepsie Gulch and ties into the Poughkeepsie road. The town of Poughkeepsie was at the head of the gulch by the same name. Poughkeepsie was described by Crofutt as "the biggest little mining camp in the San Juan Country." By 1890, the settlement was abandoned, and now only a little debris exists to show a settlement was ever there. A third jeep road comes up California Gulch from Animas Forks and then goes over Hurricane Pass to Poughkeepsie Gulch and on to Gladstone. This maze of roads in the heart of the San Juan Mountains can be a little confusing, so it is suggested that, if desiring to travel in this area, you should obtain a good map or

Chapter 9: THE RED MOUNTAIN MINING DISTRCT   ✤ 265

guide book, which will also help you to see the relationship of all the different jeep roads.

Going north again on the Million Dollar Highway in Ironton Park, on the east side can be seen the dumps of the Saratoga and Albany Mines on Brown Mountain (which is called Mount Abram at the Ouray (north) end. Mount Abram is 13,339 feet in elevation and Brown Mountain is 12,801 feet at the south end. Albany was the northern terminus of the Silverton Railroad, but there never was a town at the site. The local mines produced low-grade ore during the 1890s, which was only worth producing because of the proximity of the railroad to the mines and the resulting low transportation costs.

Hayden Mountain is the bulky, long, and tall (13,206 feet) mountain on the other (west) side of the park. Canyon Creek, Imogene Creek, and the Camp Bird Mine, are on the other side of Hayden Mountain. Hayden is named after the leader of the Hayden Survey, and Abram Cutler helped the Hayden survey team and had Mount Abram (sometimes called "Mount Abrams) named after him.

Near the northwest end of Ironton Park is Crystal Lake, partially enhanced by a man-made dam. Across the highway to the east are the concrete foundations and the brick chimney of a once attractive ski lodge that was built in the late 1930s but was destroyed by fire in the early 1950s. A workman thawing ice off the roof set fire to the lodge building, and it burned to the ground except for the cement garage and foundation and the chimney. A 1,800 foot ski lift was built at the lower end of Hendrick Gulch in conjunction with the lodge. A formal opening was held in 1940, and guests included the governor of Colorado. However a quarrel arose between the two owners, and the lodge was never operated again. The property was later taken over by the St. Germain Foundation, which occupied the property only in the summer. Members of the religious sect believe that Ironton will be one of the seven spots that God will save when he destroys the earth. Interestingly, there are several other sects that also believe that Ironton Park, or areas close by, will be saved at the Armageddon.

To the north and east of the St. Germain Foundation is Hendrick Gulch, which cuts deeply into Brown Mountain. The gulch is a large, wide, but shallow avalanche area in the winter. It runs frequently, but only covers the road with a few feet of snow. The Guadalupe Mine was about half way up the gulch and was accessed from the York and Lucky Twenty Tunnels. The mine produced mainly copper, and its surface buildings were very avalanche prone. Production continued at the mine until the 1930s, with the ore being taken out over the Million Dollar Highway in trucks.

From this point on north to Ouray, you will be traveling the "impassible canyon," as described by the Hayden Survey. With steep cliffs that rise almost straight up from the river, it is easy to see why they felt this way. The original Million Dollar Highway may have a few "tricks" left, but it has even more treats to share with you.

William Henry Jackson took this photograph of Crystal Lake at the north end of Ironton Park, with the three Red Mountains glowing in the background.

Author's Collection.

PHOTO ESSAY

There have been so many photographs taken of this section of the Million Dollar Highway over the years that it is worthwhile to pause for a moment and let the photographs speak. If a picture is worth a thousand words, then these dramatic photos, many of which were taken by some of the world's most famous photographers of the time (as well as by many ordinary tourists), must speak ten thousand words about the spectacular, original Million Dollar Highway.

Famous photographer George Beam shot this photograph of an early-day tour bus somewhere around the Ruby Cliffs about 1925. The way the bus is parked there couldn't be too much traffic.
Photo Courtesy Denver Public Library, Western History Collection, GB-5319.

Beam also took this photograph of tourists using the new overlook at Bear Creek Falls. He even managed to get a little of the falls into the picture, which is very hard to do.
Photo Courtesy of Denver Public Library, Western History Department, GB-5324

Beam photographed this scene about ten years earlier (circa 1915), before the Million Dollar Highway was upgraded into an automobile highway. This section is just north of the Riverside Slide. Note the log bridge and cribbing.
Photo Courtesy of Denver Public Library, Western History Collection, GB7588.

※ 271

Famous frontier photographer William Henry Jackson took this photograph of the Bear Creek tollgate, the toll keeper's "hotel," and the bridge over Bear Creek Falls. The photograph was taken about 1885, as there was no toll after the highway became public in 1887.
Photo Courtesy of Colorado Historical Society, WHJ 2778.

An unknown photographer took this photo of the Ruby Cliffs about 1885. Note the men in the foreground, who are double jacking — one holding a drill bit and the other using a sledge hammer. Why they are working on this rock is anyone's guess, but they were probably just posing for the photographer.
Author's Collection.

※ 273

Another unknown photographer took this photograph of the fully loaded Circle Route Stage near the Ruby Cliffs. At the far left, peering from behind his burros, is the prospector that the Circle Route Stage said you might meet on the road! From the style of the clothes and the telephone and electric lines, this photo was probably taken about 1890.

Ruth and Marvin Gregory Collection.

Yet another unknown photographer shot this photograph near the Riverside Slide on the Million Dollar Highway. Why is the man walking down the highway in front of the buggy with what looks like a suitcase in his hand? The deep ruts in the road may have actually been of comfort to many travelers. From the condition of the road, the photo was probably taken while Mears still owned it – the mid-1880s.

Photo Courtesy of Colorado Historical Society, F6303.

This is one of my favorite photos on the highway. When you enlarge the photograph, the lady on the right has a look on her face that says, "I wouldn't go back over this road for a million dollars." There is at least one person in the coach, maybe more. No one rides up top this day. The photo was probably taken about 1890.

Author's Collection.

This photo was taken for the Sanborn postcard company from the Hayden Trail on Mt. Hayden to the west of the "Impassible Canyon." It shows how the Million Dollar hugs the cliffs and even passes over a bridge that would have been unnoticeable from the highway. The photo was probably taken in the late 1920s or early 1930s, as there are guardrails (installed in 1924 and removed by 1935).

Photo Courtesy of Ft. Lewis College, Center for Southwest Studies.

This William Henry Jackson photograph was reproduced in a variety of sizes, in an early color process called chromolithography. This is the steepest portion of the highway, just south of Bear Creek. Log cribbing was again used in several spots, and a photographer shoots his own scene to the right of the stage.
                                                Author's Collection.

In doing the research for this book, I found more photographs of the Ruby Cliffs with Twin Peaks in the background than of any other section on the highway. The stone guard rails added in the early 1920s gave it a very solid look. The unknown photographer did a good job of capturing the scale of the mountains and the steepness of the gorge; and there is even a little snow on Twin Peaks.

Sanborn Postcard Company. Author's Collection.

Whoever took this photo did a good job in placing the horseback rider so that he adds some dimension to the surroundings. This photo is taken near the Riverside Slide, and the log bridge seen in some of the previous photos is at the extreme right of this scene, which was probably taken shortly after the road was built. The Colorado Historical Society identifies it as an image for use by the Ouray Stage Line.

Photo Courtesy of Colorado Historical Society, F44092.

From the car in this scene looking north at the Ruby Cliffs, and the men working on the stone barriers, we can date this photo to the early 1930s. Some of this work was done by government CCC workers during the Great Depression.
　　　　Photo from the Ruth and Marvin Gregory Collection.

This picture was taken looking south from Bear Creek Falls. Mt. Abram is in the background and the Engineer Road leads left through the gap in the mountains. The Mother Cline Slide is directly above the road in the center of the photograph. The telephone and electric lines have been moved higher above the road, but the stone guard rails are still in place, dating the photo to the early 1930s.

Marvin and Ruth Gregory Collection.

This very early color postcard was hand colored from a black and white photograph taken about the turn of the century. Postcards helped to promote the scenery along the Million Dollar Highway and drew thousands of early tourists to the area. One couple that came about 1919, could have ridden on this stage. They were Lula and Raymond Myers — the author's grandparents, who were on their honeymoon.

Author's Collection.

❊ 283

One last photo of basically the same spot on the highway shows the telephone and electric lines very prominently. Upon closer inspection it looks like they were drawn on the photograph to give some amazing looking depth to a stereo card, which made photographs appear in 3D. Now people who weren't even traveling the highway could be truly scared by it!

Underwood and Underwood Photography. Author's Collection.

Chapter 10

THE "IMPASSIBLE CANYON" AND THE CITY OF OURAY

THE THREE MILES OF THE Million Dollar Highway that lie immediately north of Ironton Park to the Engineer Road might well be called "Mears' Miles," as it is the only portion of the road totally built by him. It was this section of road that the County of Ouray avoided, and which eventually got Otto Mears involved with the road. The six mile stretch from Ironton Park down to Ouray was the section that thwarted Mears' efforts to extend the Silverton Railroad to the tracks of the D&RG Railroad in Ouray. The route was just too tough for a traditional railroad, since it had an average eight percent grade and there was little or no room for switchbacks. Nevertheless, this portion of the Million Dollar Highway is perhaps Mears' crowning achievement.

That portion of the road that crawls around the sheer cliffs of the Uncompahgre Canyon was built an average of 500 feet above the river at a cost of nearly $100,000 in 1883. So did Mears' construction crews while building it. It is said that five men died while doing work on this hazardous section of road. At the time, the construction of the shelf road was considered one of the greatest achievements in road building and engineering in the United States. Many true and exciting tales have been told by travelers on

Chapter 10: THE "IMPASSIBLE CANYON" AND THE CITY OF OURAY ❋ 285

this section of road, where the cliffs and mountains rise thousands of feet above the Uncompahgre River.

One of the more humorous stories was told by Ike Stevens, who was driving a sled over the highway in the winter about 1890 with a load of eggs, a cargo of dead pigs, and two very hung-over miners. While crossing a tilting slope, the wagon box came off the runners and shot out over the cliffs like a toboggan. It finally came to rest many hundreds of feet below near the creek. Ike had held tight to the reins and let the horses keep him from going on this "sleigh ride," but the miners rode the wagon box all the way to the bottom at an amazing rate of speed. They were fished out of the gorge, perfectly okay, but now totally sober and reportedly in "an Indian-rubber condition."

As already recounted, the first automobile came down the Red Mountain road in 1910, but the first auto didn't get to the top

Several of the routes taken over the years are visible in this photo of the switchbacks north of Ironton Park. Today's route is to the left, the old auto road of 1920 is near the middle, and the Mears toll road is barely visible down by the creek.

Author's Collection.

of Red Mountain Pass totally under its own power until June 22, 1911. Hartman Brothers, an automobile dealership in Montrose, Colorado, sponsored the event and billed it as "one of the most remarkable, perilous, and daring trips ever undertaken by an automobile on the American continent." A scout was sent ahead of the auto on horseback to make sure the way was clear, so that the car didn't have to back up.

Today, as we travel north into what the Hayden Survey called the "impassible canyon," one of the first things that meets us after the double switchback (the road originally went straight down) are two monuments that mark a more serious side of the canyon – multiple victims of the Riverside Slide, which is located about a thousand feet to the north. The monuments couldn't be placed closer to the slide or an avalanche might have claimed it. The Million Dollar Highway passes through at least sixty-three avalanche areas in the twenty-four miles between Silverton and Ouray, but the Riverside Slide is by far the most dangerous and deadly. These monuments testify to that danger. One has three crosses and memorializes Rev. Marvin Hudson and his daughters Amelia and Pauline. The other was erected in memory of three snowplow drivers who were killed at different times near the spot. All (as well as others who don't have a monument) lost their lives in the Riverside Slide.

A man-made snow shed was built at the slide in 1985, for the purpose of carrying the slide over the road and any cars that are on it, but unfortunately funding was not available to build the entire defense structure. The snowplow monument only had two names on it when originally erected. The name of the third was added after the snow shed was built. Despite man's mighty (and expensive) efforts, the Riverside Slide still remains only partially tamed.

The Riverside Slide gets its name from a mine that was located right at creek level near the slide. The original Mears road ran just slightly above the mine, but the upgrade of the road to automobile traffic in the 1920s moved the road up higher on Abrams Mountain, and the debris rock from construction now covers the mine and the earlier route. When the route was lower, the slide

Chapter 10: THE "IMPASSIBLE CANYON" AND THE CITY OF OURAY ❋ 287

could cover the road to much deeper depths, and at times it was necessary for travelers to go over the slide in the winter, but only after removing the debris of dead trees and large rocks brought down by the slide.

Several factors make the avalanche the most deadly to cross a road in Colorado – perhaps in the United States. One is that there are actually two slides – one on each side of the canyon (East and West Riverside). They sometimes run at the same time, or the release of one may set off the other. Another dangerous problem is that neither slide cannot be seen or heard until it is too late to take any action. And yet other deadly factors are that both slides have major catch basins and travel a considerable distance (the East Riverside travels 3,280 feet) downhill before hitting the road, while gaining speed all the way. Finally, the slides have no place to go when they cross the road, so they may actually go down one side, up the other, and the back to the highway.

At first some locals were fascinated by the Riverside's huge pile of debris and even made a lengthy snow tunnel through the slide. Building the tunnel (instead of just going over the slide) was not an easy task, for as Rev. J. J. Gibbons wrote that "the Riverside Slide was not just snow, but a conglomerate of broken trees and huge boulders, some obviously weighing two or three tons." All of this was compacted by the force of the slide to the consistency of concrete. The county crew bored the tunnel, which Gibbons reported "was one of the wonders of the Ouray County Toll Road that summer. It was 580 feet long and high enough for a Concord stage with six horses." It was late fall before the roof of the tunnel caved in, but its walls stood for two more years before they collapsed. The Riverside Slide may have been a tourist attraction, but it was a very deadly one. Gibbons also wrote "in the spring, which at this altitude begins about the first of May, only a mail carrier will ride a horse over the trail. Snow slides creep silently at first down the mighty slopes, and suddenly, with an awful roar, overwhelm the unsuspecting victim."

The first survival story at the Riverside occurred in February of 1897, when Jack Bell, who was the mail and express mail carrier

The tunnel through the Riverside Slide (on the right) was a tourist attraction, but the road was made to run over the slide as shown to the left in this scene. Burros, wagons, a horseback rider, and men on foot were all on the trail this day.

Author's Collection.

between Ouray and Red Mountain, was swept off the road into the canyon. Bell gave his own personal account of the incredible incident to the *Ouray Herald* on February 24, 1897. He was traveling from Ouray to Ironton in the early morning with two horses and a companion named David. Three feet of snow had drifted in some places, so he was carrying a large snow shovel. He stopped to dig a path at the Riverside Slide. When he dropped the reins to his horse, and bent down to pick them up, he remembered being swept off his feet and rolling in the darkness inside the slide; but then he passed out. David was also hit by the slide, but was left at the edge of the snow slide and soon worked his way free. He ran for help at Ironton, but because of the deep snow, it took him two hours to go about two miles. After sounding the alarm in Ironton, the rescue attempts began at once. The men probed and dug frantically, summoning more help and continuing their search. The rescuers were given some hope when one of Bell's packhorses

Chapter 10: THE "IMPASSIBLE CANYON" AND THE CITY OF OURAY ❦ 289

was found alive and well. The people in Ironton had contacted Ouray by telephone and more rescuers arrived from that town. Further probing found Bell's horse, whose neck was broken. At this point the rescuers became discouraged and discontinued their search when darkness fell.

It was finally decided that further efforts would be futile, and all of Jack's friends and relatives were resigned to the fact that he was dead. Mrs. Bell was inconsolable when told the news; but her husband, although unconscious, had actually been saved, in part by his large snow shovel, which ended up in front of his face and gave him some breathing room. He woke up, started digging the snow from what he hoped was above him, and trampled it under his feet. After a while, he hit a small hole made in the snow by the probe of a searcher and began to follow it upwards. This was the only way

A view of the snow tunnel at the Riverside Slide, looking south, shows that the tunnel has been enlarged considerably. The road over the slide appears slightly to the right of the tunnel, but seems to have been abandoned because of the melting snow.

Photo Courtesy of Colorado Historical Society, F2504.

that he could be sure he was going the right direction. The he later hit a small stream of water and followed the tunnel it had made for forty to fifty feet until he eventually came out from under the snow in the creek.

It was now twenty-four hours since the slide hit him, but somehow Bell managed to stumble downhill towards the Bear Creek tollgate, and as he approached within hailing distance of the toll keeper's cabin, he shouted for help and collapsed. When the toll keeper, Harvey Lewis, came outside and saw Jack, he dragged him into the tollhouse and then ran all the way to Ouray to get help. In the meanwhile, other men in the cabin cut Bell's clothes off and put him in bed with plenty of whiskey and hot coffee to drink. Bell had suffered only small cuts and bruises, although several of his fingers were frozen from clawing his way to freedom.

In December of 1908 Elias Fritz, a miner at the Treasury Tunnel, wasn't so lucky. He, two horses, and his dog were killed while he and two other men were trying to shovel a path so his freight sled could cross an avalanche that had come down a little earlier at the Riverside Slide. Another slide ran and killed him instantly, but his two companions escaped. It was a situation that was to repeat itself with deadly results over the years.

The three crosses mentioned earlier are dedicated to the Reverend Marvin Hudson and his daughters, Amelia and Pauline, who were caught in the slide on March 3, 1963. The family was traveling to Silverton, where Rev. Hudson was to conduct services at the Congregational Community Church. He had been asked not to come because of the potential danger from a recent, large snow storm, but he insisted and went anyway. The East Riverside had run and was being cleared by plows. Hudson unfortunately stopped in the avalanche path to put on his chains. The snowplow driver was coming to help him with his task when the slide hit. The air blast actually blew the driver and the snowplow backwards down the highway to safety. The avalanche piled up additional snow forty to sixty feet deep, and only a portion of the slide had run. Twenty men were soon on the scene to dig for the Hudsons,

The three crosses at the Hudson monument near the Riverside Slide tell the story of Rev. Marvin Hudson and his daughters, Amelia and Pauline, who all died in the slide.

Bill Fries III Photo. Author's Collection.

but they were constantly threatened by the very real possibility that another slide could run at any time. The search was called off for the night, and St. Bernard search dogs were brought in the next morning.

Hampering rescue efforts was a continuous snow, and the rescuers had to stop and shoot down the slide periodically. The rescue party used divining rods, witch sticks, long steel rods, dogs, and metal detectors in their search, but it was a week before the minister's body was found under six feet of snow. He had a broken neck and had died instantly. It was March 17 before Amelia's body and the car were discovered 600 feet below the point where they had been swept off the highway. The car was found with the doors and top torn off, but a glass bottle of cream in the car

Bulldozers and searchers looked for months in the debris of the Riverside Slide before they found all of the Hudsons' bodies and their car. Most of the time, the searchers were in very real danger since the slide could run (and kill) again.

Marvin and Ruth Gregory Collection.

wasn't broken. Not until May 30th did the packed snow release Pauline's body.

The snowplow driver monument at the Riverside Slide honors three highway department workers killed at three different times, while they were doing their job trying to clear the slide. Each time a second slide ran killing the drivers. Bob Miller, father of seven and age thirty-six, died on March 2, 1970, while clearing the slide with his D7 bulldozer. He had come from Durango to bring a Colorado Department of Transportation rotary snowplow to help in the efforts to clear a large slide that had run the previous day. He was operating a bulldozer when the other men went to Ouray for more equipment. He couldn't be found when they returned, but the men could see that the Riverside had run again and that the cat's seat and hood were on top of the snow. The cat was found just two hours later, seven feet under the snow and 300 feet from where it was evidently hit by both the East and West Riverside Slides. Miller was found two days later, 120 additional feet to the north. Fifty men worked on the dangerous rescue effort, as it was snowing the entire time. The rescuers tried shooting down the slide to lower the danger but couldn't get it to run.

Terry Kishbaugh was killed doing the same job on February 10, 1978. He was driving one of the big rotary plows, trying to clear the Riverside, when a second slide swept him away. It took a week to find the plow and three months to find Terry's body. Eddie Emil on March 5, 1992 (after the snow tunnel had been constructed) was standing near his snowplow, just outside the snow shed, when a large slide buried him and Danny Jarmillo. Neither man could initially move, but they could hear each other. Just as with Jack Bell, the rescuers gave up on them, and then Danny dug himself to safety. He took shelter in the snow tunnel, where four other people were trapped. Eddie died because he was located near the running engine of the plow. Carbon monoxide poisoning didn't kill him; it was the water from snow melted by the heat of the engine that soaked his clothes and caused him to freeze to death. The plow was still running two days later when they dug Eddie's body out.

Famous country western singer, C. W. McCall, heard of these incidents and wrote a popular song on the Riverside Slide.

> One cold black night of a Colorado winter
> It snowed on Red Mountain Pass.
> We warned everybody that the slides was runnin'
> And 550 was a mess,
> But out of the plow shed south of town
> Came a blade with a flashing blue light.
> We told that boy whatever you do
> Beware of the Riverside Slide.

Snowplow drivers and mail carriers are considered to be very special people in the San Juans. As Tad Bartimus, an Associated Press writer, wrote "they are a man paid by people he doesn't know, to perform a service they take for granted, in a place, where by the

This monument was erected in honor of the snowplow drivers who were killed by the Riverside Slide. "The lonely vigil of the night is known only to these men of courage." The slide is about a quarter of a mile north, as the monument would be destroyed if any closer.

Jan Smith Photo.

Chapter 10: THE "IMPASSIBLE CANYON" AND THE CITY OF OURAY ❋ 295

This section of the road was what stopped the Hayden Survey and made them declare it was not passable. The people and cars on the road look like toy models, while Red Mountain Creek rages below. This spot is just north of the Riverside Slide.
  Photo Courtesy of Denver Public Library, Western History Department, F46608.

laws of nature, he should not be." Snowplowing is very long, dangerous, lonely, hard, and scary work. One of the plow supervisors, Doug Stewart, when asked why the men do this kind of work, replied that they are "men who are impelled to do their best by their own sense of public responsibility and pride in their work." Mail carriers have the very same sense of obligation and face the same dangers, especially at the Riverside Slide.

A short distance north of the Riverside snow shed, a mine can be seen across the canyon to the west, clinging to a very obvious fissure vein called Silver Gulch, which runs up the steep slopes of Hayden Mountain. This is the Dunmore Mine. The mine is an old one, producing silver and some tungsten for years. In the 1930s, G. A. Franz, built a tram across the canyon from the road to the mine, which made it much easier to get the ore out. The Dunmore produced lead and zinc as by-products.

A quarter mile north of the Riverside Slide is the Mother Cline Slide, named for Captain Milton Cline's wife, Elizabeth. Cline's mine was located above the road, where the wooden chute comes down. The Mother Cline Mine was discovered in September 1874, and was a good producer that was worked much like a marble quarry with big chunks of ore being taken out of the mine and shipped in one piece. "Cap" Cline's wife was well-loved by all the local miners and often called "Mother Cline." It is unusual to name a slide after a woman, but in Mother Cline's case it was done as a sign of respect. Mrs. Cline was one of the first women to live in the San Juans and always tried to look out for "the boys" in town who had no wife or mother nearby. She would often feed them, sew up rips in their clothes, and let them rest or get warm in her cabin. Most importantly, she showed them love. She was well-loved in return and greatly admired, and her memory lives on by the naming of the slide, which, perhaps in deference to her memory, has never killed anyone.

The area where the Mother Cline Slide runs is usually more dangerous for the heavy chunks of ice (weighing two tons) that fall from the cliffs than for the snow slide, which is usually just a

Chapter 10: THE "IMPASSIBLE CANYON" AND THE CITY OF OURAY ❖ 297

few feet deep. The snow slide begins only about 300 feet above the road, and runs frequently, often stopping or even trappings traffic, but so far it has not killed or injured anyone. The March 22, 1912, *Ouray Herald* reported "the Mother Cline runs just about every time it snows, and sometimes when it doesn't." The slide has been known to run four or five times in one day.

A mile and a half north of the Riverside Slide, the Uncompahgre River rushes down the side of the canyon from the east, passes under "State Bridge," and spews out and down the mountain to the bottom of the gorge. The concrete bridge was built by the state in 1920, when the Million Dollar Highway was being upgraded. The stream was diverted through its present tunnel and the old stream bed filled in. In the canyon below, Red Mountain Creek and the Uncompahgre River make some pretty waterfalls before they join.

This is where the original trail to Poughkeepsie Gulch and Mineral Point came up out of the Uncompahgre Canyon and continued up what is now the Engineer jeep road, before Otto Mears got involved with the Million Dollar Highway. Mears brought the road up to its current level about half way up the cliffs along the river, which eliminated the steep trail from the river below; but he had only a log bridge across the creek. The bridge was one of the last projects to be finished on the original toll road. "Uncompahgre" (pronounced just as it is spelled – Un – com- pah- gre) is a Ute word for hot red water, probably a reference to the hot springs in the Ouray area and the naturally red water running off the Red Mountains.

The Engineer Road is now a difficult four-wheel drive route that follows the Uncompahgre River and eventually provides access to either Lake City or Silverton. The road has extremely rocky sections and will take all day. The Engineer Road is now part of the National Scenic Back Country Byways. The jeep trip to Lake City or Silverton (via Animas Forks) takes about four to five hours each way without stops, but it is well worth the effort. Half a dozen ghost towns, dozens of mines, and some of the most spectacular scenery in the world are located along this four-wheel drive road, but do not attempt these roads by automobile. If needed, jeep tours or rental jeeps are available in Ouray or Silverton.

The Engineer Road travels through the Mickey Breene Mine, Des Ouray Mine, and San Juan Chief Mill, among others, on its way to Mineral Point. Then, then the road forks and goes over either Engineer Pass or Cinnamon Pass to Lake City or you can go down the Animas River to Silverton. The Silver Link, Mother Cline, and Mountain Monarch were a few of the other big mines along the lower part of the road, which was called "Silver Hill" by some of the early prospectors. All of these mines were located in September of 1874. The prospectors had gotten close to the present site of Ouray in 1874, but it would be another year before they reached the bowl in which the settlement would eventually be located.

Poughkeepsie Gulch is about half way up the Engineer Road, splitting off to the south. Don't try to get all the way through Poughkeepsie, as the upper stretch is too dangerous. The gulch was named after a good-paying mine that was located in the gulch in 1873. The Poughkeepsie Mine was probably the first mine to be officially located in what is now Ouray County. The date of its locations shows that the Baker Park prospectors had spread out in 1873, or maybe even earlier, to look for mineral prospects. Supposedly, the very earliest prospectors found a long abandoned mine at the head of Poughkeepsie, indicating that Spanish or French prospectors had been there much earlier. The Old Lout is the first big dump encountered in the gulch and was eventually the largest mine in the gulch. It produced ore worth over a half million dollars. H.A.W. Tabor owned many of the mines in the upper end of Poughkeepsie. The Alaska and Como groups were his favorites. There was a mining boom in upper Poughkeepsie when prospectors heard that Tabor was buying claims there. Tabor thought that Poughkeepsie Gulch could be as big a mining district as Leadville; but, as most prospectors, he was overly optimistic.

The cliffs exposed along the section of the Million Dollar Highway from the Engineer Road to Bear Creek Falls are

Chapter 10: THE "IMPASSIBLE CANYON" AND THE CITY OF OURAY ❋ 299

The San Juan Chief Mill still stands in part at Mineral Point on the upper portion of the Engineer Road. This photo was taken in the 1960s, but several of the structures are still there.

Author's Collection.

estimated to be two billion years old. They were formed in the pre-Cambrian time. Many call this formation the "foundation" of the Rocky Mountains, as it was laid down during one of the first episodes of mountain building on earth. The road again gets especially narrow at this point. When traveling this section of road, the Rev. J. J. Gibbons reported that, "the novice is so alarmed at the sight of the abysses around him that even in the summer, when the roads are good and danger is remote, he alights from the coach and prefers to walk, not trusting himself to the best vehicle and driver." It is pretty much the same today, although not as many people get out and walk.

The "antique store" located across the canyon (the one with the wash on the clothesline) is a local prank. The "house" was part of the Natalie Mine, which operated about 1905 but was never very successful. Today, each spring, Ouray residents hike to the mine from the other side of the canyon, bringing old clothes to hang on the line, so that tourists can be puzzled by how any one would ever live in such a place, and what route one could possibly take to get to the antique store.

One more mile and Bear Creek passes under the Million Dollar Highway and falls 227 feet to the bottom of the canyon. Across the canyon can be seen an interesting but very shallow waterfall. In fact, "Horsetail Falls" usually runs in the spring and early summer or after rains when water is in Ralston Creek. The huge undulating surface is actually large ripples made from a Pre-Cambrian lakebed about 1.5 billion years ago. There is a good parking area at the bridge which allows sightseers to get out of their car and peer into the gorge to see Bear Creek Falls. Mt. Abrams is the large peak to the south up the canyon.

The Sutton Mine is across the canyon and a little south from Bear Creek Falls. The mine was accessed through the Mineral Farm Mine off the Camp Bird Road near Ouray. It used to have a 2,700-foot tram (whose cables and towers are still visible in the canyon if you look closely) that ran from its mill (which was next the highway south of Bear Creek Falls) to its mine. The Sutton Mine

Chapter 10: THE "IMPASSIBLE CANYON" AND THE CITY OF OURAY ❈ 301

The stage has stopped at the Bear Creek toll gate to allow the passengers to look at the falls. Note the pile of ore bags in front of the toll house, which is looking a little weather-worn.

Author's Collection.

was developed at four levels and produced pyrites, galena, copper sulphites, silver, and a little gold; but the margin of profit was always small. The mill was built in 1926. It had a 100-ton capacity, but the owners never mined enough ore to keep the mill running at full capacity. The Sutton Mine was rich in gold and silver at the higher levels, but the ore became poorer at the lower levels. The mill burned partially in the 1930s, and then another fire totally destroyed what was left about 1980.

Bear Creek Falls is a favorite ice-climbing spot in the winter. Look down for the climbers using their ice picks on the huge mass of blue ice. Ten or fifteen thousand years ago, glacial ice was 3,000 feet thick at this point. It ran north for twelve miles to present-day Ridgway and beyond. Bear Creek is a good spot to study many of the geological layers of rock. The groves, scratches, and polish of the glacier can still be seen throughout the area. It is estimated that the waters of the Uncompahgre River have only deepened the canyon by about fifty feet at this point.

Otto Mears' tollgate sat right on top of the falls. He had a small cabin for the toll keeper, Harvey Lewis (who actually built the cabin), and a gate made of a hinged log placed across the bridge. Mears advertised the cabin as a "hotel." Harvey actually put up a lot of travelers at his "hotel." Just south of this spot is a monument to Otto Mears, "Pathfinder of the San Juans." It was the idea of Charles E. Adams, editor of the *Montrose Daily Press*, but the State of Colorado paid for the monument. When the road was later widened, it was removed and then put back in 1961 after efforts by Joyce Jorgensen, publisher of the *Ouray Plaindealer*. Mears lived in California at the time of the original dedication and was too feeble to attend, so his daughter and grandson represented him. Mears did come later and saw his monument, but he died in 1931. His ashes were reportedly scattered at the spot.

Immediately before the tunnel (built by Lars Pilkar in 1921 along with the concrete bridge and overlook at the falls) is Bear Creek National Recreational Hiking Trail. It is open only to hikers – no motorcycles, bicycles, horses, or four-wheelers are allowed. Grand Mesa can be seen eighty miles to the north off this narrow

The Otto Mears monument was originally inset into the granite cliffs at Bear Creek, but later removed when the highway was widened. Now it sits beside the road.
Jan Smith Photo.

The tunnel built by Lars Pilkar, just north of Bear Creek Falls, was smaller than today. It is the only tunnel on the Million Dollar Highway and shows up in many old postcards.

Author's Collection.

trail. It is two and a half miles up the steep trail to the Grizzly Bear Mine, another mile and a half to the Yellow Jacket Mine, and three more miles to Engineer Pass and American Flats. One can also tie into the Horsethief Trail and travel north into through high alpine wilderness to the other side of Ouray, but this definitely makes it a two-day hike. Bear Creek was the route of one of the early trails into Ouray from Lake City, but the trail was originally down the south side of the creek. After the "Merchant's Toll Road" from Lake City to Silverton was built over Engineer Pass in 1877, the trail fell out of favor, but a new trail (the one that hikers use today) was located on the south side of Bear Creek to service the Grizzly Bear Mine. It is a very interesting and well-maintained hiking trail.

The Grizzly Bear Mine was located in June, 1875, and reached peak production in the 1880s. A small town was located at the mine (population twenty-four in 1885). The "Crazy Swede Lost Gold Mine" was somewhere a little further up this trail. Gus Lindstrom, a Swede, found extremely rich ore in 1906, while traveling in a snowstorm over the trail. He was seeking protection under a small overhang, when he noticed what he believed to be gold. The ore he brought down in his backpack assayed at over $200,000 a ton (about four million dollars a ton at today's rates). All he remembered about the location was that the vein was located at the foot of a cleft in the rocks. Others have found rich gold float in the area, but neither Gus nor anyone else could find the spot of his gold vein again. Gus searched for it for over a decade, gaining his nickname the "Crazy Swede," but never found it. The vein may have been covered over by a rock fall. Some day it may be exposed again.

Another mile north of Bear Creek Falls on the Million Dollar Highway is a broad parking area that overlooks the City of Ouray, which has been designated a National Historic Landmark. The surrounding mountains rise about 3,000 feet above the town. Twin

When Ouray County tried to build the original road to Mineral Point, they only got about this far south of Ouray before they gave up. Mears pulled the road out of the bottom of the canyon up to this level and eliminated a 20% grade.

Author's Collection.

Chapter 10: THE "IMPASSIBLE CANYON" AND THE CITY OF OURAY ❖ 305

Peaks (10,970 feet) can be seen to the northwest of town, and the amphitheatre is to the east. Both are favorite hiking spots for tourists and locals.

There is one final lost gold mine story that involves Twin Peaks. The story goes that two prospectors came to the bowl which now holds the City of Ouray in the fall of 1863. The men were very cautious because of the Utes, and made their camp alongside Oak Creek on Twin Peaks, at a spot where they could hide but also see into the bowl and up the valley to the north. They found gold float in the creek and eventually traced the float upstream to what they described as a "ledge of pure gold." Here they "mined" the precious discovery by building a fire to heat the rock and then throwing cold water on it, so as to fracture and break up the rock. The technique worked pretty well, but it also captured the attention of the local Utes. The men spied a Ute party coming up the valley from the north, waited until night, and then fled with all the gold that they could carry. No one has been able to rediscover the "ledge of gold." It could have been covered after one of Oak Creek's frequent floods, but some day it may be revealed again.

Although often mistaken for the remains of a volcano, the amphitheater is actually the remains of an ancient valley carved out by glaciers, which later was filled with ash and debris from volcanoes centered in what is now the Lake City-Silverton area. Later glaciers helped create its present shape. Shortly after the overlook, a paved road leads up to the Amphitheatre Campground, which has good facilities but is open only in the summer. There are some good hiking trails out of the campground. One of the trails leads two and a half miles up a series of steep switchbacks to the Chief Ouray Mine and a marvelous view of the area. The mine can be seen from town, if you look up and to the right of Cascade Falls. There are also some easier but scenic trails in the amphitheater (just look for signs).

Ouray has two waterfalls within the city limits. Cascade Falls is very visible to the northeast side of town. Box Canyon Falls is hidden to the west of the lookout. Four creeks (Cascade,

Canyon, Portland in the amphitheatre to the east, and Oak Creek to the northwest join the Uncompahgre River in the city limits. Horsethief Trail (one of the main routes of the Utes coming out of the San Luis Valley and going to Utah) runs just back of the amphitheatre, cuts through a notch in the north end, and then descends to the Uncompahgre River.

Just before the road enters the Town of Ouray, County Road 361 leads upwards and crosses the Uncompahgre River. Then going right will bring you to Box Canyon Falls, or staying to the left will take you into the mountains on the Camp Bird Road. Box Canyon is a slit in the rocks about twenty feet wide, two hundred feet deep, and 258 feet high. It is still being formed in the rock as

It is really hard to get a good photograph of Box Canyon, but this photographer did a splendid job. Over the years, the falls have been the water intake for the town's electric plant, the area below the falls has been mined, and now it is a tourist attraction.
Author's Collection

Chapter 10: The "Impassible Canyon" and the City of Ouray

Canyon Creek slowly cuts into the very hard rock. It has been a tourist attraction since Ouray's early days. Geologists estimate that the sculpting of the falls started 1,750,000 years ago. It was originally a mining claim, but the city bought the property in 1920. A constant mist fills Box Canyon, and the roar of the water is awesome. The sight is well worth the small admission charge.

The Uncompahgre Gorge near Box Canyon is used for ice climbing in the winter. Water from the intake pipe of the old hydroelectric plant is sprayed down the canyon walls, where it stays all winter as it is not hit by the sun. Ice climbing competitions are sometimes held in the world-class ice park.

The Camp Bird Road was finished by Otto Mears as a toll road in 1883, and connects Ouray with Imogene and Yankee Boy Basins. Although it was built over a decade earlier, it was the discovery of the famous Camp Bird Mine that gives it its name. About a half mile up the road is the Mineral Farm Mine, which was the first big mine discovered in the Ouray area. A. W. Begole and John Eckles located the mine in 1875 and then sold it in 1878 for $75,000 – a good sum of money in those days for an unproven property. Begole demanded that he be paid cash on the spot and received it. Eventually, the Mineral Farm produced over a million dollars in gold, copper, lead, and silver. Begole used his money to start a merchandise store in Ouray.

Tom Walsh discovered what would become the Camp Bird Mine while looking for flux for his Silverton Smelter. Between 1896 and 1902 his fabulously rich mine produced four million dollars in ore, much of it coming from the "waste rock" of the old mines. For many years the Camp Bird was the most profitable mine in Colorado. Walsh originally built a mill at the mine in upper Imogene Basin, but later he built a much bigger mill at the confluence of Imogene and Sneffels Creeks, two miles below the mine, which he connected to the mill with an aerial tram. Later a two-mile tunnel was driven from the mill to the mine's ore. A good size town was built at the mill, and many men also lived at the mine.

Tom Walsh and his Camp Bird Mine were famous throughout the world. Over a period of almost 100 years it produced around a billion dollars at today's prices. Now only a few buildings remain.

Author's Collection.

Walsh took very good care of his miners. Four hundred of them lived in a huge boardinghouse with steam heat, electric lights, pool tables, hot and cold running water, reading rooms, fire protection devices, porcelain bath tubs, and even marble counter tops for the lavatories. He treated his miners so well that when major labor problems broke out all over Colorado in the early 1900s, there were no major incidents at the Camp Bird.

For years the Camp Bird Mine produced $5,000 to $6,000 in profit a day for Walsh, seven days a week. Then Walsh sold the mine to a British syndicate for $5.2 million in 1902. The new owners went on to produce another $23 million in ore from 1902 to 1916, of which $16 million was profit. Over a ninety year period, the mine made over $50 million (worth well over a billion dollars today) before closing in the late 1970s.

The Revenue Tunnel is a few miles further up the Yankee Boy Road. It did very well, employing about 500 men and

Chapter 10: THE "IMPASSIBLE CANYON" AND THE CITY OF OURAY ❦ 309

eventually producing over $16 million in ore (worth about $250 million today). The Revenue Mill produced forty to fifty tons of concentrates a day that were sent to Ouray in wagons for shipment to the smelters on the railroad. The small town of Sneffels had been established on the spot before the Revenue Tunnel was started. Sneffels was originally called "Porters" for George Porter, who ran the local store. He also had a post office from 1878 to 1895, and his cabin was an early day landmark in the Sneffels Mining District.

After the Revenue, the road eventually splits and leads to Yankee Boy and Governor's Basins (dead ends) or through Imogene Basin to the upper Camp Bird and over Imogene Pass to the ghost town of Tomboy and eventually Telluride. All of these higher roads are four-wheel drive only, although an automobile can easily make it to the Camp Bird Mill site. Yankee Boy Basin offers some of the most beautiful scenery in all of Colorado. The Yankee Boy Mine was discovered by William Weston and George Barber in 1877, and

The Revenue Mine was the other really big mine up the Camp Bird Road. It produced mainly silver, and lots of it. In the foreground is the settlement of Sneffles.

Author's Collection.

produced about $50,000 in its first year of operation. In 1879, twenty-three tons of its ore averaged 1,231 ounces of silver per ton.

The Viginius Mine is located high up in Governor's Basin. It produced extremely rich silver ore and had small settlements built around its upper and lower workings. It also boasted that it had the highest post office in the United States. William Freeland discovered the Virginius at nearly 12,300 feet elevation on June 28, 1876. A shaft went down 1,100 feet, at which time the Revenue Tunnel was driven at Sneffles to strike the vein at an even lower level. The Virginius ore averaged eight ounces of gold and 150 ounces of silver per ton. Unlike most San Juan mines, the Virginius ore got richer as the mine went deeper.

The Imogene Pass Road now starts several miles up the Yankee Boy Road, as the old road through the Camp Bird Mill site is usually closed. It leads past the U. S. Depository Mine, the Yellow Rose Mine, and the site of the original Camp Bird Mine and Mill. At the top of Imogene are the rock remnants of Ft. Peabody. The Colorado State militia built it during labor troubles in Telluride in 1904. On the other side of the 13,114-foot pass are Tomboy Basin and Savage Basin (both full of old mines and the ruins of the town) and eventually the road reaches the Town of Telluride. The four-wheel drive Imogene Pass is usually only open from July through mid-September as it tops out at 13,114 feet – making it the second highest pass in the continental United States.

With the Camp Bird, the Revenue, and many smaller mines in the area producing such large amounts of gold and silver ore in the early 1900s, the Camp Bird Road was filled with activity. Two stages made the run up to the Camp Bird and Sneffles each day. A considerable number of their passengers were tourists who had come in on the Circle Route. Ouray's scenery, wildflowers, and wildlife were a wonderful draw, and the visitors loved a chance to see the rich mines being worked.

Although Americans had earlier been in the bowl that now holds the City of Ouray, it was July, 1875, when prospectors A. W. "Gus" Begole and John Eckles suddenly found themselves in the

Chapter 10: THE "IMPASSIBLE CANYON" AND THE CITY OF OURAY ❧ 311

Over the years there have been several ways that the Million Dollar Highway ran out of Ouray to the south. The original route followed close to the river. This is another route built in the early 1920s.

Author's Collection.

beautiful and then heavily-wooded little park. Near present-day Box Canyon they found good silver ore. They returned to Bakers Park and came back with other men, supplies, pack animals, and more tools. They also sent men to Saguache to bring back food and other supplies, as they were preparing to spend the winter. Other prospectors soon joined them, and a small settlement was established. Since it would become the supply town for the mines in Imogene, Yankee Boy, and Governor's Basins, the Town of Ouray grew quickly.

In October 1875 Begole and Eckles discovered the Mineral Farm Mine only a mile southwest of town. The Mineral Farm was so named because the rich ore appeared on the surface and could be mined in shallow trenches. By October 28, 1875, a post office was established in Ouray, although it was reported to be little more than a promise from the Ute agency to have the mail brought up every now and then. By November, several dozen men managed to get two wagon loads of supplies from Saguache into Ouray via the unfinished Mears Toll Road across Ute Indian Territory. The group settled in for the winter, one man writing home in November 1875 that what was to become the Town of Ouray was in "as picturesque a little spot as is to be found in America.... The only way out is to look up. The sun is a most lazy fellow – always late getting

A.W. "Gus" Begole and Gordon Kimball were both originally prospectors and were in the Ouray area from its founding. Both turned to running retail businesses as they got a little older.
    Photo Courtesy of Denver Public Library, Western History Department, F28385.

Chapter 10: The "Impassible Canyon" and the City of Ouray

up in the morning, and goes to rest soon after four o'clock at this time of year." Several women spent that winter in Ouray with their spouses, and one even gave birth to a child during that time. The people staying in Ouray weren't totally isolated, as the Ute agency was twenty-five miles to the north. A steady flow of traffic, both whites and Utes, ran between the town and the agency.

Although in 1875 a plat was drawn for a town site named "Uncompahgre," nothing came of that idea. When the post office was established in October, 1875, it used the name of "Ouray." In large part the new name was given the town to try to cement good relations between the whites and the Utes; and when the town site plat was actually filed in 1876, the city fathers used the name of "Ouray."

By 1876 there was a rush of prospectors to the Ouray area. In March of 1876, Captain Cline and thirty new prospectors joined the group that had spent the winter, and several wagonloads of ore were taken to Pueblo via Saguache. The trip took about fourteen days each way, so only the richest handpicked ore was worth sending on the long, dangerous journey. In the spring of 1876 a Mr. Randall brought in the first stock of goods to open a general store, Mr. and Mrs. Dixon started the first hotel in their log cabin, and Nat Hart opened the first saloon.

By the end of 1876 Ouray had 400 residents, 214 cabins and tents, a school, four stores, and an ore sampling works. The winter of 1876-77 was long and harsh like the previous winter, and by spring the residents were living on nothing but bread and coffee. After this alarming experience, the local merchants learned to ship in large amounts of supplies before the winter weather set in. The Barlow and Sanderson stage started regular operation to Ouray from Saguache in 1877, when the Otto Mears toll road was totally finished to the Los Piños II Agency and Mears bought and finished the road from the agency to Ouray.

Although the Fourth of July of 1876 was also the celebration of statehood for Colorado and the centennial observance of the United States, there wasn't much activity in Ouray – there was just

This is one of the earliest scenes of Ouray. The roads are crude and there aren't many buildings, but a huge American flag flies proudly on the town's Main Street. Part of the reason for the flag was to show that the town was in U.S. territory, as the Indian Reservation was just north.
Author's Collection.

too much to do in the new town. However the 1877 Fourth of July celebration was a big one. A huge thirteen by twenty foot flag was made by Mother Cline and Mrs. S. J. Parasol and was raised on a fifty-foot flagpole in the middle of Main Street and Sixth Avenue. Ira Munn built the first sawmill in Ouray in 1877, and Ouray welcomed its first paper, *The Ouray Times*.

Last but not least was the arrival in 1877 of several preachers. This brought a sense of culture and dignity to the community. The Reverend George Darley arrived on March 14, 1877 to organize a church, but soon left. Supposedly, Rev. C. L. Libby preached the first sermon in Jesse Benton's half-finished saloon. By summer's end, Darley was back and started building the Presbyterian Church building on June 24, 1877 (Darley was a carpenter before he was a preacher). Later, Darley came over Engineer Pass from Lake City, in waist deep snow for over half the distance, to dedicate the new church building in Ouray. The roundtrip was 125 miles and took him five days. Libby supposedly arrived in town half frozen and holding on to the tail of his burro, as he had gone snow blind coming over Engineer Pass, but half the preachers in Colorado reportedly arrived in the same manner in various other towns.

Ouray had the typical mining town rowdiness, but a lot of the shootings were done by the sheriff, Jesse Benton, who gained a reputation for shooting first and asking questions later. One of the few lynching of a woman occurred in Ouray. Margaret and Michael Cuddigan had mistreated their ten-year old adopted daughter so badly that she died. It was determined that when she died, her hands, feet, and legs were bruised and frozen, and that she had evidently been raped. The couple was hung almost immediately from a tree in what is now Ouray's hot water park.

The Bank of Ouray was founded in 1877, and the Miner's and Merchants Bank followed in 1878. The Dixon Hotel expanded their hotel in late 1877 to a large, two story building, and the hotel became the regular stage stop for the Barlow and Sanderson stage

William Henry Jackson took this photo about 1885. It was early in the town's existence, but electricity had arrived. The burro on the left carries a huge bellows for a blacksmith.

Author's Collection.

An 1885 photo shows Ouray's Main Street to be quite built up with businesses. The hose cart for the fire department is on the left. Many of these buildings were saloons.

　　　　　　　　　　　　　　　　　　　　Author's Collection.

from Lake City and the Los Piños Indian Agency. By early 1878, Ouray had a population close to 800. Daily mail service began in July, 1878, the same year the town began to remove stumps from its streets, grade the roads, and build plank sidewalks. In the early 1880s rich ore was found in the Red Mountain Mining District. This was followed by the discovery of gold on Gold Hill, just north of Ouray, and later at the Camp Bird Mine in Imogene Basin.

　　　Word quickly spread about the natural wonders of Ouray — its spectacular setting, the mild climate, the cascading waterfalls, the health-giving hot waters, and the beautiful trees, shrubs and flowers. Early-day tourists stayed in hotels like the Dixon House, Delmonico, and the Sanderson, which were followed a little later by the Beaumont, Western, and the St. Elmo Hotels. After it arrived in 1887, the D&RG Railroad heavily promoted Ouray, and excursion trains frequently brought hundreds of tourists a month. The

Chapter 10: THE "IMPASSIBLE CANYON" AND THE CITY OF OURAY ❖ 317

railroad's brochure pointed out that from Red Mountain, "The old-fashioned stage, with all its romantic associations is rapidly becoming a thing of the past.... Here in the midst of some of the grandest scenery of the continent, the blue sky above and the fresh, pure, exhilarating mountain air sending the blood bounding through one veins, to clamber into a Concord coach, and be whirled along a splendidly constructed road, drawn by four fiery horses, guided and controlled by a typical Western stage driver, is surely a novel and delightful experience." Many of the finest buildings in Ouray were built during the 1880s, and the city's population went from 864 in 1880 to 2,534 in 1890.

But like all early-day Colorado mining towns, Ouray had its seedier and rougher side. Ouray's bawdy houses were on 2nd Street, generally between Seventh and Eighth Streets. The Temple of Music, Bon Ton, Bird Cage, Clipper, and Monte Carlo were just a few of the drinking and gambling establishments. Over a hundred women reportedly worked as prostitutes along the street. John Vanoli's "220"

The Beaumont Hotel had just opened on this fine summer day in 1888. The flagpole still stood, but a band and speaker's platform had been added. The town now had electric street lights.

Ruth and Marvin Gregory Collection.

was on Main Street by the Ashenfelter barns. It was one of the roughest establishments in Colorado. His complex contained the Gold Belt dance hall and the Roma saloon, as well as a large collection of small cribs. Vanoli went to prison for killing one of his customers. However he only served eight months of his time, as most of Ouray's citizens felt the dead man was nasty enough that he deserved killing and petitioned the governor to reduce his sentence. It didn't seem to matter that Vanoli had shot first, or that his second shot hit the victim while he was lying helplessly on the floor.

The saloons in town were basically on the west side of Main Street, which was the dividing line between the "good" (east) and "bad" (west) parts of town. Putting the saloons on Main Street allowed the "good men" to go to the saloons without getting too far into the "bad" district. The saloons had names like The Bank, The Free Coinage, The Bucket of Blood, The Corner, The White House, The Capitol, and The Cabinet. The Beaumont Hotel also had a bar for the "better class."

By the end of the 1890s, it was evident that the San Juan silver days were coming to an end, since the repeal of the Sherman Silver Purchase Act in 1893 had devastated Colorado's silver industry. Times got tough. Even old Gus Begole, town father and major storeowner, had to go out of business. In July, 1893, Ouray turned its electric street lights off in an attempt to save money. Municipal salaries were cut by twenty percent for all employees, the city stopped spreading water on the streets to keep down the dust, and merchants were allowed to pay there license fees in installments. Fortunately, Ouray was spared the fate of many Colorado settlements that became ghost towns almost overnight. The Revenue Tunnel was finished in 1893, and produced such large amounts of silver that it could be mined profitably even with the low price of silver. Ouray and the other San Juan camps now had cheap transportation with the arrival of the D&RG Railroad, and there was the large gold discovery made by Tom Walsh in 1895 at the Camp Bird Mine, and rich, but smaller, gold discoveries made earlier on Gold Hill, which actually adjoins the Ouray city limits.

Most of the Victorian homes in the town were built in the 1890s or 1900s, and are still a source of real pride to their owners and the town. The brick for the Beaumont Hotel, Wright's Hall, the Elks Club, the County Courthouse, and many other buildings came from the Francis Carney brickyard near the present-day swimming pool.

Even though the town was in its "golden years," there was still a rowdy element, so the county built a new brick jail behind the county courthouse. In 1895 Vanoli spent time in the jail when he shot another customer at the Gold Belt. No charges were brought this time, even though he shot the man three times, one of which was in the back as the man was fleeing. Vanoli committed suicide just six months later. Like all the San Juan towns, the 1900s in

William Henry Jackson took another photo of Ouray about 1890, which shows that it had grown to be large and was near the peak of its prosperity. The amphitheater is in the background.

Author's Collection.

By the 1890s, the D&RG had expanded its faculties in Ouray to several spurs, a roundtable, a depot, and several warehouses for freight. The red light district was just across the river to the left.
    Photo by McClure, Courtesy of Denver Public Library, Western History Collection, McC2198.

Ouray were a time of a slow fall into depression, as metal prices slid. Ouray's population fell from 2,196 in 1900 to 1,165 in 1920.

If Ouray hadn't been surrounded by such beauty, it possibly would have died. In order to attract more tourists, the town decided to "clean up its act." Most of the bars, dance halls, and brothels were shut down. Dancing halls were made illegal in 1902, gambling halls in 1903. The neighboring towns complained that many of the gamblers and prostitutes moved to their towns. Hot water was found to seep into the pits Frances Carney had dug to get the clay for his bricks, and some of the resulting ponds were planted with gold fish. In 1926, one of the gold fish ponds was enlarged and made into a large, outdoor hot water swimming pool, which ranges in depth from two to ten feet and is 150 feet by

Chapter 10: THE "IMPASSIBLE CANYON" AND THE CITY OF OURAY ❖ 321

280 feet in size. The pool is now open year-round and is a major winter attraction for the city. At one time, the swimming pool was advertised as "the largest and most radioactive swimming pool in the world."

Trails were built into Box Canyon and the municipal hot springs pool and many smaller spots like Buchanan's Bath House were promoted as being able to cure almost any ailment. Don't worry about the radioactivity; there never was very much.

From the day it was opened, a major attraction of Ouray was the Million Dollar Highway. Just as today, many people traveled the road for its amazing scenery, but in those days they did it on horseback, stage or carriages instead of the comfort of an automobile. Exploring the mountains on the four-wheel drive roads is now one of the main summer attractions. Ice climbing and the hot springs pool have become the major attractions in the winter.

The tourist business has always been important to Ouray, and the hot water swimming pool helped after it was built in 1926. The alligator's part of the pool is to the far left.

Author's Collection.

Ouray's tourist business now brings in over 100,000 visitors a year. C. L. Hall, a mining engineer of the beginning of the twentieth century, wrote: a fitting description, "Ouray is peerless. She will be famous as a mountain resort when many of the now famous watering places are abandoned and forgotten." "Watering places?" Did he mean the saloons or the hot springs?

Ouray is the end of our trip over the Million Dollar Highway, but if you are just now discovering the beauty of its mountains and the quaint towns along its route, we hope that this is just the

Someone went to a lot of effort to get this shot of Ouray from Twin Peaks. A great variety of roads can be seen in the right hand section of the photo – the original "County" road on the immediate left of the river, the Million Dollar Highway higher up, and the present highway at the left. The Camp Bird Road and some of its variations can also be seen at the far right.

Photo Courtesy of Denver Public Library, Western History Department, F11525.

beginning of a love affair that will last for years to come. You will never regret the time you spend here, and you will never forget the awesome sights that you see. Another reason for the name of the Million Dollar Highway might be that many people would give a million dollars to live in or visit this moving and inspiring land.

Epilogue

THE SAN JUAN MOUNTAINS are undoubtedly some of the most rugged and beautiful in the world. The Million Dollar Highway allows almost anyone to enjoy this beauty. Even in a vehicle, it takes a long time to explore the San Juans. There are people who have spent their entire life poking around in these mountains, yet have not come close to seeing it all. The Million Dollar Highway should whet your appetite, but there is much, much more. It is my hope that this book will stimulate your curiosity, inspire an even greater love for this prime example of God's creation, and provoke a spirit of adventure.

Take time to stop and savor this country. It refreshes the soul and stimulates the mind. It may sound sentimental or simplistic, but use all your senses and your imagination. Listen to the wind blowing in the trees, the gurgling of the creek, or the call of the hawk. Smell the fresh, clear air or the fragrance of the evergreens. Taste a wild raspberry or feel the stones polished by glaciers and water. Imagine what it was like to live here in a log cabin in 1860, or what it was like to "Strike It Rich!"

The heritage of the San Juans is that of mining, which is today seen by many as "raping the land." Our land is too beautiful to be ravaged, but it also has a history of sharing great wealth. Historian Duane Smith wrote, "Damned and praised, mining is not yet dead in the San Juans; some day it will reemerge." Meanwhile it is important that we learn from the past, while we travel into the future. Or as Winston Churchill put it, 'The further backward you can look, the farther forward you are likely to see."

The spirit of the San Juans is a feeling that seeps deep into your soul. It is something that writers and photographers have unsuccessfully tried to capture for years. It is a country where the most delicate beauty and the most horrible hazards exist side by side. Its people hold tightly to their past, but realize that they have a grand future ahead.

Even though it is bound to fall short, perhaps it is appropriate to add poetry to the attempts of written prose and photographs to convey the ineffable qualities of these mountains—such as that articulated by Alfred Castner King, the poet of the San Juans. King was blinded in 1900 by an explosion in the Calliope Mine near Ouray. He later wrote of the San Juan Mountains as he remembered them, as perhaps no one else has written before or since:

AN IDYLL

I love to sit by the waterfall,
And listen to its laughing story,
As it fearlessly leaps o'er the rocky wall,
From the mountain peaks stern and hoary;
Or watch the spray as the colors play,
When the glorious sunlight kisses,
And tints confuse into rainbow hues
To embellish the wild abysses.

I love the rose and the columbine,
Whose delicate beauty pleases;
I love the breath of the fragrant pine,
As it floats on the morning breezes;

I love the sound from the depths profound,
When the Thunder-God is bringing
His crystal showers, to the tinted flowers,
In their sweet profusion springing.

I love the lake in the mountain's lap;
Without a flaw or error
Recording the clouds, which the peak enwrap,
And the trees, as a crystal mirror;
The wild delights of the mountain heights
Thrill my breast with a keen devotion,
As songbirds love the blue arch above,
Or the mariner loves the ocean.

Life in the San Juans is one of ironic twists. This beautiful land will attract millions of people in the future, but those who come to enjoy the peace and beauty may, in fact, destroy it by their very presence. Tread lightly on our land. Help to preserve our history. Help to save it for others, but most of all, enjoy and savor the special time that you spend here.

BIBLIOGRAPHY

Armstrong, Betsy R., *A Century of Struggle Against Snow, San Juan County, Colorado,* Boulder, University of Colorado, 1976.

_____, *Avalanche Hazards in Ouray County, Colorado, 1877 to 1975,* Boulder, University of Colorado, 1976.

Baars, *The American Alps,* University of New Mexico Press, Albuquerque, 1992.

Bauer, W. H., J. L. Ozment, and J. H. Willard, *Colorado Postal History,* Crete, Nebraska, J.B. Publishing Co., 1971.

Blair, Rob, editor, *The Western San Juan Mountains,* University Press of Colorado, Niwot, Colo., 1996.

Borland, Lois. "The Sale of the San Juans," *Colorado Magazine,* Vol. 28, No. 2 (April 1951).

Brown, Robert L., *An Empire of Silver: An Illustrated History,* Denver, Sundance Publications, 1984.

Bureau of Land Management, *Frontier in Transition,* U. S. Government Printing Office, Washington, D.C.

Chronic, Halska, *Roadside Geology of Colorado,* Mountain Press Publishing, Missoula, Montana, 1980.

Cornelius, Temple, *Sheepherder's Gold,* Sage Books, Denver, 1964.

Crofutt, George A., *Crofutt's Grip-Sack Guide to Colorado,* Omaha, The Overland Publishing Co., 1885.

Cross, Whitman and Esper Larsen, *A Brief Review of the Geology of the San Juan Region of Southwestern Colorado,* 1935, USGS Survey Bulletin 843, Washington, D.C., 1935.

Crum, Josie, "Three Little Lines", *Durango Herald News,* Durango, 1960

Cummings, D. H. "Toll Roads of Southwestern Colorado," *Colorado Magazine,* Vol. 29, No. 2 (April 1952).

Dallas, Sandra, *No More than Five in a Bed,* University of Oklahoma Press, Norman, Oklahoma, 1967.

Daniels, Helen Sloan, *Adventures with the Anasazi of Fall Creek,* Ft. Lewis College, Center for Southwest Studies, Durango, 1976.

Daughters of the American Revolution, Sarah Platt Decker Chapter, *Pioneers of the San Juan Country,* Colorado Springs, Colo., Outwest Printing, 1942.

Darley, Rev George, *Pioneering in the San Juan,* Western Reflections Publishing Co., Lake City, Colorado, 2008.

Denver and Rio Grande Railroad, *Around the Circle,* Denver, Denver & Rio Grande Railroad, 1892.

Eberhhart, Perry, *Treasure Tales of the Rockies,* Swallow Press, Athens, 1961.

Ferrell, Mallory, *Silver San Juan,* Boulder, Colo., Pruett Publishing Co., 1973.

Fossett, Frank, *Colorado, Its Gold and Silver Mines,* New York, C.G. Crawford, 1880.

Gibbons, J. J., *In the San Juan Colorado,* Chicago, Calumet Book and Engraving Co., 1898.

Griffiths, Thomas M., *San Juan Country,* Boulder, Colorado, Pruett Publishing Co., 1984.

Gregory, Marvin, and P. David Smith, *Mountain Mysteries,* Ouray, Colo., Wayfinder Press, 1984.

_____, *The Million Dollar Highway,* Ouray, Colo., Wayfinder Press, 1986.

Gulliford, Andrew, editor, *San Juan Sampler,* Durango Herald Small Press, Durango 2004.

Hafen, Leroy R., "Otto Mears, Pathfinder of the San Juans," *Colorado Magazine,* Vol. 9 (March 1932).

Hall, Frank, *History of the State of Colorado,* Chicago, Blakely Printing Co., 1890.

Hayden, F. A., *U.S. Geological and Geographical Survey of Colorado,* Washington, D.C., 1874, 1875, 1876.

Hungerford, John B., *Narrow Gauge to Silverton,* Hungerford Press, Reseda, California, n.d.

Ingersoll, Ernest, *The Silver San Juans,* Reprint, Olympic Valley, Calif., Outbooks.

_____, *The Crest of the Continent,* Glorieta, New Mexico, The Rio Grande Press, 1883.

Jarvin, Marion, *The Strater Hotel Story,* self-published, 1963.

Jenkins, John, *Colorado Avalanche Disasters,* Western Reflections Publishing Co., Ouray, Colo. 2001.

Jocknick, Sidney, *Early Days on the western Slope of Colorado,* Western Reflections Publishing Co., Ouray, Colo., 1997.

Kaplan, Michael, *Otto Mears, The Paradoxical Pathfinder,* Silverton, Colo., San Juan County Book Company, 1982.

Keilt, Maureen, *Durango,* Desert Dolphin, Inc., Durango, 1993.

Kindquist, Cathy, *Stony Pass, The Tumbling and Impetuous Trail,* San Juan County Book Company, Silverton. Colo., 1987.

Kushner, Ervan F., *Otto Mears, His Life & Times,* Frederick, Colo., Jende-Hagan Bookcorp, 1979.

Lendle, Leith, *Trimble Hot Springs,* Published by Trimble Hot Springs, Durango, 1985.

Marshall, John, and Jerry Roberts, *Living and Dying in Avalanche Country*, John Marshall Publisher, Silverton, Colo. 1992

McConnell, Virginia, "Captain Baker and the San Juan Humbug." *Colorado Magazine*, Vol. 48, No. 1 (Winter 1971).

Monroe, Arthur, *San Juan Silver*, Montrose, Colo., Self Published, 1940.

New Mexico Geological Society, *Guidebook to the Southwest San Juan Mountains*, Colorado, 1957.

Nossaman, Allen, *Many More Mountains*, Volumes 1,2,3, Sundance Books, Denver, Colorado

Osterwald, Doris, *Cinders and Smoke*, United Printing and Publishing Co.

Petersen, Freda Carley, *Death in the Snow*, Ferrell Publishing Co., Silverton, Colo., 2003.

Rathmell, Ruth, *Of Record and Reminiscence*, Ouray County Plaindealer, n.d., 1976.

Rhoda, Franklin, *Report of the Topography of the San Juan Country*, Washington, D.C., 1901.

Rice, Frank, *A History of Ouray and Ouray County*, Feb. 1961, Unpublished manuscript.

Ridgway, Arthur, "The Mission of Colorado Toll Roads." *Colorado Magazine*, Vol .9, No. 5 (September 1932).

_____, The Stony Pass Road, *Colorado Magazine*, Vol. 16, No. 2 (March 1939).

Rockwell, Wilson, *Sunset Slope*, Ouray, Colorado, Western Reflections Publishing Co., 1998.

_____, "Portrait in the Gallery, Otto Mears – Pathfinder of the San Juans," 1967 *Denver Brand Book*, Vol. 23, Denver, Colorado, Denver Westerners, 1967.

Sabin, Edwin, *Around the Circle*, Colorado Springs, 1913.

San Juan Forest Service, *San Juan Forest History* (ongoing publication).

Sloan, R.E., *The Silverton Railroad Companies*, Mega Publications, Northglen, Colorado, 1975.

Sloan, R. E., and Carl A. Skowronski, *The Rainbow Route*, Denver, Colo., Sundance, Ltd., 1975.

Smith, Duane, *Quick History of Silverton*, Western Reflections Publishing Co., Ouray, Colorado.

_____, *Rocky Mountain Boom Town*, University of New Mexico press, Albuquerque, New Mexico, 1980.

_____, *Quick History of the Durango-Silverton Train*, Western Reflections Publishing Co., Ouray, Colo, 1998.

_____ "Silver Coquette – The San Juans 1860-1875," *Denver Brand Book* 1965, Vol.25, The Denver Westerners, Denver, Colo. 1970.

_____, *Song of the Hammer and Drill*, Golden Colo., Colorado School of Mines Press, 1982.

Smith, P. David, *Exploring the Historic San Juan Mountains*, Wayfinder Press, Ridgway, Colo., 2004.

_____ *Mountains of Silver*, Western Reflections Publishing Co., Ouray, Colo., 1994.

_____, *Ouray: Chief of the Utes*, Ouray, Colorado, Wayfinder Press, 1986.

_____, *Quick History of Ouray*, Western Reflections Publishing Co., Ouray, Colo. 1990.

Spencer, Frances, *The Story of the San Luis Valley*, Reprint of San Luis Valley Historical Society, Alamosa, 1975.

Stone, Wilbur Fisk, *A History of Colorado*, S. J. Clark Publishing Co., Chicago, Ill., 1918.

Tucker, E.F., *Otto Mears and the San Juans*, Western Reflections Publishing Co., Montrose, Colo. 2003.

Wheeler, George, *U.S. Survey of Territories West of the 100th Meridian*, Washington, D. C., 1876.

Wiley, Marion C., "The High Road," Colorado Division of Highways, Denver, 1976.

Williams, Henry T., *Tourist Guide and Map of the San Juan Mines of Colorado.*

Williamson, Ruby, *Otto Mears, Pathfinder of the San Juans*, Printed by B&B Printing, Gunnison, Colo. 1981

Wolle, Muriel, *Stampede to Timberline*, Chicago, Swallow Press, 1974.

_____, *Timberline Tailings*, Chicago, Swallow Press, 1977.

Index

Abiqui – 33, 34, 36, 41, 50
Abram, Mt. – 265, 281
Alaska Mine – 298
Albany Mine – 265
Alpine Loop – 201, 202
Amphitheatre – 305
Anasazi (Ancestral Pueblo) – 20, 22
Anderson, Chet – 189
Andrews Lake – 198
Animas Canyon – 57, 64, 89, 143, 183, 198
Animas Canyon Toll Road – 85-87, 139
Animas City – 37, 39, 41, 44-46, 64, 89
Animas City (Second) – 148, 165-167, 170, 175
Animas City Mountain – 176
Animas Forks – 72, 73, 77, 159, 160, 218
Animas Forks Railroad Car – 160, 222, 223
Animas River – 20, 25-27, 33, 37, 41, 46, 114, 173, 176, 183
Animas Valley – 22, 64, 148, 176-178
Antelope Park – 66, 67
Anza, Don Juan – 27
Arkansas River – 27, 31
Arlington Saloon – 211, 212
Arny, William – 46
Arrastra – 47
Arrastra Gulch – 47, 48
Ashenfelter, John – 98
Autobees, Charles – 28

Baker, Charles – 32, 34-36, 39, 40, 46, 48, 49, 53, 56-58, 64, 67, 73, 78, 158, 200
Baker, Charlie – 192, 193
Baker, Jim – 42
Baker City – 36
Baker, Sull – 192, 193
Baker Brothers Seam – 192, 193
Baker's Bridge – 37, 46, 64, 184, 185
Baker's Park – 32, 34-40, 46, 48, 49, 53, 56-58, 64, 67, 73, 78, 158, 200
Baker's Party – 46
Bandora Mine – 228
Bank of Ouray – 315
Bank of the San Juans – 166
Barber, George – 309
Barlow and Sanderson Stage – 71, 77, 88, 315
Basketmaker Culture – 20
Barr, Jim – 251
Barstow Mine – 257
Bear Creek – 64, 73, 300, 301
Bear Creek Falls – 121, 124, 269, 271, 281, 300, 301
Bear Creek Hiking Trail – 302, 303
Bear Creek Tollgate – 93, 95, 301, 302
Bear Creek Tunnel – 122, 131
Bear Mountain – 234-236

Beaver – 231
Beaver and Belfast Mine – 261
Beckwith, Lt. Edward – 42
Begole, A. W. "Gus" – 73, 307, 310-312
Bell, Jack – 287-290
Bell, Siding – 149
Bell, W. A. – 168
Benton, Jessie – 315
Bent's Fort – 33, 42
Bergman, Lt. Col. E. H. – 44-46
Bishop (town) – 188
Bitter Root Mine – 155
Black bear Mine – 242
Black Bear Road – 242, 243
Black Canyon – 43
"Black Kid" – 209
Blackmore, Frank – 144
Blair, Thomas – 47, 206
Blair Street – 217
Bland-Allison Act – 81
Blue Mesa – 74
Bolam Pass – 189
Boulevard, The – 173, 175
Box Canyon Falls – 305-307
Bradford, I. J. and Milton – 118, 119
Bradley, E. C. – 73
Bradshaw, Charles – 146
Brenna, Thomas – 251
Brewster Stage Company – 88
Bristlecone Pine – 2
Brooklyn Jeep Road – 101
Brooklyn Slide – 234
Brower, George – 210
Brown Mountain – 265, 266
Brunot, Felix – 50, 52
Brunot Treaty – 49, 52
Bullion City – 48
Bullion King Mine – 236
Burns, Tom – 179, 180
Burros – 58
Burro Bridge – 83, 87, 229, 231, 244
Burrows Park – 72
Butte City – 244

California Gulch – 69
California Trail – 28, 29, 33, 42, 73
Camp Bird Mine – 226, 307, 308, 310
Camp Bird Road – 306-310
Camp Pleasant – 37, 39
Canon City – 63, 77
Capitalists (definition) – 16, 17
Carney, Francis – 320
Carson, Kit – 28, 50, 69
Carson, Levi – 193, 194
Carson Lost Mine – 193, 194

Cascade (town) – 155, 190
Cascade Creek – 37, 39, 64, 190
Cascade Falls – 305
Cascade Tank – 154
Castle Rock – 37
Cebolla River – 70
Cement Creek – 65, 87
Chase, Charles – 215
Chris Park Campground – 186
Champion Mine – 86
Champion Slide – 200
Chattanooga – 87, 100, 220, 231-234, 244
Chicago Basin – 156
Chief Ouray Highway – 135
Chief Ouray Mine – 305
Christ of the Mines Shrine – 225
Circle Route Garage – 118
Circle Route Highway – 118
Circle Route Stage – 108, 119, 224, 228
Circle Route Tour – 118, 135, 174, 179
Clear Lake – 228
Cline, Elizabeth – 296, 314
Cline, Capt. Milton – 296, 313
Clovis Culture – 20
Coal Bank Hill – 64, 113, 135
Coal Bank Pass – 192
Cochetopa Pass – 31, 40, 42-44, 70, 71, 74
Colorado Automobile Road – 111
Colorado Boy Mine – 261
Colorado Good Road Association – 111
Colorado Highway Commission – 111, 112, 116
Colorado Highway Department – 122, 131
Colorado Trail – 182
Comanche – 24, 27
Como Mine – 298
Compton, Bill – 124
Comstock Sampling Works – 226
Congress (town) – 240-244
Congress Mine – 90, 101, 239-241
Conejos – 69
Continental Divide – 12, 14, 198
Copper Glen – 244
Corkscrew Gulch – 221, 264
Corkscrew Turntable – 259
Coronado – 23
Crater Lake – 198
Crawford, George – 224
Crazy Swede Mine – 303, 304
Crooke Smelter – 67
Crosby, L. G. – 114
Croxton- Keeton Auto – 113
Crystal Lake – 265
Cunningham Gulch – 159
Cunningham Pass – 39, 53, 56, 65, 66, 86
Curry, John R. – 208
Cutler, Abram – 265

Darley, Rev. George – 88, 314
Day, Dave – 4
Day, Victoria – 181

Dead Man's Gulch – 200
Del Mino – 100, 244
Del Norte – 34, 49, 52, 66, 67, 70, 72, 77
Denver – 30, 70
Des Ouray Mine – 298
Denver and Rio Grande Railroad - - 67, 75-77, 87-90, 101, 114, 117, 126, 137-158, 163, 164, 166, 167, 170, 179, 209, 212, 316, 320
Denver and Rio Grande Western RR – See D&RG Railroad
Dickerson, W. B. – 66
Dixon House – 313, 315
Dodge City Cowboy Band – 213
Dolan, Jack – 234
Donald, John – 119
D.S.O. (Durango-Silverton-Ouray) Highway – 128, 130
Duncan, Ray – 189
Dunmore Mine – 296
Durango – 89, 142, 165-176
Durango Mountain ski area – 189
Durango Trust – 167-169
Durango-Silverton Railroad – 146-164

Earp, Wyatt – 211, 212
Eckles, John – 307, 310, 311
Edwards, John – 194
Elbert Creek – 64, 189
Electra Lake – 64, 153, 188
Elk Park – 156, 157
Emil, Eddie – 293
Engineer Mountain – 188, 191, 192
Engineer Pass – 73, 77
Engineer Road – 79, 81, 83, 281, 297-299
Eolus Mtn. – 153
Escalante-Dominguez – 25, 26
Eureka – 77, 159

Fall Creek – 178
Federal road Aid Act – 121, 124
Fish Lake – See Molas Lake
Fisher Brewery – 225
Fisher, Charles – 225
Folsom Culture – 20
Forest Service (U. S.) – 111, 112, 117, 121, 122
Fort Garland – 34, 40, 69
Fort Massachusetts – 32
Fort Peabody – 30
Fort Plummer – 44, 46
Fort Uncompahgre – 28
Freeland, William – 310
Freemont, John C. – 42, 43
French, Abnah – 47, 48
Fritz, Elias – 290

"G.W." – 35
Garfield Peak – 156
Galloping Goose – 174
Genesee-Vanderbilt Mine – 251
Gibbons, Rev. J.J. – 108, 180, 188, 233, 249, 287, 300
Gibbs, Charles – 159

INDEX

Gilpin, Gov. William – 70
Gladstone – 87, 218
Gold Hill – 316
Gold King Mine – 160-162
Gold Prince Mine – 159
Golden Fleece Mine – 72
Goldsmith, Warren – 251
Good Road Bill – 122
Gold Belt Theatre – 317, 319
Goulding Creek Trail – 188
Governor's Basin – 309, 310
Grassy Creek – 66
Grand Turk Mountain – 198
Greene, George – 168, 206, 207
Greene Smelter – 168
Greene Mountain Mill – 159
Greene Smelter – 65, 207
Greene Street – 217
Grizzly Bear Mine – 303
Grizzly Peak – 191
Guadalupe Mine – 266
Gunnison, Capt. John W. – 41, 42
Gunnison River – 20, 31, 42
Guston – 244, 253, 254
Guston Mine – 253-256

Hamilton, E. M. – 48
Hammond Tunnel – 255
Hanson, Rasmus – 79
Harker, O. H. – 40
Hart, Nat – 313
Hart, Sen. Thomas – 42
Hartman Brothers – 286
Harwood, Bill – 86
Haviland Lake – 46, 57
Head, Lafayette – 69
Henderson, H. T. – 188
Hendrick Gulch – 255, 256
Henson Creek – 77, 182
Hermosa (town) – 148, 149, 181, 182
Hermosa Creek – 178
Hermosa Creek Toll Road – 187
Hermosa House – 180, 181
Hermosa Valley – 189
Hidden Valley – 178
"High Line" – 140, 151, 152
Hogue, Parson – 171
Holladay, Doc – 210, 212
Hoosier Boy Mine – 232
Horseshoe Curve – 234
Horsetail Falls – 300
Hotchkiss, Enos – 70, 72
Hotchkiss Mine – 72
Howard, Mr. – 86
Howardsville – 53, 77, 159, 206
Hub Saloon – 161
Hubner, Martin – 231
Hudson, Marvin, Amelia and Pauline – 286, 290-293
Hudson Mine – 246

Ice Lake – 228
Ida L. Mine – 261
Idaho Gulch Slide – 200
Idarado Mine – 128, 255, 256
Ignacio Lake – See Electra Lake
Imogene Basin – 309
Imogene Pass – 309, 310
Impassable Canyon – 91, 276, 283-302
Influenza Epidemic – 123, 123
Ingersoll, Ernest – 57
Ingram Pass – 242
Ironton (town) – 262, 263
Ironton Park – 93, 110, 244, 261, 162, 165

Jackson, William H. – 57
Jaramillo, Danny – 293
Jennison, "Widow" – 77
Johnson, Miles – 47
Joker Tunnel – 224, 257-259
Jones, J. T. – 73

Kampfshulte, Mary – See Mary Mears
Kansas Territory – 28
Kearn, William – 206
Kellogg, S. B. – 32, 36
Kendall Mountain – 199
Kendall Mountain Slide – 200
Kimball, Gordon – 312
King, Alfred Castner – 325, 326
Kishbaugh, Terry – 293
Knob, The – 99, 247

La Garita Mountains – 42, 43
La Loma – 34, 49
La Plata County – 206
La Plata Mountains – 25, 26, 45, 46
La Veta Pass – 27, 33, 34, 69, 77
Lake City – 61, 62, 67, 68, 71, 72
Lake City and Antelope Park Toll Road – 72
Lake Durango – 176
Lake City – Silverton Toll Road (See Merchant's Road – 73, 77
Lake Fork of the Gunnison River – 72-74
Lake Emma – 217
Lamert, Hugh – 178
Larson Brothers Mine – 261
Larson, Harry – 261
Larson, Milton – 261, 263
Leroux, Antoine – 28, 42
Lewis, Harvey – 95, 302
Libby, Rev. C. L. – 314, 315
Lime Creek – 39, 64, 196
Lime Creek Burn – 88, 124, 193-196
Lime Creek Road – 122, 124, 190, 191, 194, 195
Linstrom, Gus – 303
Little Burro Mine – 231
Little Giant Mine – 47, 48, 50
Little Molas Lake – 198
Liverpool – 244
Lockwood, Bob – 124

"Long Walk" – 69
Longfellow Mine – 239
Lookout Mountain – 231
Loring, Col. William W. – 42
Los Piños I Agency – 70, 71
Los Piños ii Agency – 73, 74
Los Piños Pass – 70
Lost Gold Mines – See Baker's Seam, Carson Mine, Crazy Swede Mine, Lost Shepherds' Lode, Lost Twin Peaks Lode
Lost Shepherds' Lode – 197, 198
Lost Twin Peak Lode – 300
Louisiana Purchase – 27
Lucky Twenty Mine – 266

Manifest Destiny – 49, 137
Marcy, Randolph – 26, 42
Marmot – 257
Marshall, Jim – 155
Marshall Pass Toll Road – 75
Masterson, Bat – 210, 212
Martha Rose Smelter – 226
McCall, C.W. – 294
McDonald, John – 98
McGiney, Barney – 251
McGuire, John – 113
McNichols, Robert – 231
Meldrum, Andy – 260, 261
Meldrum Tunnel – 260, 261
Mears, Mary – 70
Mears, Otto – 50, 52, 68-78, 85, 90, 91, 95, 98, 100, 101, 108, 109, 114, 119, 120, 159, 161, 221, 222, 301, 302, 307
Mears Highway – 136
Mears' Toll Road (Red Mountain) – See Ouray-Red Mountain Toll Road
Mecure, Henry – 31, 35
Mechling, David – 113
Meeker Massacre – 75
Melton, John – 118
Merchant's Toll Road – 76, 77
Messerole – 151, 187
Mexican-American War – 151, 187
Micky Breene Mine – 298
Mill Creek – 235
Mill Gulch – 234
Miller, Bob – 293
Million Dollar Highway (name) – 3, 4, 128, 130, 132
Mills (defined) – 17
Mineral Creek – 202, 231
Mineral Farm Mine – 307, 311
Mineral Point – 160, 296, 299
Miners (defined)—16
Miners and Merchant's Bank – 315
Missionary Ridge – 182, 183, 185
Model T Ford – 125
Molas Lake – 88, 198, 199
Molas Pass – 198
Molas Trail – 199

Mormon War – 42
Mother Cline Slide – 133, 281, 296, 297
Mountain, James – 83, 230
Mountain Monarch Mine – 298
Mules – 58, 59
Muleshoe Slide – 234
Munn, Ira – 314
Murnane – 151, 187

Natalie Mine – 300
National Belle Mine – 239, 247, 248, 250
Navajo – 69
Needle Mountains – 152, 153, 198
Needles, The – 189
Needles Wilderness – 152
Nellie Creek – 73
New York and San Juan Smelting and Mining Co. – 207
Newberry, J. J. – 46
Newman, Paul – 185
Nilsen, Sven – 230, 231
North Star Mill – 226
North Star Mine – 87, 226

Old Lout Mine – 298
Old One Hundred Mine and Mill – 159
Old Spanish Trail – See California Trail
Ophir Pass – 83
Ophir Pass Road – 229
Ophir Toll Road – 83, 84, 230, 231
Ornate, Juan de – 24
Osgood, Clayton – 209
Otto Mears Monument – 302
Ouray (town) – 73-75, 84, 304-322
Ouray, Chief – 49-53, 76, 184
Ouray to Los Piños Toll Road – 73-75, 81
Ouray, Mineral City and Animas Forks Toll Road – 81
Ouray and San Juan Wagon Road – 81, 83-85, 92-99, 109
Ouray-Red Mounatin Toll Road – See Ouray and San Juan Wagon Road
Ouray Hot Springs Pool – 320, 321
Ouray Times - 294

Pagosa Springs – 46
Palmer, William J. – 137, 168
Parasol, Mrs. S. J. – 314
Pathfinder of the San Juans – See Otto Mears
Patton, Joe – 100
Perrin, Charles – 168
Pfeiffer, Albert – 31
Pidgeon Peak – 189
Pikes Peak – 29, 111
Pikes Peak Gold Rush – 30-32, 39
Pilkar, Lars – 131, 302
Pinkerton, Charles – 184
Pinkerton, James H. – 183, 187
Pinkerton-in-the-Pines – 184
Pinkerton Hot Springs – 37, 183, 184

Index

Pioneer Stage Co. – 88, 149, 150
Pitcher, James – 161
Pole Creek – 56
Pollack, Thomas – 36
Poncha Pass – 31, 69, 75, 77
Porphyry Basin – 236
Porter, George – 309
Porter, John – 168, 206, 207
Porter Fuel Co. – 168
Poughkeepsie Gulch – 87, 298
Poughkeepsie Mine – 298
Powderhorn – 71
Prospectors (defined) – 16
Prostitution – 169, 170, 246, 317
Province of New Mexico – 23
Pueblo (town) – 60
Pueblo Indian Revolt – 24
Purgatory Park – 189
Purgatory Ski Area – See Durango Ski Mountain

Quality Hill – 211
Quintana, Juan – 194

Rainbow Route – 217, 225
Ralston Creek – 300
Randall, Mr. 313
Ransome, F. L. – 41
Red Mountain City – 239-242, 244-246
Red Mountain Creek – 91
Red Mountain Mining District – 84, 90, 102, 104, 109, 219, 223, 224, 237-266
Red Mountain Pilot – 249
Red Mountain Review – 249
Red Mountain Pass – 220, 241, 242
Red Mountain Railroad, Mining, and Smelting Co. – 259
Red Mountain Task Force – 239
Red Mountain Town – 220, 242, 243, 247-250
Red Mountains – 239, 243, 244
Redford, Robert – 185
Reese, Dempsey – 47, 48, 206
Revenue Mill – 309
Revenue Tunnel – 308-310
Rhoda, Franklin – 56-58, 73, 153
Rice, F. R. – 36
Rico House – 151
Rico and Durango Toll Road – 151, 185-187
Ridgway, Arthur – 76
Rio Grande Pass – See Cunningham Pass
Rio Grande River – 20, 24, 25, 27, 52, 63, 66
Rio Grande Southern Railroad – 118, 173, 174
Riverside Slide – 133, 270, 274, 279, 286-296
Riverside Snow Tunnel – 107, 287-289
Rivera, Juan – 24-26
Roberts, Robert – 231
Robinson Mine – 252
Robidoux, Antoine – 28
Rock Creek Trail – 23
Rockwood (town) 64, 140, 149, 150, 185, 186
Rockwood to Dolores Wagon Road – 187

Rockwood, Thomas – 149
Rocky Mountains – 27
Rocky Mountain Stage Co. – 88
Roff, Roy – 124
Rogers, Jack – 244
Rogersville – 244, 245
Roma Saloon – 318
Rough and Ready Smelter – 208
Ruby Cliffs – 82, 85, 268, 272, 273, 278, 280, 282, 283
Ruby Cliffs – 82, 85, 268, 272, 273, 278, 280, 282, 283
Ruffner, Lt. E. F. – 46

Saguache (town) – 67-70, 77
Saguache Chronicle – 70
Saguache-Ouray Toll Road – 72-75, 81, 312, 313
Saguache and Natrop Toll Road – 70
Saguache and San Juan Toll Road – 70, 73, 312
Salfisberg, Fred – 124
Sangre de Cristo Mountains – 27
Sangre de Cristo Pass – 33, 34, 36, 42
San Juan Dome – 11-14, 18
San Juan Excitement – 39
San Juan Chief Mill – 299
San Juan Herald – 249
San Juan Mountains – 3, 10-18, 24, 27, 121,
San Juan National Forest – 18, 152, 242
San Juan and New York Smelter – 168
San Juan Smelting and Mining Co. – 168
San Juan Triangle – 15, 16
San Luis Valley – 23, 24, 27, 31, 32, 34, 36, 40, 63, 66, 69, 70
Santa Fe – 23
Saratoga Mine – 265
Savage Basin – 310
Schneider, Pete – 207
Scotch Creek Pass – 151, 185, 189
Scout Lake – 190
Searcy, W. N – 119
Shelton, William R. – 229
Shenandoah-Dives Mine – 215
Sheridan Pass – 239
Shining Mountains – 22
Short, Luke – 212
Sierra de las Guillas – 27
Silver Belle Mine – 259, 260
Silver Crown Mine – 232
Silver Falls – 154
Silver Gulch – 296
Silver Ledge Mill – 233, 234
Silver Ledge Mine – 233, 235, 236
Silver Panic of 1893 – 71, 214, 223, 249, 318
Silverton (town) – 64, 65, 67, 72, 88, 89, 140, 158, 162, 165, 200, 201, 204-217
Silverton and Hermosa Turnpike Co. – 187
Silverton Commercial Club – 117
Silverton, Gladstone and Northerthly Railroad – 87, 217, 218
Silverton Jockey Club – 210

Silverton Northern Railroad – 78, 159, 160, 217
Silverton Railroad – 109, 110, 128, 129, 166, 169, 219-225, 235-237, 239, 240, 250, 259
Silverton Railway – 224
Silverton Xtreme Ski Area
Silverton Visitor's center – 202, 203
Silverton-Red Mountain Toll Road (Mears) – 99-102
Sinclair, Jack – 213
Sky City Union – 248
Slattery, Jack – 161
Slumgullion Pass – 67, 72
Smelters (defined) – 17
Smuggler Mine – 169
Sneffles (town) – 309
Snowden, Francis – 204, 205
Snowflake Hiking Trail – 199
Solid Muldoon – 249
South Fork – 66
South Mineral Creek – 64, 226
St. Germain Foundation – 265
St. Paul Mine – 240
Spring Creek Pass – 72
State Bridge – 297
Stevens, Ike – 285
Stevenson, J. J. – 46
Stockton, Clint – 209
Stoiber, Ed – 159
Stony Pass – 20, 39, 41, 48, 52, 56, 57, 65, 66, 86-88, 113, 120, 206, 216
Sulton Mine – 226
Sultan Mountain – 58, 64, 198
Summit (town) 239, 244
Summitville – 49
Sunnyside Mine 159, 215, 216
Sutton Mine – 300
Sweetville – 244

Tabor, H. A. W. – 87, 88, 149, 298
Tacoma – 153
Tall Timber Resort – 154, 155
Taos – 33, 34
Teft Spur – 155
Telescope Slide – 234
Telluride (town) – 243, 310
Texas, Republic of – 28
Thousand Mile Circle Route – 125
Three Forks of the Animas – See Animas Forks
Tierra Amarilla – 33
Tabasco Mill – 72
Tobins, Tom – 28
Toll Roads – 62-64, 68, 70
Tomboy Mine – 31-
Tower, Mr. – 206
Trappers – 28
Trappers' Trail – 33
Treasury Tunnel – 128, 255
Trimble, Frank – 179
Trimble Hot Springs – 148, 179-181
Trust for Public Land – 239

Tulley, Thomas – 112
Turret Peak – 189
Twilight Peak – 193, 194
Twin Peaks – 305, 322
Twin Peaks lost Gold Mine – 305

Ulford, L. L. – 207
Uncompahgre Canyon – 79, 81, 139, 297-305, 307
Uncompahgre National Forest – 18, 242
Uncompahgre Peak – 73
Uncompahgre River – 20, 31, 73, 85, 297
Uncompahgre (town) – 313
Upper Animas Valley – 188
U. S. 550 – 134
U. S. Depository Mine – 310
U. S. Land Office – 172
Ute Indians – 22-25, 28, 35, 39-41, 45-47, 49, 50, 52, 69, 174
Ute Treaty – 1863 – 50
Ute treaty – 1868 – 50
Ute Treaty – 1873 – See Brunot Treaty
Ute Treaty – 1880 – 75

Vanoli, John – 317-319
Verde Cuerno – 2
Virginius Mine – 310

Wagon Wheel Gap – 66
Wallace, Joseph – 85
Walsh, Tom – 226, 307, 308
Walsh Smelter – 226, 227
Walsen, Fred – 91
Walton, William – 28
Waterfall Ranch – 148, 178
Watson, Squire (W.D.) – 65, 66
Weir Toll Road – 88, 112
Weminuche Wilderness Area – 15
West Needle Mountains – 153
Weston, William – 309
Wigglesworth, Thomas – 99, 179
Wightman, James – 85, 113, 139, 140, 151, 155
Williams, "Preacher Bill" – 42
Wilson Range – 230
Windom Peak – 153
Wolf Creek Pass – 27, 116, 117
Wood, Dave – 77, 95
Wood, George – 171
Wootton, "Uncle" Dick – 28
Wyman, Louis – 98, 113

Yankee Boy Basin – 309
Yankee Boy Mine – 309, 310
Yellow Jacket Mine – 303
Yellow Rose Mine – 266
Yvonne Pass – 77

Zaldevera, Juan – 24

www.ingramcontent.com/pod-product-compliance
Lightning Source LLC
Chambersburg PA
CBHW060457170426
43199CB00011B/1240